From Sophie to Sonia

A HISTORY OF WOMEN'S ATHLETICS

By Noel Henry

Contents

ACKNOWLEDGEMENTS

Irish Women's Athletics by Peter Pozzoli (1972);
Women of Ireland by Kit and Cyril Ó Céirín (Tír Eolas 1996); *Irish Olympians* by Lindie Naughton and Johnny Watterson (Blackwater Press 1996); *Irish Runner Magazine,* Editor Frank Greally;
Marathon Magazine, Editor Fr Liam Kelleher;
The First Fifty Years – Blackrock Athletic Club by Tom Kelly;
John Cussen, Newcastle West, Co. Limerick; Mary Scanlon, Limerick (re: Sophie Pierce);
Bord Lúthchleas na hÉireann

PRODUCTION TEAM
Frank Greally: Greally Publications
Editor: Richard Gallagher
Layout and design: Alex Tuohy & Mary Guinan
Cover design: Mary Guinan
Photograph of Noel Henry: Dave O'Connor
Additional Photographs: Fionnbar Callanan, John Mulvihill, Steve Humphreys, John Sheehan, Joe Fanning, Terry O'Rourke, Sportsfile, Allsport
Cover photographs: Sportsfile

Printed by: Vision Print, Brookfield Terrace, Blackrock, Co. Dublin.

Introduction

I am greatly honoured to be invited to pen my thoughts as an introduction to this splendid book recording the feats of Irish women athletes down through the years. What better inspiration could there be for today's young hopefuls than to read about the women who led the way in showing the world that a small country like Ireland could compete at the highest level?

Great sporting moments and great achievements provide lasting pleasure; lovers of sport will remember and talk about Catherina McKiernan's brilliant cross-country running for the rest of their lives.

Sometimes people describe to me where they were or what they were doing when I won the World Championship 5,000m. Often the details are so vivid, it's like a slideshow of that particular moment in time.

These are the things that make winning a race or breaking a record really worthwhile for me – the joy and excitement in the eyes of somebody who has shared in the achievement, even if only by cheering at a television screen thousands of miles from the actual scene of the event.

That joy and excitement is very much a two-way thing. It gives me a warm feeling inside, a feeling that I often draw on when I'm tired or alone or debating on a cold and windy evening about putting on the trainers and facing into a long run.

As I reflect on the World Cross Country Championships this year (1997) in Turin, I know that Catherina, Una, Valerie, Pauline, Maureen, and myself made history. We finished third in the world, beaten only by the fabulous Kenyan and Ethiopian women. I had always dreamt of being part of a medal-winning team at this great championship – and the first time always means the most, so Turin 1997 will forever remain a cherished memory.

Hard work and commitment never fail to produce worthwhile results. If something is easy to achieve, then it is probably not worth having. I'm sure that the long hours and diligent research put into this book by Noel Henry will be richly rewarded in the years ahead by the sheer enjoyment people get from reading it.

From Sophie to Sonia. A history of women's athletics. The exploits of Maeve, Ann, Mary, Claire, Deirdre, Caroline, Aisling, Catherina, Susan, and many more. Just the book for a cold and windy evening, curled up beside the fire. But what about that long training run? Not to worry – I can always do the few extra miles tomorrow!

Sonia O'Sullivan
31 August 1997

Foreword

Irishwomen have come a long way since the forties, the time that, as Nuala Ó Faoláin says in her autobiography, *Are You Somebody?,* was 'a living tomb for women'.

In that patriarchal society a woman had few rights: she was banned by law from employment in the public sector after marriage; she had no entitlement to the family home, which could be sold over her head; wife-beating was tacitly accepted.

In his book *Dublin Tenement Life,* Kevin C Kearns recalls the terrible hardships inflicted on women in the thirties and forties by their husbands and other menfolk. Many wives of the time desperately wanted to limit the number of their pregnancies; often their very lives depended on it. But according to the Catholic Church, a woman who refused her husband's sexual advances was committing serious sin, even if she already had more children than she could feed and care for.

In the same book, Mary Doolan remembers what it was like in the confessional: 'Women were often chastised rather than consoled by the priest. If you went into confession (and) said you wouldn't have sex with your husband – but we didn't call it "sex" in them days – you wouldn't get absolution. You'd be put out.'

As for premarital pregnancy, it was regarded as utterly scandalous, a moral blight on the family. Pregnant girls were forced to leave home. Some went into prostitution; others were taken into orphanages, where their babies were put up, often against the mother's will, for adoption. In the face of such cruelty, more than one despairing young woman took her own life.

Mary Doolan recalls another barbaric practice: 'Following childbirth the mother had to be "churched", which involved ... kneeling at the altar rail before the priest, with a lighted candle, and being blessed.'

As Mary says, the belief was that sexual intercourse and childbirth had contaminated even the married woman in the eyes of God. Until she had been 'purified' by churching, she was forbidden to prepare food for the family, even take up a knife and cut bread.

Few women at the time questioned the moral basis of the ritual, but half a century later Mary expresses the keen resentment that many still feel: 'The way it was, you were like a fallen woman ... I thought I was dirty because I had the child ... It was a living disgrace.'

Neanderthal attitudes extended also to the sports arena. Not only were women not encouraged to participate – they were actively discouraged.

In the late sixties women began to gain social and political recognition. The women's liberation movement gathered momentum; the Equal Pay Act began to come into force; women started to play sports previously barred to them.

Of course, girls have always played camogie and hockey in certain schools. Hockey has boomed in recent years, and in 1995 history was made with the highly successful staging of the World Cup at Belfield.

Camogie, the sister of hurling, has been popular since the forties. The annual All-Ireland Championship culminates in the high-profile final in Croke Park.

The Irish Ladies' Football Association was founded in 1973 and has grown enormously. The national team ranks 17th in Europe. The goalie is Sue Hayden of Verona FC and Greystones, superfit at age 34 and approaching her 50th cap.

The Women's Gaelic Athletic Association was set up in 1974. By now almost every county fields a team in the All-Ireland. The 1996 final brought together Laois and Monaghan, went to a replay (15,000 attended both games), and was won with style by Monaghan. Incidentally, the action here was in clean, refreshing contrast to the macho fracas between Meath and Mayo a few weeks previously.

The final of the 1996 Women's Rugby Championship was won by a team from Creggs, Co. Roscommon. This tiny village with a long sporting tradition made history by defeating the much-fancied Blackrock (Dublin).

Our women handballers celebrated their 25th anniversary in 1996 by winning world titles in the USA.

Irishwomen have now been embraced (or forced entry) into all sports (with a few diehard exceptions). Some have scaled the heights of excellence: Michelle Smith, our triple Olympic and double European swimming champion; Sonia O'Sullivan, our world track champion; Catherina McKiernan, our cross-country and marathon champion. We even have a world boxing champion, the brilliant and articulate Deirdre Gogarty of Drogheda – those who know about the sweet science tell me she is the best pound-for-pound fighter anywhere.

It is fair to say that dramatic gains have been made since the bad old forties. Even that longtime bastion of sexism Fitzwilliam Lawn Tennis Club has woken up. On 8 December 1996, after 120 years of exclusivity, it voted to admit women to full membership.

But not all is equality and light. A number of golf clubs continue to discriminate. And even the Oireachtas, which should be leading by example, seems stuck in a time warp. The Members' Bar in Dail Éireann was refurbished at a cost of £380,000 and reopened in December 1996. We have more than 20 female TDs and several female senators, but the magnificent new Members' Bar has no ladies' toilet – only a gents'!

Sadly, violence against women shows no sign of going away – indeed it seems to be increasing and, like some other crimes, to be partly accepted by the authorities. I am reminded of a comment by the great Listowel novelist and playwright John B Keane: *Ireland is not a safe place for women to walk alone. The chivalry and dignity for which we were once noted have evaporated. When a community loses its chivalry there is little left.*

Perhaps that poignant judgment is a little too severe. Any country that has the wit to elect Mary Robinson as its President cannot be without virtue. In the face of prejudice and inertia, that marvellous woman turned a retirement home (Áras an Uachtaráin) into a real, living powerhouse and did us proud all over the world.

But it is true that though much has been gained by and for women, some other things have been lost or damaged. I suppose we can only embrace the good and keep on trying to overcome the bad. And in that ongoing battle between progress and ignorance,

I believe sport is paramount.

Anyway, my aim in this little book has been to trace the growth of women's athletics in Ireland during the past 75 years and to remember and salute those women (and a few men) who were and are central to that development.

Noel Henry
1 January 1998

Part one

The global and historical context

The fight for acceptance

Although women competed in track and field at the 1928 Olympic Games in Amsterdam, we had to wait until the 1960s before women's athletics was accepted in Ireland. One of the main reasons appears to have been Catholic Church opposition to women competing in a sport which demanded physical exertion.

This narrowminded attitude prevailed not only in the Church but also in society at large. An *Irish Times* editorial of 4 May 1928 headed 'Women Athletes' supported the stance of Pope Pius X1 on the subject. It pointed out that the Pope was not a spoilsport and did not condemn traditional forms of sport for women, such as lawn tennis, golf, and swimming.

It went on: *His censure, we may believe, is reserved for certain developments with which Ireland has become familiar through illustrated newspapers. In France, Germany, Italy and even England, many girls are devoting themselves to public sports which demand violent exertion and sometimes, it would seem, a notable scantiness of clothing.*

They compete for 'records' in hundred yards and quarter-mile races; they vie in high jumping, long jumping and the throwing of heavy weights. These performances are done before crowds of male spectators. His Holiness is surely in the right when he says that they are irreconcilable with women's reserve and that in this matter Christian Europe ought not to be less modest than pagan Rome. Furthermore, the extreme exertion that is required by such sports as track racing, weight throwing and competitive rowing must be bad for even the most robust women.

The topic of women in athletics appears to have been seldom aired in the 1930s. The dreadful split in Irish athletics (1936) and the war of 1939-1945 did nothing to encourage women in sport.

A further *Irish Times* editorial appeared on 12 March 1944 under the title, 'Ban on Women Athletes'. It included the following: *Women are now forbidden to take part in athletic events at meetings conducted by the National Athletic and Cycling Association of Ireland, and a new and separate women's sports association may be formed.*

A joint meeting of the General and Joint Councils of the NACAI refused to carry into effect a recommendation of the association's recent congress, 'that championships for women be held in a limited number of events, and that one event for women be inserted in each of open Meetings throughout the country.'

The NACAI Congress had provoked much protest, the foremost expression of disagreement being from Dr John Charles McQuaid, President of Blackrock College, who wrote to the NACAI in the following terms: 'I protest against this un-Catholic and un-Irish decision. I hereby assure you that no boy from my college will take part in an athletic meeting controlled by your organisation, at which women will compete, no matter what attire they may adopt.'

Mr McManus of the Dublin Board NACAI protested that women were already taking part in different kinds of sport all over the world. 'I don't see why we should hinder them here,' he said, 'or allow anyone else to stop us helping them. It is very unfair if the women are to be driven out of sport.' A retort to Mr McManus was, 'We cannot flout public opinion.'

This attitude towards women in sport would continue for the next three decades. McQuaid would become Archbishop of Dublin, and his conservative views would delay the acceptance of women's athletics until the 1960s.

Crusaders was the first club to have a women's section. It was formed after a famous meeting held in Moran's Hotel, Talbot St, Dublin, in November 1963. Maeve Kyle travelled from Ballymena. Billy Morton of Clonliffe Harriers and Louis Vandendries of Crusaders were also present. The consensus was that it was high time women's athletics began in the Republic of Ireland.

The breakthrough was not achieved without opposition: two well-known Crusaders athletes actually walked out of the meeting in protest. The motion was carried, however, and the first female section was formed.

Clonliffe Harriers now followed the Crusaders example – and also had their teething problems. Two meetings voted against progress. At the third attempt, Alec Sweeney's motion in favour of a women's section was carried. New women's clubs were now forming all over the country, and the first international match was held, against Scotland.

But as late as 1970 we had what now seem incredible incidents of discrimination. When women arrived that year at Maynooth College for the annual Intervarsity Cross Country, the college authorities forbade them to profane the hallowed grounds – the women had to find another venue.

The NACAI were just as slow to accept females. Kilkenny's Sean Byrne was the first in the association to champion women, in the early sixties. But the County Board chairman at the time would have none of it – and said some hard things against the idea of women in athletics. Sadly, there was no seconder for Sean's proposal.

It was 1965 before the NACAI saw the light and formally decided to allow women compete in athletic events. At long last women's athletics had become officially recognised – and was well on the way to being generally accepted.

Pioneers and revolutionaries

Back as far as the 1850s some European countries were trying to educate the ordinary people in the benefits of sport. England commenced making efforts to properly organise sports under standard rules that would eventually become rules for all countries. Ireland was in the throes of recovering from the ravages of the Famine and the loss of over a million people.

In the period from the 1870s the only official Irish sports meeting was organised by Trinity College Athletic Club. The Civil Services Athletic Club was formed to take part in the two-day event, which was known as The College Races and was held each year in the early summer.

These gatherings were not only noted for athletics; they were quite a social occasion, at which the ladies assembled to show off their finery in front of attendances reported at 10,000 over the two days.

Class distinction was one of the most serious drawbacks to athletics; indeed it was one of the reasons for the eventual emergence in 1884 of the Gaelic Athletic Association, in Thurles, Co. Tipperary. The early College Races, otherwise known as Trinity Sports, were a real 'closed shop'; only 'gentlemen athletes' were allowed to take part. This exalted brotherhood was restricted to 'any person who has never competed in an open competition or for public money or at any period of his life taught or assisted in the pursuit of athletic exercises as a means of livelihood or as a Mechanic, Artisan or Labourer'. The prizes, by the way, included Gold Pins, Loving Cups, Silver Inkstands, Picnic Stands and Baskets, and Silver Topped Walking sticks.

Of course we have progressed since then, though when you look at the magnificent golf courses springing up around Ireland with all kinds of obstacles to membership for the ordinary person, you realise that there is still ground to be won.

Anyway, the GAA provided vital sporting opportunities for the ordinary youth of the country at that time, at least for the young males.

The earliest newspaper mention I can find of a woman competing in an athletics event in these islands is in the English *Times* of 11 July 1795. It reports that at Wrothan, Kent, an unnamed lady ran a distance of one mile in five minutes and 28 seconds for a pound (sterling) wager. If the details are accurate, she was an extraordinary talent.

On 8 August 1891, Eva Francisco was reported to be the first Irishwoman to run 100 yards; her time was 13 seconds. Seemingly, a famous foreign circus, Hengles, was performing in Dublin. As part of the entertainment, the women's sprint was organised during a sports meeting. Perhaps Eva was a member of the circus. The date was 8 August 1891.

On 25 June 1898 two Dublin women, Misses Nolan and M.A. Guinness, dead-heated in a 100-yard race, in a time of 12 seconds, equalling the record set by two Americans, Maria Thornton and Mary Morgan. This time of 12 seconds was to stand as the official

World's Best until 1921. Yet it would be many decades before women in this country would be welcomed in athletics.

In the 1920s a certain Sophie Pierce emigrated from Limerick to England and became a world-class athlete. Her career is chronicled elsewhere in this book.

Enid Shankey, Maeve Kyle's mother, attended Trinity College in the 1920s and took part in women's races within the College grounds.

In 1947 Queens University Belfast had the distinction of forming the first women's athletic club in Ireland. They competed in a triangular tournament against teams from Glasgow University and St Andrews. Queens had one scoring athlete on this occasion, Viva Shepherd taking runner-up in the hurdles, high jump, and long jump.

In the same year, Billy Morton, Ireland's great organiser of athletics, promoted an athletics meeting at Lansdowne Road, the headquarters of the Irish Rugby Football Union. Surprisingly, the programme included a women's 100 yards. England's Maureen Gardner won. Dublin's D. Saunders finished second.

In 1948 Billy Morton continued his encouragement to women by inviting the legendary Francina Blankers-Koen (known as Flying Fanny), who had recently won four Olympic gold medals in London. Fanny duly won the 100- and 200-yard races.

It was around this time that the Archbishop of Dublin, John Charles McQuaid, was in full cry against women athletes. His 'hell and damnation' sermons against the moral dangers of 'scanty' athletics clothing now sound laughable (especially in the light of current styles), but they were taken seriously at the time – and would postpone the introduction of women's athletics in the south of Ireland for another 15 years.

In the meantime, Northern Ireland's women were becoming established, and in July 1950 the NIAAA (Northern Ireland Amateur Athletic Association) held their first championships. One year later they could boast nine women's clubs.

Perhaps the most significant happening in this context was the arrival up north of Kilkenny's Maeve Kyle. With her husband, Sean Kyle, Maeve formed what would become one of the most progressive clubs in all of Ireland, Ballymena AC.

In 1955 and 1956 Maeve won five NI titles, and in the years 1957 to 1962 the Ballymena club had 40 championship wins. The great Mary Peters would win 18 NIAAA titles for Ballymena.

Having battled vainly for many years against Southern indifference, Maeve Kyle found success in Northern Ireland. Her ultimate triumph came when, at last, the Amateur Athletic Union of Éire were shamed into awarding an Olympic vest to a woman, for the first time.

And so, in November 1956, Maeve flew to Australia to join two other Irish Olympians, hurdler Eamon Kinsella and metric miler Ronnie Delany, who would cover himself and Ireland in glory by scampering away with 1,500m gold. Maeve was eliminated in the heats of the 100m and 200m.

In 1958 Maeve again wore the green vest – this time with the red hand of Ulster instead of the shamrock – as she teamed with Thelma Hopkins, Mary Peters, and Bridget Robinson at the Cardiff Commonwealth Games. None of the foursome qualified for finals, but at least it was a step forward to have four women financed to a major championship. The future was looking brighter.

In 1960 Maeve Kyle (now Irish record-holder at 220yards, 24.5) was again selected to represent Ireland, this time in the Rome Olympics. Again she failed to qualify but had the satisfaction of posting a personal best in the 200m heats.

Maeve, now 34, was selected for the 1962 European Games at Beograd. In her heat and semifinal she registered 55.1 and 55.4 for 400m. Alas, the effort took its toll and a 57.5 in the final was good enough for only sixth place.

November 1963 saw the historic meeting in Moran's Hotel, Dublin, at which it was resolved to bring women's athletics to the Republic of Ireland. The Northern women in those early days gave great encouragement to their sisters in the South.

The first match between the two bodies involved five events. Joan Atkinson, Thelma Hopkins, and Lorna McGarvey scored wins for the North; Jackie Spence and Margaret Barry Murphy took sprint and field events for the South. Maeve Kyle played a dual role as a member of both bodies.

The first triangular international, with Belgium and Scotland, was held in Brussels in 1964. Ireland fielded a combined NIAA/AAUE team. The North sent Maeve Kyle, Lorna McGarvey, and one Mary Peters, whose double in the high jump and shot sealed an Irish victory. The Southern representatives on that historic occasion were Jackie Spence, Peggy Hogan (Crusaders), and Clonliffe's Claire Dowling, one of our all-time greats.

Mary Peters was born in England (6 July 1939) of English parents but had lived in Northern Ireland since she was twelve years of age. Technically she was probably ineligible for that triangular, but she showed her heart was in the right place by supporting her sister athletes in the circumstances. Mary would of course go on to win Olympic gold in Munich.

1965 and 1966 would be the last years we would see our friends from over the Border compete in AAUE championships. Maeve Kyle took five titles: hurdles and pentathlon in 1965 and, versatile as ever, 80m hurdles, 440yds, and long jump in 1966.

Tokyo 1964 saw the 36-year-old Maeve in her third Olympic Games. She reached the semifinals of 400m and 800m with Irish records of 54.5 and 2.11.3. Over the years the 400m mark had come down in eight stages from 60 seconds, Maeve being the record-breaker every time.

After over 30 years of division, the athletics bodies in the Republic at last got together. In March 1967 The Amateur Athletic Union Éire (AAUE) and the National Athletic and Cycling Association of Ireland (NACAI) merged to form a new body, Bord Luthchleas na hÉireann (BLE), which was recognised by the International Amateur Athletic Federation (IAAF) and would bring more athletes into the fold. It was directed in the main by former AAUE officials and had most of the members of the two old associations. The merger was not, however, total: a small breakaway group rejected BLE on the political grounds that its jurisdiction was confined to the Republic; they set up a new NACAI.

In the summer of 1964 Claire Dowling was the first AAUE and Clonliffe woman to gain international honours; she competed against Scotland. The first AAUE track and field championships were held in Dublin in 1965, and Claire was Clonliffe's lone star, winning three titles: long jump (17 feet 2.5 inches), 220yds (26.2) and 440yds (57.6).

Crusaders took most of the honours at that meet, with Hazel Tennison and Tipperary's Peggy Hogan excelling in the half-mile and mile events. In the following year Peggy surprised the cream of England by her shock victory in the British intermediate cross-country championships.

Clonliffe's Ann O'Brien was by now progressing well in training. A very strong-willed little lady, Ann trained hard in the spring of 1966 with the first all-Ireland track championship in view. Her sights were set on the double: half-mile and mile – but the defending champions, Hazel Tennison and Peggy Hogan, would take some beating.

Ann's months of dedicated training and planning with some of her male clubmates in Santry Stadium paid off handsomely. In the space of one glorious hour she completed the great double and made history by becoming the first Irishwoman under five minutes for the mile; her times were 2.16.1 and 4.59.2.

The first all-Ireland women's CC championships were held in 1967. Peggy Hogan won the individual title and Clonliffe the team event.

From 1965 to 1972 the Clonliffe pair Claire Dowling and Ann O'Brien dominated Irish athletics, winning no less than 37 national senior titles between them. Ann represented Ireland at the 1968 European Games in Athens. Claire competed at the 1971 European Indoor Games in Sofia, where she registered 2.07 for 800m, and in the 1971 Outdoor European Games at Helsinki, where she reached the 800m final. Her times in the three Helsinki races were 2.08.6, 2.06.1, and 2.03.4. At the Munich Olympic Games in 1972, Claire was eliminated in the quarter-finals with a time of 2.09.

It is important to remember that Claire achieved these exceptional times while domiciled in Collooney, Co. Sligo. Most of her interval training was done on the road near her home.

Claire won Irish senior titles in 100, 220, 440, 880, long jump, pentathlon, and cross-country. Ann O'Brien for her part won titles in 440yds, 880yds, 800m, 1,500m, mile, high jump, and cross-country and amassed a total of nine International (World) CC singlets. She was the first woman in the world to compete in eight successive World CC championships. Both Claire and Ann won British AAA medals in the early seventies.

Due credit must be given to these pioneers of women's athletics now that our womenfolk have taken their rightful place on the international athletics stage.

Ireland competed in the first Home Countries International at Barry, Wales, on 18 March 1967, and finished second to England. The Irish scorers were Peggy Hogan (3rd), Ann O'Brien (7th), Brenda Bailey (12th), and Maureen Conlon (13th).

The next International Cross Country was held at Blackburn on the 23 March 1968. England were again the victors; Ireland placed fourth. Ann O'Brien (8th) and Ursula

Kennedy (10th) were the leading Irishwomen.

On 22 March 1969 at Clydebank, Scotland, Canada and New Zealand gave the field more of an international look. Ireland again placed fourth, led home by Ann O'Brien (5th), Peggy Hogan-Mullins (10th) and Ursula Kennedy (20th).

On 21 March 1970 the International CC was held at Frederick, USA. It was the first time for our women to compete in the States. The long trip was rewarded with third place. Ann O'Brien finished ninth, Peggy Hogan-Mullins tenth, and young Deirdre Foreman an impressive 12th on her international debut. This latter lady would make a huge impression on the Irish scene in the next two decades. Other team members were Jean McNicholl (17th) and Nuala Bowe (29th).

In March 1971 at the European Indoor Championships, Claire Dowling-Walsh posted third in her 800m semifinal (2.07.4).

The San Sebastian International CC attracted Morocco, Belgium, Italy, Holland, New Zealand, Spain and the home countries. Once again, Ann O'Brien (19th) led the Irish. The improving Deirdre Foreman was 25th, Kathryn Moroney was 34th, and Beatrice Lambert was 36th. Ireland took seventh in the team event.

The European Championships where held at Helsinki, Finland, in August 1971. Claire Dowling-Walsh performed heroically, finishing second in her quarter-final of the 800m (2.06.1) and fourth in her semifinal (2.03.4). She was desperately unlucky to be impeded in the final but managed sixth in 2.08.6. At the same championships, Margaret Barry-Murphy long-jumped 5.73 for 16th place.

Ann O'Brien won her last National CC title in 1971. Mary Lynch of Raheny won the same title in 1972, Mary Tracey in 1973, and Deirdre Foreman in 1974, 1975, and 1976.

Tracey was prominent throughout the seventies. She won the National 1,500m in 1972 and booked her passage to the Munich Olympics, which will be remembered as the Games at which two of the Israeli team were murdered by Palestinian terrorists in the Olympic village and nine more, taken as hostages, died in a botched rescue attempt at the airport.

Mary Tracey and Claire Dowling-Walsh were eliminated in the quarter-finals of the 800m. Mary's time for fourth was 2.04.2, while Claire registered 2.09. Mary also reached the 1,500m quarter-finals, where she finished sixth in 4.16.4 and was eliminated. Margaret Barry-Murphy was eliminated in the 100m hurdles, sixth in her heat in 15.89.

Ireland took eighth place in the 1973 International CC, at Waregem. Mary Tracey, Deirdre Foreman and Mary Lynch were the scorers. In a six-nation European Cup at Copenhagen in 1973, Aideen Morrison (54.1 400m) and Mary Tracey (2.02.9 800m) were the only Irish winners.

The 1974 International CC was staged at Monza, Italy. Competing teams had now increased to twelve. Deirdre Foreman (23rd), Mary Lynch (29th), and Ann O'Brien (46th) were best of the Irish.

January 1975 saw Ireland achieve a notable international victory – the Home Countries CC at Coltsbridge. Vera Sherry (Monaghan) and Deirdre Foreman were in excellent form, finishing second and third.

January 1976 was another good month. Mary Tracey (Purcell) led an Irish team to second place at an international cross-country at Rawtenstall. Also in 1976 twelve countries, including the USA and the USSR, competed in the International CC Championships at Chepstow. Ireland took eighth place; Deirdre Foreman was 14th, Mary Tracey 22nd.

At the Montreal Olympics Mary Tracey finished fifth in her 1,500m heat, but her time of 4.08.63 was not good enough to qualify.

Mary Tracey had consistent success at the British AAA championships, winning 800m (2.03.00) in 1972, 800m (2.03.3) in 1973, and 3,000m in 1975 and 1976 (9.08 in both races). She also posted second in the 800m in 1974. Our women were now making a strong impression on the British scene; Mary Tracey Purcell was leading the effort.

Part two

Focus on the greats

Sophie Pierce with some of her trophies - this photo was taken in 1923

Sophie Pierce-Evans

Sophie Pierce-Evans was born in Knockaderry, Co. Limerick, on 17 November 1896. Her father farmed 350 acres, much of it in apple trees. Sophie got a taste for farming and began studying agriculture in Dublin in preparation for farming in South Africa. But when she interrupted her studies to take a job in London, agriculture took a back seat to her two new interests, athletics and aviation.

Her international athletics career spanned the years 1922 to 1926, and she was a real all-rounder, an accomplished horsewoman, tennis player, golfer, and athlete. Besides which she achieved probably most note as one of the world's first woman aviators. Physically, she was a veritable amazon, standing almost six feet, weighing eleven stones, and well proportioned with it.

Sophie was a despatch rider in a unit attached to the Royal Flying Corps from 1915 to 1918. In 1919 she married a British Army officer, Elliott Lynn, but the marriage ended in divorce. In 1928 she married a Lord James Heath and from then on was known as Lady Heath.

Sophie made a significant contribution to the campaign for recognition of women in sport, particularly in athletics. But that contribution has until now been largely overlooked or underestimated. Her address to the Olympic Congress on 30 May 1925 in Prague coupled with the wider social factors of the time led to the acceptance by the IOC of women's track and field in the Olympic Games.

From its foundation in 1894 by Baron de Coubertin, a French noble and its sole financier, the IOC was clearly an association of gentlemen amateurs whose original purpose was to promote the cause of amateur sport by gentlemen. This ethos, coupled with de Coubertin's vehement opposition to women in sport, ensured that women's involvement in Olympic competition was kept to a minimum until de Coubertin's retirement in 1925.

The situation was not helped by the attitude of the mostly male medical profession, whose serious doubts about the effects of strenuous exercise on women, particularly in the context of childbearing, produced a protracted debate.

Sophie was not deterred by male prejudice or medical ignorance. Her athletics career commenced in 1921. She excelled in several events, including the high jump, in which she set a world record at Brentwood, England, on 6 August 1923 with 4'10.5" (1.48). Maeve Kyle was the first Irishwoman to best Sophie's mark.

Sophie competed for Britain in two World Games, placing fourth in the javelin. Her best performance was at Stamford Bridge on 28 June 1924, when she threw a world record 173'2" for the Greek two-arm aggregate event then in vogue. This mark was to stand for 14 months.

Competing in the last Monte Carlo Games, in1923, this amazing athlete contested no less than eight events: 60m, 250m, 65m hurdles, high jump (third with 4'7"), long jump, shot, javelin (third with two-arm aggregate 142'11") and pentathlon (third).

Sophie competed for Aberdeen University while working there in 1921 and was elected chairwoman of the new Women's Amateur Athletic Association when it was set up in 1922. The WAAA began with one club and 25 women. By 1925, its membership had risen to 25,000 women and 500 clubs.

Sophie's approach to fitness for women caused such an interest that she was requested to deliver talks on BBC radio and in venues throughout England. She wrote a coaching manual, *Athletics for Women and Girls,* which was published in 1925. It remains even today one of the most sensible and comprehensive books of basic training for would-be female athletes. Certainly this lady from County Limerick was years ahead of her time. To think that the Republic of Ireland had to wait a further 40 years to witness women competing in athletics!

Sophie set marks for six events which were in effect all-Ireland records: high jump, 4'10.5". which stood from 1923 until 1943; long jump, 12'11.5", which stood from 1923 until 1944; shot putt, 30'2.5", which stood from 1923 until 1951; discus, 64'3.25", which stood from1924 until 1951; javelin, 107'9", which stood from 1924 until 1958;100m hurdles, 16.00, which stood from 1923 until 1964.

Sophie's activities with the WAAA and her writings on sport absorbed most of her time, and given her position within the WAAA, the high esteem she was held in by the sporting world, and her commonsense approach to training and exercise, it was not surprising that she was asked by the International Athletics Federation to submit the case for women's inclusion in track and field events in Olympic competition from 1926.

As a result of Sophie's submission on behalf of the IOC, women were admitted to three athletic events in the 1928 Amsterdam Games. Although it would be many more years before women were accepted into all Olympic sports, the early groundwork was done by Sophie.

Having achieved what she set out to do in Prague, Sophie flew back to London. Enroute she sat beside a Captain Reid of the Royal Air Force. Inquisitive as always, Sophie engaged Captain Reid in a lengthy discussion on the technical aspects of flying. He promised to introduce her to the Light Aeroplane Club in London and arrange for her to have flying lessons.

This was a challenge Sophie could not resist, and so she embarked on an avocation that would become a lifelong passion and would lead her to break new ground for women and to set new aviation records in inter-war Europe.

Sophie took up the rights of women in aviation just as she had campaigned earlier for women in athletics. During 1926, 1927, and 1928 she proved that women were men's equals if not their superiors in the air. She took up professional stunting and gave exhibition flights.

Sophie was selected to represent England as a judge in the 1928 Amsterdam Olympics. But she was denied the opportunity of witnessing an English team compete – they withdrew in protest that the number of women's events was inadequate, a decision much regretted by the other participating countries.

Presenting her judge's badge on arrival at the stadium, Sophie, now Lady Heath, was refused permission by an over zealous official because she had mislaid her entrance ticket! Undaunted, she fetched her plane from a nearby airfield and was soon circling dramatically over the packed Olympic stadium, dropping leaflets threatening that unless admitted immediately she would land in the centre of the arena. Within minutes Lady Heath was taking her place with the other international judges. Sophie Pierce had shown that she retained her fighting Irish spirit!

Sophie continued her flying career until 1930 – and created aviation history by making the first solo flight from Cape Town, South Africa, to London.

Among her more ambitious attempts was a flight to discover how many aerodromes it was possible to visit in one day. If no aerodrome was available, she would settle for a likely field near a town. Taking off from Manchester, She called at 50 aerodromes and landed in 17 fields, refuelling six times along the way.

Sophie was a regular competitor at air races all over the world and had many offers from leading British manufacturers to demonstrate the reliability of their aircraft. She eventually became a pilot with KLM, the Royal Dutch Airline, and regularly flew the London-Amsterdam route. Her flying career came to a halt in Cleveland, Ohio, after a serious crash from which the brave lady never fully recovered.

She divorced Lord Heath in 1930, returned to Ireland in 1931, and bought out Iona National Airways and Dublin Air Ferries, which subsequently went bankrupt in 1935, whereupon Sophie returned to London.

Lady Sophie Heath, celebrated Irish airwoman and athlete, died tragically in a road accident in London in 1939, aged only 42 years.

For all her wonderful achievements, the name Sophie Pierce is hardly known in Ireland today. That is a great pity.

Peter Pozzoli knew more about women's athletics in the sixties and seventies than any living person. An Italian married to an Irishwoman and living in England, he edited some splendid books on women's athletics.

Peter liked to call a spade a spade and oftentimes severely criticised BLE's treatment of women. He has since passed away – and BLE has become a little more enlightened. Perhaps some day soon we may see a Sophie Pierce trophy being contested by our women athletes. No Irish athlete better deserves to be remembered.

Sophie Pierce plaque at Allied Irish Bank, Newcastle West, Co. Limerick

Maeve Shankey (Kyle)

Maeve Kyle will go down in history as the one who put women's athletics on the map in Ireland, and indeed in countries all over the world. Born Maeve Shankey in 1928 in Kilkenny, where her father was headmaster in Kilkenny College, she showed early athletic talent. Encouraged by her two sportsmad brothers, she played many sports but excelled especially at running and could outsprint most of her childhood peers whether male or female.

Incidentally, Maeve's mother, then Enid Shankey, took part in athletics in Trinity in the twenties. Of course such unladylike activities were then permitted only within the discreet confines of college!

Maeve still has a silver medal won by Enid in a race in Trinity. That medal, now mounted, is dated 1923. It may well be the first (or perhaps the second) track medal ever won by a woman in Ireland.

Maeve was a first-class hockey player; while still at school she won Leinster senior representative honours. At Trinity College she gained the first of 58 Irish caps. The summit of her hockey career was the winning of the Triple Crown in 1950, when the Irish team played for the first time at the famous Wembley Stadium.

While at Trinity, Maeve won colours not only at hockey but also at tennis and sailing. She organised a women's athletic club in the college, and when Billy Morton invited the famous Fanny Blankers-Koen to run in Lansdowne Road, Maeve and her hockey colleague Joan O'Reilly provided the opposition to the quadruple gold medallist of the London Olympics 1948.

Shortly after this event Short and Harlands, Belfast, moved to form Ireland's first athletics club for women.

In 1953 Maeve met Sean Kyle, whom she describes as 'an athletics nut'. Sean, with the aid of fitness instructor Joe O'Keeffe, reshaped her training schedules. Maeve won the 100yds and 220yds in the RUC Coronation Sports, at Ravenhill, Belfast. She also guested in the Northern Ireland championships, again winning both sprints.

In 1954 Maeve married Sean, and together they founded Ballymena Athletic Club the following year.

When winning the British Women's AAA championships in 1956, Maeve set Northern Ireland records in 100m and 200m. She went through the season unbeaten and was rewarded by selection on the small athletics team to represent Ireland in the 1956 Olympic Games in Melbourne, Australia. This was the first time a woman had been selected on our Olympic team, and not everyone approved. Maeve herself came in for much criticism.

Financially, the Amateur Athletic Union was in dire straits at that time, because it comprised only six or seven clubs in the Dublin area. The NACAI, outlawed by the International Association of Athletics Federations, controlled athletics in the rest of the country. Consequently, athletes bound for Melbourne had to contribute £200 toward their expenses. For the newly married Kyles, with a young child, Shauna, this presented a huge obstacle. We tend to forget that 40 years ago £200 was for many a year's salary.

Melbourne 56 was an eye-opener to someone used to the small crowds at hockey games and athletics events in Ireland. The sportsmad Australians were witnessing their first ever Olympics, and the pressure on our home-based athletes, hurdler Eamon Kinsella of Donore Harriers and Maeve, were enormous. Curious fans crowded the Athletes' Village and made it very difficult for the contestants to get on with their training. Ronnie Delany was least affected of the Irish; he had been training and racing on the US circuit and was accustomed to the adulation.

Maeve was eliminated in the heats of the 100m and 200m but was still able to savour Ronnie Delany's wonderful victory in the 1,500m. Written off by most of the so-called experts, Ronnie surprised a class field, sprinting from the back of the pack in the final 300 metres and finishing well clear of his rivals. Maeve told me that she shed tears of joy as Ronnie received his gold medal and stood proudly for the National Anthem with the Tricolour flying high.

Maeve represented Northern Ireland in the 1958 Commonwealth Games at Cardiff, Wales, the AAUE having passed her over for the European Championships the same year. But by the time the 1960 Olympics came round she was back in favour with the Irish selectors and was picked for her second Games, in the beautiful city of Rome, Italy.

The torrid atmosphere in the new Olympic Stadium was not favourable to athletes from Ireland's green and misty climate. Nor did the luck of the draw help Maeve – she was pitted straightaway against superstars like America's Wilma Rudolf and Australia's Shirley Strickland. Maeve again bowed out in the heats, placing fifth in both 100m and 200m.

Maeve put the disappointment of Rome behind her and continued to dominate Northern Irish and British sprinting in 1961, 1962, and 1963, setting several new records. She now looked forward to being picked for a third Olympic Games, Tokyo 1964.

Maeve reckoned she was never so well trained for her events – this time she was concentrating on the 400m and 800m – but she had quite a job convincing the selectors. Even though she had posted qualifying times on 12 occasions, she was not informed of her selection until the very last minute. This upset Maeve's preparation. She reached the semifinals of the 400m and 800m but felt she could have qualified for both finals if she had been selected earlier.

Maeve ran in the European Games of 1966 and the Commonwealth Games of 1970, qualifying for the finals of the 400m and relay, some achievement for a woman of 42!

From 1974 to 1981 this marvellous athlete entered international masters' (veterans') competition and won, literally, a sackful of gold and silver medals, 30 to be exact, in the following cities: Toronto, Christchurch, Helsinki, Gothenburg, Hanover and Viareggio. By the way, the great Sonia O'Sullivan is not Ireland's only female world record holder. According to *National Masters News* (USA) of January 1996, Maeve Kyle holds world best times for 100m in the 40-45 (12 seconds flat) and 45-50 (12.5) age groups.

Not content with her competitive achievements, Maeve has served in the administration of athletics since 1959, as committee member, secretary, chairman, and current president of the Joint Federation. She has been a British Amateur Athletics Board (BAAB) member for over 20 years. She is also a Britain team manager and selector.

Sean and Maeve Kyle are qualified coaches and have trained scores of record-breakers at the Ballymena club, where every athlete is welcome. They are indeed a husband and wife team who have unselfishly dedicated their lives to Irish and British athletics.

Maeve admits to a certain personal pride and satisfaction at the modern achievements of Sonia, Catherina, Sinéad, Susan, and their likes – she knows that the courage and effort of the pioneers of the fifties and sixties, herself included, prepared the way for today's stars.

Maeve has, by the way, kindly endorsed this publication, which she describes as 'a unique record of the development and progress of Irish women athletes and a fitting tribute to those who strove, often in the face of apathy and prejudice, to pursue and perfect the sport they loved and believed in'.

She offers a further testimonial, which I am delighted to reproduce:

'As you read this fascinating history, with its record of courage, tenacity, success, failure, and shining talent, be thankful that the author, himself a former outstanding athlete and coach, had the patience and enthusiasm to explore and trace the path from the early days of local trial and tribulation to the modern international glories of Irish women athletes.'

The AAA Indoor Championships, Wembley Stadium, 1962 - Maeve Kyle leads on the final lap on her way to a world's best for 400m

Ann O'Brien (Cummins)

When 20-year-old Ann O'Brien arrived home after work one evening in November 1963, her mother welcomed her with a piece of news: 'Billy Morton of Clonliffe Harriers is starting a women's section. If you go down to Moran's Hotel next Friday night, they'll tell you all about it.'

That was how Ann was introduced to athletics. She was among the first recruits to the new female section of Ireland's oldest running club. She was to bring great honour to that club during the next decade.

Ann was coming to the sport of athletics as a late starter. Very few schools at that time taught physical education, and successive governments had generally shown little interest in the athletic development of the youth of Ireland.

Ann herself sums up the situation: 'There was nothing in the schools at that time and we had no Community Games or BLOE, which came much later to nurture and prepare aspiring young athletes. Nowadays, athletes have a much better chance to improve themselves and to avail of scholarships at home or in the United States of America, where many of our athletes have furthered their careers both athletically and academically.'

Ann continues: 'In the early days there was little recognition from men for the women athletes. Male club members from both the AAUE and BLE showed a lack of interest. At track meetings in Santry the one or two races for women were relegated to the end of the programme, by which time most of the spectators had departed to the pub! It was not until 1968 that the attitude toward women was changing – officials were beginning to show an interest and more women's sections were cropping up.'

Despite all the discouragement, Ann says, she 'never doubted that it would happen eventually and that women athletes would be accepted'.

There was no real background of track and field athletics in the O'Brien family. Christy, Ann's father, had been an international boxer. Her mother was an inter-county camogie player. Noel, Ann's eldest brother, played Gaelic football with the Dublin minors and did become a fine distance runner with Metropolitan Harriers. But it was the four O'Brien sisters, Ann, Nuala, Ursula, and Antoinette, who created all the athletics interest around the Finglas area.

All four worked in Addis at Finglas and represented the firm in the annual Business Houses Cross County Championships. They made a great squad – Addis took the team title five years on the trot!

Nuala would be named as a reserve on international teams, but it was Ann who had the major international career added to many domestic successes on track, road, and country.

Ann did most of her early training with her sisters and spent many weekends in Ballymena, where the home of Maeve and Sean Kyle offered a welcome to all aspiring athletes.

Maeve and Sean were founders, with Corkman Fergus O'Donovan, of The Bears Club at Gormanston College (1964). Hundreds of athletes, male and female, have spent valuable coaching weekends there and benefited from the advice of leading Irish and British coaches.

One such coach was Londoner Colin Young, who was also an international walker. Colin offered to help Ann, and from then on his monthly training schedules were eagerly received in Finglas. I commenced training with Ann at that time, and we dutifully adhered to Colin's guidelines.

Ann's dedication (40 miles per week) was considered by some a trifle excessive. But it paid off when she started winning Irish titles. She won her first AAUE mile in 1966 and from then until 1970 continued her winning of 880 and mile titles.

Possibly the most satisfactory of those doubles was in 1968. Ann had broken the magic five minutes for the mile a few times in training. She entered the National Championships in confident mood and surprised her two great rivals, the Crusaders pair Peggy Hogan and Hazel Tennison, in both mile and 880, officially breaking five minutes for the first time. This was a milestone (no pun intended) in Irish athletics. Unfortunately, the media hardly noticed it. Incidentally, the English international Diane Leather had received banner headlines in the British press a few years previously for a similar breakthrough.

Ann was the first BLE woman to win a gold medal in the British women's AAA Championships. She took the 3,000m in 1970, retained the title in 1971, and also took 1,500m silver in 1971.

Ann won the National Cross Country title every year from 1968 to 1971 and wore Irish vests in nine International (World) CC Championships, a record at the time.

Like all internationals at that time, she paid her own expenses when competing abroad. Travelling team managers were unheard of in those early days. Selected for the European Games in Athens, Ann had to find £200 to make the trip.

We in Clonliffe arrived at a novel idea to raise the necessary funds: the first ever sponsored run – 82 miles from the GPO, Dublin, to The Anchor Hotel on the banks of the Shannon in Lanesborough, Co. Longford. One man, Noel Henry, versus 12 women from Clonliffe Harriers running in relay.

Leaving Dublin at 9am we all arrived to a bonfire welcome in Lanesborough twelve hours later and £600 richer – tired but extremely happy and satisfied. After deduction of all expenses, I was able to send Ann's monies to BLE. I still have the receipt from The Anchor Hotel – B & B for 12 women at 10/6 (55p) each. That was 1968 – the good old days.

Ann has many happy memories to look back on: outstanding match races against two of the world's best – a mile at Santry against Doris Browne of the USA and a 3,000m in Formia, Italy, against Paulo Pigni. In each race Ann had to give best to her world-class rivals.

Another race Ann recalls was the 3,000m British Championship at Manchester 1970. Ann's running gear was mislaid on the flight from Dublin. She was lined up, prepared to race in bare feet, jeans, and T-shirt, when an announcement came over the loudspeaker – a harassed airline official had turned up with the precious spikes, shorts, and vest.

The start was delayed to allow Ann change. Undeterred, Ann ran a great race, set a new British all-comers' record, and left one of England's foremost runners, Madeleine Ibbotson, some 20 yards behind. The course commentator was understandably impressed and described the Irish girl as 'real gutsy'. It was a good description of a very brave little lady.

Ann has great admiration for Mary Purcell, who took over as Ann's career was coming to an end. She especially likes Mary for her forthrightness: 'She does not go behind the door about anything and just speaks out.'

Unfortunately, Ann's own honesty brought disappointment on at least two occasions, when her criticism of BLE got Press coverage and resulted in unfair international team selection.

When BLE refused to host the Home Countries International in Dublin, Ann's (and my own) critical remarks were highlighted in the British *Athletics Weekly*. Again, in 1974, Ann openly and rightly criticised poor BLE management at the International CC in Monza, Italy. Following a newspaper report, Ann was omitted from the Irish team. In any event, the Irish were well beaten. Two weeks later, Ann answered the selectors by winning the Eastern Regions CC Championships, leaving most of the Irish team behind her.

Ann now admits that that injustice was what caused her to give up athletics. She expresses her delight at the progress in women's athletics in the meantime, and is thrilled to see Sonia O'Sullivan and Catherina McKiernan competing with the world's elite.

Ann O'Brien has left her own special mark on Irish athletics. With 18 national titles, one at 440yds, five at 800yds/800m, seven at 1,500m/mile, four at cross-country, and one at high jump, she so dominated women's running in the early years of BLE that defeat for her was almost unthinkable. She ran with tremendous grit and determination and, had the road boom come a few years earlier, might well have achieved a great marathon time.

All through her career she showed exceptional strength of character, coping along the way with her brother's death in the boxing ring. Gerard, having only his second amateur bout, took a knockout punch from which he never recovered. Coming from a close-knit family, she often had to look after older or ailing relatives. At such times her running tended to take a back seat.

Ann came out of 'retirement' to run in the 1981 Dublin City Marathon with her 'old' training partner and friend Noel Henry and coasted to an easy 3.30.

Now in the early fifties, Ann lives with her husband, Stan, and son, Gerard (21), a promising Gaelic footballer.

Ann O' Brien with Kip Keino of Kenya, and the author, Noel Henry, at Santry Stadium in 1968

Claire Dowling (Walsh)

Claire Dowling and Ann O'Brien (Cummins) both joined Clonliffe Harriers in 1963. Though both late starters, in their early twenties, this duo would be Ireland's foremost pioneers in women's athletics.

Claire, already very fit from horseriding and show-jumping, immediately made her presence felt by winning Clonliffe Harriers' first race for women, 600 yards down Santry Avenue.

Hugh Cooney and Noel O'Rourke were generous with their time and supervised training twice a week. Claire won her first AAUE title in 1964 – the pentathlon. The same year she won the first of her many Irish singlets, when she competed in Ayr, Scotland. Two weeks later Ireland created history by winning a triangular international v Scotland and Belgium. Claire helped by winning the 200m

Training in those days was not nearly as demanding as nowadays, but good results came from hard sessions indoors, even though the methods and equipment were makeshift. A women's changing room was built under the stand – the luxury of hot showers would come later. No training was permitted on Billy Morton's beloved cinder track during the winter months. All races were across country or on the roads.

Claire won numerous AAUE titles at 100m, 200m, 400m, long jump, and pentathlon in the 1964/1974 era. In December 1970 she made her debut indoors; the race was an 800m in Berlin; the experienced German Hildegarde Falck was in the field. Claire surprised herself and the crowd by winning in 2.10.9.

In the AAA 800m she took silver, defeating the British Olympian Lillian Board. Tragically, that was to be Lillian's last race – she died of cancer the following year.
Claire was selected for the European Championships in Helsinki, where she easily qualified for the 800m semifinal by running up in her heat in 2.06.01. In the semifinal, she again ran smart, posted a brilliant 2.03, and became the first Irishwoman to contest a European final.

In the final, Claire was well positioned at the bell, reached in 58.04. But Gunhild Hoffmeister and Hildegarde Falck, the race favourites, tripped each other and fell in front of Claire, who had to check and sidestep the fallen bodies. Vera Nikolic of Yugoslavia took advantage of the pile-up and sprinted to victory in two minutes even. The two Englishwomen Patricia Lowe and Rosemary Stirling took silver and bronze. Claire never made up the 20 metres she had lost and finished eighth in 2.08.06. While disappointed at the result, she was elated at having reached the final.

Claire and family were now living in Collooney, Co. Sligo, where her husband, Brian, was an accountant with Shannon GWI. She was training in isolation, without the company of other athletes, and doing her speedwork on the road near her home. Some preparation for the 1972 Olympics! Sometimes she travelled to Claremorris, Co. Mayo, to use the track there.

To compound Claire's problems, she had some illness prior to Munich. Not surprisingly, she failed to do herself justice at the Games and was eliminated in the 800m first round (2.08.98).

What should have been a great Olympics for Claire was further ruined by the massacre of 11 members of the Israeli team. Palestinian terrorists broke into the Israeli quarters in the village, murdering two athletes and taking nine others hostage. As the world watched its TV screens in horror, 15 hours of negotiations failed to satisfy the Palestinians. Eventually, a helicopter took terrorists and hostages to the airport – where things went drastically wrong. German sharpshooters opened fire, and in the ensuing melee all nine of the hostages died when a hand grenade exploded. Two of the terrorists and one policeman also died. After a 24-hour suspension and a memorial service in the main stadium, the Games resumed – the Israelis wanted it that way.

Claire competed in the Rome European Games in 1974 and ran a 54-second quarter but failed to qualify. She continued to compete internationally, in European Cups, for example, while gradually winding down an athletics career on which she can now look back with immense pride. Her 400m Irish record was eventually wiped from the books by Caroline O'Shea before being improved on by a certain Patricia Walsh (now Ó Cléirigh), who just happens to be Claire's daughter. Patricia's time of 53.06, posted 6 Aug 1987 in Santry, is still intact at the time of writing.

Mary Tracey (Purcell)

Mary Tracey was born in Dublin into a family of six boys and five girls. At school she played interprovincial hockey. One summer while holidaying in Curracloe, Co. Wexford, she joined the lads for a soccer game; among the players was one Peter Purcell, who was then coaching Guinness Athletic Club. Peter was deeply impressed with the young lady – especially her penchant for speedy dashes up the wing. Sure that he had discovered a future star, he immediately urged her to take up running.

Mary declined the invitation to take up running, but she and Peter started dating. 'Peter was always late for our dates,' says Mary. 'His excuse was that he got held up in training. So one night I decided to go up to Guinness's and see just what this training amounted to. My first run was up the road in the Phoenix Park.' This was in 1970.

In her first track season Mary clocked 25.5 for 200m, 56.5 for 400m, and 2.09.6 for

800m. She was already being spoken about as our most promising ever runner, and it was no surprise to followers of athletics when, on a bleak June evening in 1972, the Guinness girl clocked 2.04.2 for 800m, which qualified her for the Munich Olympic Games. A pathetically small attendance at Santry had seen a new running legend emerge.

Before commencing her final preparation for Munich, Mary took the British AAA 800m title in 2.03. Then Mary and Peter headed off for six weeks of Olympic preparation under the blue skies of St Moritz.

'This was financed by monies from various sources,' says Mary. 'I was working in Leo Laboratories. Everybody there was marvellous. They each paid in tenpence per week for so many weeks, and that helped a lot. Peter paid his way out of his own pocket.'

Mary's training in St Moritz was tremendous – or so it seemed. 'Many of the English squad were also in St Moritz. They were amazed at the type of training I was doing. Many of them felt I was certain to win a medal in Munich.' Unfortunately, it didn't work out that way.

'When I went to the Olympics I felt completely lethargic. I have always run well after altitude training, but it was wrong for Munich. I ran 2.04.18 for fourth in the 800m heat and felt terribly sick after it. I didn't feel like going out at all for the 1,500m, but Peter advised me to just go around. I ran 4.16.4 and failed to qualify.'

Between Munich 72 and Montreal 76, Mary Purcell took seven national titles and was never beaten by another Irishwoman. She successfully defended her British 800m title in 1973 and looked poised to do so again in 1974 but stumbled on the last bend and lost out to Leslie Kiernan.

Mary made many forays abroad and scored many international triumphs. These included the South African de Beers Open 800m of 1973 (2.05.2), the 1973 Europa Cup 800m (2.02.9), the 1,500m (4.18) at the Golden Spike Meet in Ostrava, Czechoslovakia, in 1974, and the 1,500m at the Sparta Games in the Hague in 1975. Along the way she outran such major stars as the Russian Braghina and Glenda Reiser.

By the time the 1976 Montreal Olympics arrived, Mary Purcell was an international athlete of high repute. But again she suffered Olympic disappointment – and blames her own 'lack of adventure' for her failure to reach the semifinals of the 1,500m.

'Our heat was slow-run and I should have gone 300 metres out, but I waited with the bunch until the final straight and got outrun by the first four.' She finished fifth in 4.08.63 and was eliminated.

After Montreal Mary went into temporary retirement to have her first child. Kara was born in May 1977.

In 1978 Mary was back to domestic invincibility. She won the National 1,500m for the sixth time and set an Irish record 8.58.4 for 3,000m in Oslo. But she was suffering from a virus at the European Championships in Prague and could not do herself justice.

Of all Mary's record-breaking exploits around this time, the one that attracted most publicity was her run in a certain race at Belfield. Having decided to concentrate on the 3,000m, she reckoned she needed sterner competition than what her female contemporaries could offer – she resolved to run the first 3,000 metres of the men's 5,000m.

The BLE officials were outraged and probably scandalised. They forbade her to run.

Mary defied them – and set off with the lads.

Thus affronted, the officials resolved to show their authority; they instructed the announcer to make no mention of her during the race. Undaunted by this piece of censorship, Mary posted a brilliant time of 8.51.4. It was never ratified as a record.

Mary's next target was Limerick and the World CC Championships, which she hoped to contest for the first time. She prepared for it with an outstanding display on the American and Canadian indoor circuits. Of the eight mile races she contested she scored four wins, two seconds, and two thirds. Her victories included a win in the prestigious Maple Leaf Games.

The omens were good for Limerick, but Mary's dream of a medal was again shattered, though she ran an absolute blinder in the mud to post sixth and be first Irish finisher.

Mary's courage on Limerick Racecourse was somewhat eclipsed by a certain John Treacy, who retained the world title he had won in Scotland. The same John would go on to thrill us all with Olympic Marathon silver in Los Angeles 1984.

Mary took third in the European Indoor 1,500m in 4.14 and in 1980 had more success on the Canadian indoor circuit before arriving home to take the BLE CC title, which she had last won in 1973. She beat all the leading women of the day in that race in the Phoenix Park, including Carol Meagan, Deirdre Nagle, Fionnuala Morrish, Siobhán Treacy, Vera Duffy, Carey May, Jean Whiston, and Jean's sister Patricia Appleby.

After good 1,500m wins in the Cork City Sports and the National Championships (4.14.4) at Belfield, Mary refused to go to the Moscow Olympics on conscientious grounds. Again she went into retirement, this time to have her second child. Jan was born in 1981.

In 1982 Mary turned her sights on the marathon and clocked a splendid 2.38.49 when winning the BLE title. Her time was less than two minutes outside Carey May's Irish record.

Later that year, in the Dublin City Marathon, Mary looked on target at 20 miles to break that record – then things started to fall apart. Debbie Mueller of the USA passed Mary and went on to win in 2.40.58. A shattered Mary eventually slipped back to sixth.

Ever the great fighter, Mary was back the following October for another encounter with the Dublin City Marathon. Always with the leading group, she ran strongly until the 21-mile mark but then began to tie up. The finish was nail-biting. Spurred on by her Dublin supporters, she dug deep and managed to hold off the great challenge of England's Julia Gates. She reached the sanctuary of St Stephen's Green and the tape in 2.46.09.

In an article in *Irish Runner* in August 1986 Olympian Dick Hooper acknowledged Mary Purcell as Ireland's most famous female runner:

She burst onto the scene with her 2.04.2 800m in 1972 and with her penchant for breaking records and notching up titles dominated Irish distance running for the next decade.

It is fair to say that if you asked the average athletics fan to name the only woman to have won the Perfect Five national championships – 800m, 1,500m, 3,000m, cross country, and marathon – most people, without pausing to give it much thought, would nominate Mary.

They would be wrong. For somehow, somewhere along the line, Mary omitted to win the 3,000m. This despite the fact that she was national record-holder and a pioneer over the distance.

To a certain Deirdre Nagle goes the title of Ms Versatility: The DCH and previously Guinness stalwart has during a magnificent career annexed all five of the above mentioned events. Her magical haul consists of 800m in 1979, 1,500m in 1981, 3,000m in 1980 and 1981, mid-seventies trio of CC titles, and a somewhat controversial marathon in 1984 (of course, the singlet she wore that day in Cork has now gone out of style).

Besides having won eight national titles, Deirdre is also by far the most experienced Irishwoman in the World CC Championships, having won selection on 13 occasions. It's enough to drive any husband into officialdom.

Deirdre's and Mary's careers have always been closely entwined. They started out as club-mates with the now defunct Guinness AC; both married their coaches; both have been friends and rivals for a long time.

Mary's national titles total eleven: a single 800m, a single marathon, two cross-countries, and seven 1,500s, five of them consecutive (1972-1976). By the way, Mary's streak of five in the blue riband followed hard on a similar feat (1967-1971) by the great Ann O'Brien-Cummins. So it took until 1977 and the 11th running of the event for a third name, Jean Appleby, to be added to the illustrious list.

Deirdre Foreman (Nagle)

Deirdre Foreman has been part of the athletics scene for almost 30 years, has won honours at events varying from 800m to marathon, and has proudly worn the Irish singlet on numerous occasions on road, track, and country.

Commencing athletics in 1968 at the age of 18, Deirdre made the first of many appearances in the International (World) CC championships, in the USA, in 1969. In 1971 she ended Ann O'Brien's great reign, when she won the 1,500m title in a record time at Guinness Sports. The lead changed four times during this race, Deirdre just holding off her Clonliffe rival at the finish.

In 1974, the year she married Dermot Nagle, Deirdre won the National Intercounties CC, the National Interclubs CC, and the British Women's CC.

In 1980 she ended Mary Purcell's eight-year run unbeaten against Irishwomen on home tracks. The following year she combined with Carol Meagan, Fionnuala Morrish, and Carey May to win the Home Countries CC Championships.

Her debut marathon was Dublin City 1981, where she recorded 2.49.40 and finished second to her DCH clubmate Emily Dowling. She repeated that second placing in Dublin 82, this time giving best to Debbie Mueller of the USA. Deirdre's consolation was a PB 2.42.08.

Deirdre and Jerry Kiernan won the National Marathon in Cork 1984 but were stripped of their titles over a trivial issue concerning logos on club singlets. Runner-up Dick Hooper was presented with the men's trophy – which he promptly handed to Jerry to loud applause from the assembled athletes. There was no national trophy for the women's victor, but adidas, who sponsored the event, presented trophies to Deirdre and Jerry.

In 1983 Deirdre ran her best ever marathon, recording 2.37.05 in London. This time places her sixth in the Irish rankings, headed by Catherina McKiernan (2.23.44) and Carey May (2.28.07).

Continuing to impress on road and country, Deirdre was a member of the Dublin City Harriers team that made history by taking the European Clubs CC Championships in 1985 and 1986. She also shared in many of the 17 consecutive Interclub CC titles won by DCH.

Now retired from top-class competition, Deirdre still enjoys her runs in Dublin's Phoenix Park and has taken to orienteering. This fit lady in her late forties has played a huge part in athletics, as has her father, Brendan Foreman, and her husband, Dermot, both former athletes and holders of various BLE offices.

The Nagle family have two teenage sons, Lorcan and Damien, and live in Blackhorse Avenue, conveniently near their beloved Phoenix Park.

Emily Hopkins (Dowling)

Emily Hopkins ran her first race at 15 years of age. By 17 she had represented Ireland at the Home Countries International in Barry, Wales. The daughter of veteran Donore Harrier Tom Hopkins, the precocious Emily was propelled straight into senior level – because the schools at that time did not encourage young girls to take part in athletics. Emily's brother, Tom Hopkins, was also an international runner.

After the 1967 Cross Country International, the host country presented each competitor with a small gold plaque. Ten years later at Chepstow, Emily and a Scottish runner were presented with a special plaque as the only two women to have represented their countries on both occasions. Having worn Irish vests at three world championships and many more Home Countries internationals, Emily says she seems not to win races but 'always to figure in the placings'. Emily was attached to several Dublin clubs – Avondale, Guinness, Donore.

The Frank Duffy Memorial 10 Miles, run in Dublin's Phoenix Park, set an Irish precedent for the admission of women into a distance event. It was one of Emily's favourite races. She won it in 1978 and 1979 in 62 minutes and in 1981 set a record of 57 minutes when preparing for the Dublin City Marathon that October.

Having run her first marathon the previous year with a viral illness – and suffered the shattering experience of having to drop out at 17 miles – Emily was not going to make the same mistake again.

Advised by her husband, Mick Dowling (a former Olympic boxer), and by Donore's Dr Terry Maguire, Emily was convinced she could run a good marathon. She trained diligently; on long runs, she accompanied her male clubmates.

On the big day, everything went to plan. Running at even pace, she covered the first five miles in 32 minutes, the next five in 31, and the next ten in 62. Despite slowing over the last six miles, she had more than a minute to spare over Deirdre Nagle at the finish. Her time was 2.48.22.

Thirty years on from her first footrace, Emily is still competing. Her daughter Lisa is also a fine athlete and in recent years has competed alongside and against Emily in national championships.

Michele Walsh (Carroll)

Michele Carroll was not called the Queen of Irish sprinting without good reason; she is one of our finest sprinters of all time. She successfully represented Ireland on many occasions abroad and won a record 31 national titles in the 19 years 1977 to 1995, including her most recent hat trick of 100m, 200m, and 800m. The main domestic opposition to her was in the early 1980s, when the talented Amond sisters from Carlow, Patricia and Mary, shared some of the sprint titles.

Michele's introduction to athletics came through the Community Games, where she won silver in the Co. Dublin finals. At 16 years of age she created a sensation by breaking 12 seconds for 100m with a national record 11.8.

One of Michele's greatest disappointments was missing out on the Moscow Olympics, despite having run the qualifying time. These games were preceded and surrounded by political controversy, and the Irish Government wanted them boycotted. Mary Purcell was selected at middle distance but declined for personal reasons. Michele was put on standby but was never called.

Michele took up an athletics scholarship at the University of Arizona, in Tucson, and became a key member of their relay team. Every summer she travelled home to add to her collection of national titles. Meanwhile, she was also excelling academically – and graduated with a degree in Graphic Design in 1985. For the next year she concentrated on her new career, working in an advertising agency in Tucson, and did a minimum of training.

During this time Michele maintained contact with Ronnie Carroll, an international colleague and fellow Dub who had graduated from Arkansas University and then moved on to Texas University as assistant coach. Ronnie and Michele married in 1987. Two years later they settled back in Ireland and established their own graphic design business, RMC Design.

A serious leg injury forced Ronnie, a former National CC champion, to retire from competitive athletics. Their first child, Eoin, was born in 1991, and a second boy, Ruairi, arrived in 1994. A little girl, Cliona, arrived in December 1996.

Notwithstanding these extra responsibilities, Michele continued winning national championships until 1995, when following her hat-trick of titles, she decided, at age 34, to retire from competitive running.

Michele was and is a delightfully cheerful and unassuming character who can look back on her wonderful career with immense pride.

Patricia Quinn (Griffin)

Patricia Quinn (born 5 Mar 1955) got her introduction to athletics nearly 30 years ago at a race in her local Ballinamore, Co. Leitrim. Coming from a sporty family (her late father was involved in athletics and Gaelic football, and her sisters and brothers were all athletes – Mickey was Leitrim's first All Star), Patricia was soon to make a name for herself, especially at schools level, where she gained international selection.

She joined the newly formed local club, set up by Mayoman Pádraig Griffin. Pádraig had come to teach in Ballinamore and discovered there was an abundance of athletic talent in the area. A supremo of athletics at national level, the founder/editor in 1963 of *Marathon* magazine, with a dynamic and passionate personality, he had a rousing effect on club members. And so when Patricia Quinn joined Ballinamore AC she met a human dynamo on a one-man crusade for the betterment of Irish athletics.

During the late sixties and early seventies athletes from Ballinamore made an indelible impression. The Leddy brothers, P.J. and Eddie, were to the forefront of distance running; Patricia was also making a name for herself. Her career at national level really took off when she won silver for the exacting pentathlon event.

With her schooldays over, Patricia set out for Dublin and a job with Irish Permanent Building Society. Most of her training was now coached and motivated by Tommy Coyle of Raheny Shamrocks. Regular runs up the Hill of Howth laid the foundation for future success on track, road, and country. Patricia had not, however, lost touch with her first coach. In fact their relationship blossomed; they were married after Patricia moved back to Ballinamore in 1978.

In 1981 Patricia was on the team that won the Home Countries International CC. There followed a couple of non-competitive years, which wasn't surprising – sons Coilín and Ronán were born in 1982 and 1983.

Patricia has been winning titles for over 25 years and has represented Ireland about 30 times in almost as many countries. She has competed in every distance from 100m to marathon. Her biggest win in terms of profile was perhaps that in the Evening Press Women's Mini Marathon of 1988 – when she led home a world record 16,000 women. Her time for the ten kilometres was a PB 33.57. A few months after that victory she was named Best Home Based Athlete of 1988. She retained her Mini Marathon title in 1989 (34.28).

Patricia has pleasant memories of her many trips abroad with the late Ursula Noctor.

She was very close to Ursula when Ursula's illness was diagnosed in 1991; the pair travelled to, and roomed together at, the Ekiden Relays. They also ran the Chicago Marathon the same year. Patricia posted 2.42.28 for seventh; Ursula finished fourth. Despite her illness Ursula travelled to Ballinamore in 1992 to win the BLE Half Marathon. Patricia says of Ursula, 'She was a great example to all of us and bore her illness with such courage and dignity.'

The Griffin boys, Coilín (born 3 Aug 1982) and Ronán (born 30 Nov 1983), are following in their mother's footsteps – both are BLOE national champions. The two girls are Níamh (born 15 Oct 1992)) and Gráinne (born 27 Aug 1996).

Coach/husband Pádraig has spent over 30 years in athletics administration, including a spell as BLE President; he has also written and published an important study of the politics of Irish athletics.

Louise McGrillen

Louise McGrillen was a late starter in athletics, but made an immediate impact when, after four years studying in Maynooth College, she was spotted by the Donore coach Tony Farrell, who saw her potential and offered to take her under his wing.

Tony was noted for his hard schedules, including long runs, sprints, and lifting 8cwt sacks of flour in O'Leary's Bakery! Louise responded well – and gained her first Irish vest in the 1981 Home Countries CC at Mallusk, where Ireland won the team event for the first time. On track, she gained a vest for the triangular international in Skopje v Yugoslavia and Greece.

Louise posted a great win in the National CC in 1983, leaving a string of the leading women behind and qualifying for the World CC in New York, where the Irish team ran superbly to finish fourth. Regina Joyce posted 21st, Roisin Smyth 22nd, Monica Joyce 26th, and Louise 36th.

Come the track season, and Louise was in great form. She clocked 9.13 for 3,000m in Wales and thereby qualified for the European Championships in Athens.

The event was held as a straight final and was fiercely contested. Louise appeared to be in contention until an injection of pace with 800m to go put her out of the reckoning.

In 1984 Louise was determined to make the Olympic team for Los Angeles. At Kilmacow, however, she relinquished her national CC crown after a titanic battle with Derry's Roisin Smyth.

A super-confident Roisin (21) again beat Louise in a 1,500m on the grass of Trinity College. But Louise bounced back to win the BLE 3,000m. Better still, she posted an Olympic qualifier – nine minutes even.

The decisive clash came in the Cork City Sports 3,000m, in June. Louise never got to grips with the race and had to give best to the Looby sisters and Kay Carter, whom she had more than matched over the country. She eventually slipped to fifth place. Roisin Smyth won in a fine 8.57.94 – well inside the qualifying time for Los Angeles.

Louise had dominated middle-distance running for much of the previous season and was bitterly disappointed at not being selected for the Olympics. But she did the next best thing to competing: accompanied by her husband, John, she set off to cover the Games as athletics correspondent for *The Irish Press* newspaper and *Irish Runner* magazine.

The following year, Louise regained form and won the Dublin CC, the National Intercounties CC, and the National Interclubs CC titles. It was the first time this treble had been achieved. She also led DCH to their marvellous European Clubs Cross Country medals – silver in 1983 and 1984 and gold in 1985 and 1986.

Louise has two marathons to her credit: Berlin 1989 (2.58) and Dublin 1991 (2.56).

In the late eighties Louise suffered a number of injuries. These, and probably the conspicuous lack of encouragement from BLE, ended her career. She did make a few comebacks but failed to reignite the spark of earlier years.

The highlights of her career were her involvement with her club's European successes and her wins in the De Loughrey Cup down the Main Road of the Phoenix Park. Her 1984 record, 13 seconds below the previous mark, was special.

Louise was associated with the Evening Press Women's Mini Marathon for 12 years, until the *Press* closed down, and reckons the event contributed hugely to the real liberation of Irishwomen in the past 20 years.

Running is still an integral part of her life; she jogs recreationally all year round.

Carey May (Edge)

Carey May first came to prominence at orienteering. She turned to mainstream athletics in 1978, winning the Eastern Regions 110m hurdles and also showing great promise as a long jumper.

In the early eighties she took to cross-country and narrowly failed to win a place on the Irish team. After this disappointment, she was advised by the late Jim Dowling to have a run in the Ulster Marathon in Letterkenny, Co. Donegal, on 21 August 1980. The race was to change her career.

Using her orienteering experience, she reeled off consistent 6.30 miles on a hilly course and created marathoning history by becoming the first Irishwoman to break the magic three-hour barrier, with a time of 2.53. It was a glorious follow-on to the pioneering efforts of Jean Folan, Bridget Cushen, and Mary Butler.

Two months later, with some excellent advice from Donore's great coach Eddie

Hogan and some steady mileage and fartlek training, Carey found herself installed as favourite for the first Dublin City Marathon. It was her first experience of a large marathon; she found it exhilarating and emotional. The warm support of the spectators and the generous encouragement of other runners lifted her – and she breasted the tape in a fine time of 2.42.11, first woman, 50th overall, and 11 minutes faster than her debut at Letterkenny. The race made Carey's mind up: she had been bitten by the bug – and was now committed to run marathons worldwide.

BLE's first official marathon championship for women was held at Cork in June 1981. In appalling weather – cold winds and heavy rain – Carey ran most of the race on her own and became the first national champion at the classic distance. Her overriding memory of the event, which attracted only a small field, is the desire to reach the finish line. Nevertheless, her time of 2.42 qualified her for the Avon All-Women's Marathon in Ottawa.

Carey prepared well for Ottawa, with plenty of mileage and a few track races. Unfortunately, she suffered a stomach upset and struggled to finish a disappointed 16th in 2.49. It was a hard lesson.

Carey now accepted an athletics scholarship from Brigham Young University, Utah, where the coach was Patrick Shane. Following a successful cross-country season, during which she finished second in the National Collegiates, Shane changed Carey's training schedule with the upcoming Fiesta Bowl Marathon in view. Carey rewarded his tutelage by winning in 2.36, her fastest time to date.

Carey's next marathon was the Avon, this time, in San Francisco. The gun fired at 7am, but already it was sunny and warm. Carey and Lorraine Moller of New Zealand were always with the leading group. Lorraine forged ahead in the final few miles to win in 2.36.12. Carey, looking fresh, held off Laurie Binder for second place in 2.37.31.

Next came the European Championships in August 1982 at Athens. In the birthplace of the classic distance, Carey had the disastrous experience of missing her bottles at several water stations. She then made the mistake of accepting drinks from others – and suffered the consequences. With the heat and humidity, it was all she could do to finish in one of her slowest times. She returned to College in Utah and another successful cross-country season.

An invitation to compete in the famous Japanese all-women marathon in Osaka in January 1983 concentrated coach Shane's mind. He prepared a special schedule combining speedwork and distance. To prepare for the time difference, Carey went to bed early and rose to train at 4am. A last week of easy running and the plan was to go out and stay with the leading group.

Carey was determined to put the Athens disaster behind her. She became confident that she could beat Regina Joyce's Irish best of 2.32 and actually go under 2.30.

Marathon running enjoys a high profile in Japan. In Osaka, over a quarter of a million spectators lined the route. Race day, Sunday, dawned cool and breezy; the forecast was for a few showers. I will let Carey herself take up the story:

We got to the stadium at 10.15am and chatted with the other runners until it came to warmup time. It was then I discovered that we had to warm up on the track in front of

25,000 people! However, the Japanese crowd were marvellous – I cannot think of anywhere where the people admire women's athletics so much.

The first mile was run on the track. The pace was ideal for Charlotte Taske and I, who had earlier agreed to run a steady pace together. Also in our group were Joyce Smith (England), Rita Marchisio (the previous year's winner) and Akem Masuda.

By the 10k mark Charlotte and I were clear of the group and gradually increasing the gap. At 14k I sensed she was beginning to struggle, and I was still feeling strong. I decided to break away. It felt a little strange being out there alone. I had never envisaged being in such a position, although Coach Shane had told me I could win again and I was in form to go under 2.30.

The time car ahead showed 57 minutes for ten miles and 1.54 for 20. I knew then that I could beat my previous record. The support along the course was tremendous. People were three and four deep the whole way, with little children waving flags – it made you feel like running well just to please them.

The sun had become very warm, and the last six miles were just as tough as any other marathon. At this stage I was glad I had taken water at every station. I kept trying to force my pace, fearing somebody might creep up on me. With the support of the 25,000 crowd in the stadium I was able to sprint the last two laps on the track to reach the finish line in 2.29.23, a course record, a PB, and an Irish record.

I cannot really describe the way I felt. I had often thought about winning, but had never even dreamt about running that time. What made it all the more special was the way the other athletes were so pleased and full of congratulations. I'll never forget the look on Al Guy's (BLE official) face as he fought his way through the officials onto the track. I was sorry to hear Mary Purcell had problems and had to pull out of the race – she had trained hard, and it must have been very disappointing for her.

The race was given tremendous coverage, and the rest of the day was spent giving interviews and attending the closing ceremony.

Carey continued her marathon victories by winning Toronto 1983. At the end of 1983 she was ranked seventh in the world, third in Europe, and eighth in the all-time lists. Her many international wins were, however, scarcely rating a few lines in the Irish papers, and her Toronto wins of 1983 and 1984 slipped by with hardly a mention.

The inaugural women's Olympic marathon took place in Los Angeles in 1984. Regina Joyce finishing 23rd (2.37.57). Carey May came 28th (2.41.27). Both had suffered in the intense heat.

Carey spent November and December 1984 building up for her second visit to Osaka. She followed the same training pattern that had brought her success two years before. At Osaka Airport she and Julie Isphording of the USA were met with flowers and photographers. Then the race organisers ushered the marathon ladies to taxis, which brought them to their hotel. The excitement of the upcoming race was evident everywhere.

Again I let Carey describe the race:

As I had received a lot of media coverage before the race, I made up my mind that I was going to go out and give it everything. I was fit and could have no excuse whatever for having a bad run. I expected the main threats to come from Lisa Larsen, Carla Beurskens (both from Holland), Karolina Szabo of Hungary, and Rita Marchisio of Italy, all of them with 2.33 or better PBs. Lisa announced to everyone that she was going to win, which I think put too much pressure on her and contributed to her dropping out at 26k when running second.

I ran early on in the group behind Lisa, and we caught her by the 10k mark (35.10). By 11k I had dropped Gabriella Anderson and Laurie Crisp and was out on my own. I reached halfway in 1.13.31 and 20 miles in a fast 1.52.

For the last 7k I was running scared, praying that no-one would come up to me. It seemed to take an eternity to reach the track. I had visualised it so many times – coming into the stadium, hearing the crowds, and crossing the finish line. It was just like a dream come true. It's hard to describe the elation I felt – I had done it again!

My time was another course record, a PB, and an Irish record – 2.28.07. Carla Beurskens took second in 2.31.11. Rita Marchisio outkicked Szabo for third in 2.36.

The reception I got was incredible. Apparently there were 500,000 spectators on the course and some five million watching live on television.

The people of Osaka took Carey to their hearts; her victory was seen as a classic. Early in 1996 Osaka New Airport held their celebration marathon. Over 40 of the world's most famous athletes were invited, including Grete Waitz (Norway), winner of three World Marathons and seven New York Marathons. Carey May accompanied Lasse Viren in a gentle 26-miler.

In her brilliant career Carey ran 25 marathons and still holds two of the three best Irish times. Her national record 2.28.07 stood from 1985 until September 1997, when Catherina McKiernan clocked 2.23.44 in Berlin. In 1995 Carey ran two 'appearance' marathons: Seattle (2.53) and Los Angeles (2.45).

Carey is married to David Edge, a Commonwealth Marathon silver medallist. They live in Seattle with their twins, Nicholas and Brittany.

Carey wins Osaka 1983 in a P.B. and Irish record 2:29:23

Regina and Monica Joyce

The most talented sisters to represent Ireland on track, road, and country, Regina and Monica were born in Cawley, Sussex. Their father, Michael Joyce, from Westport, Co. Mayo, was a noted athlete before he emigrated to England.

Both girls showed early athletic promise. Regina at 14 set an age world best 4.36 for 1,500m; Monica finished fifth in the AAA (British) Championships. Both won titles at schools level and later accepted athletics scholarships to San Diego University, USA.

In 1978 they decided to avail of their dual nationality. Unfortunately, their application to BLE was delayed by a postal strike in Ireland, and Regina ran for England in the 1979 World CC Championships at Limerick. Despite Regina running the fastest 1,500m and 3,000m in Britain in 1981, the AAA refused to select her – they disapproved of American scholarships. Monica and Regina opted to run for Ireland, coming home to compete in major races.

The talented sisters certainly made their presence felt in the early eighties. Monica won Irish titles at 1,500m in 1982 (4.10.48) and 1983 (4.18.90); Regina won the 3,000m in the same years (9.03.83 and 9.13.15). They finished first and second in the 1983 AAA 5,000m, Monica taking the gold. That August, Regina achieved a unique treble: on a Saturday she won the Westport 10k; the next day she won the Mullingar Lakeland 15; later in the week she flew to the USA to win the Fiesta Bowl Marathon in a PB 2.32.56, an improvement on Carey May's Irish record.

It was around this time that Regina showed her incredible resilience – twice. Competing in a road race in Gasparilla, Florida, she was knocked down by a car and suffered a broken collarbone but got up and went on to win. Amazingly, a few weeks later, she was again knocked down by a speeding car, this time in the TAC 10k – again she recovered to win.

The women's marathon at the inaugural World Track and Field Championships, Helsinki1983, attracted huge interest. On a warm day, the kind marathoners dread, Regina Joyce threw down the gauntlet to the world's best, including Norway's Grete Waitz, Portugal's Rosa Mota, and England's Joyce Smith. After ten kilometres, the bold Regina was 100 metres clear of the field, a lead which she held until halfway.

When Grete Waitz eventually took over, it was obvious Regina could not stay the increased pace. But though she lost places over the last few miles, she gamely registered 2.33.52 and a proud seventh place – the greatest achievement by an Irishwoman in a championship marathon. Carey May, the other Irish competitor, struggled in the heat but gamely finished 13th.

March 1984 and the Meadowlands Arena, New Jersey, was the venue for the 12th World CC Championships. Ireland fared splendidly, finishing their scoring four in the first 36 places and thereby taking a noteworthy team fourth place. As expected, Regina was team leader (21st), followed by national champion Roisin Smyth (22nd). Monica Joyce placed 26th and Louise McGrillen 36th. The best ever result by an Irish cross-country team had been in 1970, when Clonliffe's Ann O'Brien led them to third overall.

Regina Joyce came to Dublin in June 1984 and was a very impressive winner of the Evening Press Mini Marathon. Taking the lead at halfway, she went on to record the fastest time ever for the great event: 32.34.88. Second was Carey May; third was Laura de Wald of the USA. Regina defended her title successfully in 1985 (33.33). This time the Frenchwoman Veronique Marot and the American Debbie Mueller filled the minor placings.

Los Angeles was the venùe for the 1984 Olympics – and the overall standard of the first women's Olympic marathon was exceptional. Norway's Grete Waitz was favourite. Joan Benoit (USA), Rosa Mota (Portugal), and Ingrid Christiansen (Norway) were also fancied. In the intense competition and the intense heat, Regina Joyce and Carey May found it difficult to produce their best and were disappointed with 23rd and 28th placings.

The World CC Championships were held at Lisbon on 24 March 1985. Again the Irish team finished an excellent fourth. Monica Joyce posted 12th, Louise McGrillen 40th, Anne Hilliard 59th, and Deirdre Nagle 78th. The non-selection of an in-form Regina Joyce for this event provoked anger among athletics followers, many of whom felt her inclusion would have placed Ireland among the medals.

Monica Joyce

Regina Joyce

Caroline O'Shea

Caroline O'Shea (born 13 Dec 1960) was ten years old when she joined Crusaders AC, and by 1976 she had registered 12.1 seconds for 100 and 24.2 for 200m. She won BLOE and Schools titles and two British Junior AAA titles. She won nine 400m National Senior titles and clocked 53.24 to erase Claire Dowling's national record. Subsequently, Claire's daughter Patricia set a mark of 53.06 which still stands.

Caroline raced over 800m for the first time when she won the Dublin Championships in 2.08. Then at Cork Sports in June 1984 two Russian women, Trina Podjalovskaya and Lubov Gourina, pulled Caroline through to a 2.07, a second inside the Olympic qualifying time. The following is Louise McGrillen's report in *Irish Runner* magazine of Caroline's Los Angeles heroics.

On the opening day of the 1984 Olympic Track and Field programme in Los Angeles and before a near capacity crowd of 88,000, Caroline had the presence of mind to compose herself, steer clear of trouble and get a free run home. From the gun, Caroline belied her inexperience at this event by staying well clear of trouble in lane two, and feeling comfortable with a 400m split of 59 seconds, she bided her time to the last bend and coasted up the home straight to finish second to Doina Melinte in a time of 2.03.6. As Caroline ran, the story-writers delivered a message to US athletes: 'USA going for gold', which cheered the crowd but failed to unnerve the athletes.

The semifinal next day was no easier, and Caroline came in for some rough treatment, but once again she breezed up the home straight to finish in fourth place and qualify for the final in a time of 2.02.7, thus becoming the first Irishwoman to make an Olympic track final.

This was by far the hardest semifinal and also a messy race. Caroline was tripped at the 200m mark when all eight runners bunched together for the pole spot. Coming up to the 400m mark, all eight were spread across the track, the intermediate time being 61 seconds, but Caroline had the presence of mind to compose herself, steer clear of trouble and get a free run home. As the pace increased down the back straight, Caroline responded instantly and clinched her final place in the last 80 metres. It was a fine race and an equally fine indication of untapped potential. After a very short spell at 800m running, Caroline had been jettisoned to world class level without having served an apprenticeship, and somehow she makes it all look so easy.

In the 800m final, held at 5.30 in the evening and 82 degrees fahrenheit, the pace was as hot as the weather. Gabriella Dorio of Italy led Doina Melinte at the bell (57.28), with Caroline seventh at 58.04 and looking strong. Going down the back straight Melinte made her move and pulled away with every stride in the final 50 metres to win from Kim Gallagher (USA) and Lovin. Caroline finished eighth in 2.00.77, just hundredths of a second outside her Irish record.

It was a marvellous performance, and what really counted was the effect on the TV audience back in Ireland. Caroline came home to a reception which would scarcely have been bettered had she won a medal.

Caroline finished the 1984 season by defeating Mary McKenna over 800m at the Dundrum Sports and besting her American rival Kim Gallagher in the Cork Sports 800m.

Caroline's first race of 1985 suggested she was returning to peak form: she beat Elly van Hulst of Holland in a fast 800m (2.01.1) at Reutlingen, West Germany. But tragedy struck only weeks later when at the Nice Grand Prix, France, she fell and broke her shoulder. That was to be her last race; in its aftermath, she developed serious achilles tendinitis, which caused her retirement in 1988.

During her brilliant career Caroline held Irish records for 800m (1984 to 1994) and 400m (1978 to 1987).

Caroline O'Shea, 1984 Olympian, caught by the lens of Ray McManus, Sportsfile. Titled 'The Change', this picture was Sports Photo of the Year 1984

Ursula Noctor

In 1980, Ursula Noctor decided she would tackle the first Dublin City Marathon. Insofar as 1,400 others were of like resolve, the Celtic AC runner was in good company. Ursula was, however, different from most – she was still only 14 years young. As it happened, the brave teenager was introduced to DCH coach Jim Kilty, who persuaded her to hold fire on the great event. Jim then took over as Ursula's mentor – and found himself coaching one of the country's finest athletes.

In her final year at school, Ursula figured prominently on both track and country. In her first senior race, the Jack Hartigan Memorial Cup in Naas, she defeated such experienced internationals as Emily Dowling and Ailish Smyth.

On track, Ursula served notice of her rich promise by winning the National Junior 1,500m in 4.29. And in a mile at Belfield, she was pipped by Monica Joyce; but Louise McGrillen and Siobhán Treacy were behind her.

In the Cork Mini-Marathon (10k) in 1983, Ursula broke clear of the field at halfway and won convincingly from her DCH clubmate Anne Hilliard and Castlepollard's Marese Cullen. She then won the inaugural BLE 5,000m track championship and set course records at the Enniskillen and Crumlin 10k races.

For many seasons Ursula was an ever present on the successful DCH teams that won so many National CC team titles (the club won 17 such titles consecutively from 1976 to 1992). She was also on the teams that won the European CC title in 1985 and 1986. She represented Ireland in the 1986 World 10k in Madrid and the same year won the Waterside Half Marathon and the Northern Ireland 3,000m title.

By 1990 Ursula was setting her sights on the full marathon distance. Her debut, at Columbus, USA, was impressive – third place in a time of 2.39.25. (She would run Columbus again in 1991 and post seventh.)

There followed Ursula's first bout of illness, after treatment for which she felt in good enough shape to travel to the Chicago Marathon and record a fine 2.41.20 for fourth place. Her teammate, Leitrim's Patricia Griffin, ran a PB 2.42.36 and finished seventh.

In January of 1992 Ursula won the Raheny Five in a record 26.42 (Connie Kelly's old mark had been 27.18). February saw Ursula winning the London Half Marathon in 75.32. She also reduced her 10k PB to 33 minutes. Her form was so good that she began to eye the Barcelona Olympics.

A recurrence of illness, however, put paid to those Olympic hopes. Nevertheless, the indomitable Ursula determined she would run another marathon. And so in Chicago, in October of 1992, she ran what would be her farewell marathon. She posted a remarkable 2.41.50 in fourth place.

Four months later, in February 1993, Ursula expressed the wish to visit the Divine Mercy Convent Shrine, outside the Polish town of Krakow. A former nun at this convent, a Sister Faustina, was later beatified. Ursula's father, Gerry, accompanied her on her last journey abroad.

Ursula Noctor died peacefully on 4 April 1993.

Two trophies commemorate this popular and courageous athlete. The first, commissioned by her club, Dublin City Harriers, is a unique bronze replica of the Phoenix Monument (not far from which Ursula lived). This trophy, made from threepenny pieces, was first presented to Finn Valley in 1994.

The second is commissioned by Charleville AC, Co. Cork, for whose annual ten-miler Ursula Noctor holds the race record. The trophy will go to the first woman to improve on Ursula's 56.17.

Ursula's clubmate Roy Dooney contributes the following appreciation.

What most people forever will remember about Ursula was her willingness to help others and her total lack of selfishness. Athletics is an individual sport, and as such demands a degree of selfishness from its participants, especially those who compete at international level. Ursula was unique in that she was never selfish in a way that intruded on others – she always went out of her way to help friends and fellow athletes.

When DCH needed someone at short notice to compete in a walk (or even a javelin throw) in the qualifying rounds of the National League, Ursula would always oblige. She was the first person to come up to you after a race to know how you got on – never to tell you about her race first.

But behind her charm and warmth there lay a fierce competitive spirit, which she used to inspire her teammates and colleagues. She competed with distinction for her country and her club, winning and participating in more national and international championships than most athletes even dream of. She adored running and athletics, as much for the people involved as for the competition itself.

Ursula was immensely popular, having travelled to races in every corner of Ireland and in many places abroad. She was always the same – modest in victory, gracious in defeat, but above all, clearly enjoying the company of other athletes. She had a keen eye and a sharp sense of humour and was one of the funniest commentators on the sport and some of its officials.

I ran with Ursula in her last competitive race, the Chicago Marathon, late October 1992, and two aspects of her character still stick in mind. The first relates to the desire of the local media to interview her about her illness and the fact she had undergone major operations for cancer since she had been in Chicago in 1991. The papers wanted to build up the story; Ursula was understandably reluctant to be distracted on the eve of a big race. But her kindness and compassion got the better of her – she agreed to do all the interviews because she said it might help somebody else reading her story to fight as she had done.

My second memory of Chicago is from the race itself which, for the second half, is largely out and back on the same highway with a turn at the 20 miles. I was at 23 miles when I met Ursula running in the opposite direction at about eighteen and a half. She shouted encouragement to me from the far side of the road. It was typical that from the midst of her own struggle she could still encourage someone else.

On the evening after Ursula died, and following the removal ceremonies in Chapelizod Church, a group of us went for a run in the Phoenix Park. There can hardly be a trail or pathway anywhere in the Park that Ursula did not run. On that blustery, sunny, spring evening it was hard to believe that someone who had been such a faithful part of running life in the Park would never be seen there again.

But as long as Ursula's many running friends and clubmates are training in the Park, I believe her spirit will watch over them. They in turn will always remember her as having been, in every sense, one of the best.

Ursula Noctor leads in the National Cross Country Championships

Róisín Smyth

Róisín was born in Derry but lived for ten years in Lifford, Co. Donegal, before returning to her native city. She is the eldest of three children, and both her younger brothers are active in school athletics. Her father, Noel Smyth, was Co. Louth sprints champion and has run a few marathons (PB 3.20).

Róisín was spotted as a 14-year-old at Thornhill College by coach Paddy Devine. Highly impressed by her running, he persuaded her to join Sparta. Soon, she was one of the best junior athletes in Ireland, making the Irish Schools CC teams for Inverness in 1979 and Coolmine in 1980 and representing Northern Ireland at Longchamps (schools international) in 1980.

Róisín then gave up running for two years but resumed in October 1982 with University College Dublin AC and with Paddy Devine as coach. She took second to Mary Friel in the Varsities CC Championships. Her first track race was in a match with UCD, Dublin City Harriers, and Crusaders. In an exciting 1,500m she defeated such formidable opponents as Patricia Appleby and Ursula Noctor.

Róisín's next big performance was a spectacular 1,500m victory at the Trinity Races on the grass track in College Park. Against some of the country's leading track runners, she pushed the pace and won by a handsome margin from Siobhán Treacy, Ailish Smyth, and Anne Hilliard.

Róisín finished fourth in the Northern Ireland 1,500m championship and second (behind Monica Joyce) in the BLE 1,500m, posting a Northern Ireland record of 4.22. She then rounded up her first successful track season by running up to Aisling Molloy in the Dundrum Sports 800m.

Róisín won the BLE National CC title in Kilmacow, 1984. Later that year she went to Los Angeles and posted 9.01 and ninth position in her Olympic 3,000m heat, failing to qualify. Among her many other achievements, she won the BLE 3,000m title in 1989.

Dogged by injuries, Róisín retired from competition in 1991. She now teaches school and lives in Dublin.

Christine Kennedy

If it had not been for the Dublin City Marathon, Christine Kennedy might never have taken up running. In 1981, she sat feeding her young baby down in Corofin, Co. Galway, and watching the TV pictures of Emily Dowling cross the finish line, first woman in the Dublin City Marathon.

'I suppose Emily's great marathon win motivated me,' a delighted Christine said shortly after coasting to victory in the 1990 Evening Press Women's Mini Marathon (10k). 'I saw that it was possible for an ordinary housewife and mother of young children to achieve success in sport. There and then I decided that running was for me.'

Sport had actually been part of Christine's growing up; she had tried several sports and had played Gaelic football for Galway. But she drifted out of action when she married James Kennedy and so was a very late starter when, at 25, she took up running.

Christine was one of six children born to resilient parents who both suffered the handicap of being deaf and dumb.

'My parents were very special to me,' she says. 'My father, in particular, must have been immensely strong psychologically when he came as a stranger to Corofin to work as a tailor with the handicap of not being able to hear or speak.

'Early communication with our parents must have been very difficult for older members of the family, but the neighbours rallied behind Mam and Dad and helped the communication process. The same neighbours also learned the use of sign language.'

Christine herself never found communication with her parents difficult. Today her own daughters, Fiona and Michele, can talk with their granny in sign language. Christine's father, Thomas, died in 1988. His passing left a big void in Christine's world.

Throughout her athletics career Christine has shown much of that remarkable resilience and strength of character which she so admired in her parents. Her first marathon took three-and-a-half hours, but she has since whittled almost an hour from that mark, to 2.35.05.

Christine was helped and encouraged as a novice runner by Emily Dowling, who devised her first training schedule. Liam Kavanagh would also play a big part in shaping her career. Much later, the former Irish CC and marathon champion Donie Walsh would add coaching backup. Hard work and dedication to training have been the secret of Christine's emergence from jogger to international athlete and Irish champion on road, track, and country.

Christine won her first National Marathon title in 1984 amid controversy: Deirdre

Nagle finished first (2.48.26) in Cork but was disqualified for wearing an oversized logo on her vest; Christine came in second (2.49.46) and was awarded gold.

Christine and family went to England when James's job in the computer industry promoted him there. She ran with the Parkside club and came home to win the National CC title in 1989. Further promotion took James to Paris, France, where Christine joined Racing Club de Paris. Unfortunately, while out training she was hit by a car and had only partially recovered when finishing sixth in the 1990 Nationals. She was selected for the World CC, where she was third Irish finisher.

In April 1990 Christine (now coached by Brendan O'Shea) travelled home to win her first National Marathon, in Clonmel. Her time was 2.38.05. She again flew home the following October to win the 1990 Dublin City Marathon (2.41.27). She retained both titles in 1991, when the National was incorporated with Dublin; her winning time was 2.35.56.

Christine now resides in California.

Aisling Molloy

Ballymahon-born Aisling Molloy was a great prospect at an early age, winning the All-Ireland Junior 800m at 14 and clocking 2.16. In 1979/80/81 she took All-Ireland U/16 800m titles. And at the tender age of 17 she startled many by winning the Cork City Sports 800m in 2.09. No wonder she was picked out by Brigham Young University of Utah and became in 1982 one of the first Irish females to accept a US athletics scholarship.

During that period Aisling registered PBs of 55 seconds for 400m, 2.03.12 for 800m, and 4.15 for 1,500m. She won the Conference Championship 800m and 1,500m in 1983, 84, and 85 and the American National Collegiate 1,500m. She was three times Indoor 1,500m champion and a member of the Brigham Young relay team that won the USA Championships in 1984 and 85.

Aisling returned to Ireland in 1986 and won the BLE 800m title in 2.05.99 – she would win this title on five other occasions. She won 800m titles again in 1987 and 1988, finished second in the AAA (British) Indoor Championships, and set an Irish record 2.05 in the European Indoors (she lowered this mark to 2.02.8 in 1990).

At the European Championships in Split, Croatia, she qualified for the 800m semi-final with a PB 2.01.14 but disappointed in her semi, finishing eighth in 2.04.20. It was around this time that the former AAA 800m champion Noel Carroll predicted Aisling would be the first Irishwoman to break two minutes.

Injuries in 1992/93 seriously disrupted Aisling's career, but she returned to win the 1994 National 800m (2.04.50) and went to Helsinki for the European Championships with high hopes. An 8am start and excessive heat, however, contributed to a disappointing eighth place in 2.08.46.

More injuries followed, but Aisling retained her National 800m title in 1995, posting a fine 2.03.51, which sent her off to the World Championships in Gothenburg with some expectation. Once again, however, true form deserted her, and she was eliminated, finishing sixth in her heat in 2.04.15.

Aisling prepared for Olympic year 1996 with a stay in Capetown, South Africa. Coming home for the Irish Championships in June, she looked on course to win the 800m title at Santry when tragedy struck on the final lap and she limped home dejected in second place holding her damaged hamstring (Freda Davoren of UCC won in 2.05).

Aisling Molloy, who in 1991 set an Irish record 4.27 for 1,500m at the Cork City Sports, and beat Sonia O'Sullivan into the bargain, has been perhaps the most elegant and stylish of Irish track runners through all of the eighties and much of the nineties.

Sinéad Delahunty

Sinéad Delahunty showed early promise at athletics and from 14 to 17 years of age won BLOE and Schools All-Ireland titles on track and country. And so it came as no surprise when in 1989 the Kilkenny girl accepted a four-year athletics scholarship to Providence College, Rhode Island, USA.

Sinéad had a successful career at Providence, both athletically and academically. She was NCAA Div 1 All-American on six occasions. In her senior year, 1993, she was voted Providence College Female Athlete of the Year. Back home she won the National 1,500m title (4.14.63) in 1994 after a tense battle with her Kilkenny/Providence colleague Geraldine Nolan, the 1993 800m champion.

Selected for the 1994 European Championships in Helsinki, Sinéad was rather unlucky not to progress beyond her 1,500m heat after recording a PB 4.12.16. A year later, at the World Championships in Gothenburg, she moved up to 5,000m, posting 13th and 16.18.61 in her semifinal.

Back in the USA, she took second in the National Indoor 3,000m, before returning to Ireland and running up to Sonia O'Sullivan's 4.10.4 in the National 1,500m at Santry. Sinéad then registered one of her career highs when she posted 4.25.2 for victory in the prestigious Fifth Avenue Mile, New York City. In a sprint finish she just held off England's Paula Radcliffe and France's Blodine Bitzner Ducret.

After a splendid seventh place (first Irishwoman) in the 1995 European CC Championships at Durham, England (where Paula Radcliffe took gold), and a 1,500m PB 4.08.75 at Linz, Austria, in August 1995, Sinéad appeared to be on course for the 1996 World CC in Capetown, South Africa. But she was hit by a car in February 1996 while training in Brighton, USA, and had to withdraw from the championships. A visit to Gerard Hartmann, Limerick's world-famous physiotherapist now based in Gainesville, Florida, proved beneficial, and Sinéad continued her preparation for the Atlanta Olympics. She again ran second to Sonia O'Sullivan in the BLE 1,500m at Billy Morton Stadium.

In Atlanta, Sinéad ran a clever 1,500m heat to qualify in fifth place (4.10.20). In the semifinal, she remained at the back of the field early on but surged to the front after two laps and stayed there to the bell. But when the little Romanian Szabo led the last-lap charge, Sinéad lacked the necessary acceleration and slipped down the field to place ninth in 4.12.52. After Atlanta, Sinéad raced on the European circuit and in late 1996 posted a splendid 4.07.27 for 1,500m in Brussels.

In preparation for the 1997 World Championships, Sinéad ran several Grand Prix meets, including Paris in July, where she recorded an excellent 4.27.8 when finishing fifth behind Carla Sacramento (Portugal) in the mile. She also took bronze (2.07.99) behind Amanda Crowe (Lisburn) in the National 800m at Santry.

In Athens Sinéad finished eighth (4.10.45) in her 1,500m heat but made it through to the semis as a fastest loser. She ran splendidly in the semifinal to post her fastest time of the year (4.07.46), finish seventh, and miss qualification for the final by four tenths of a second.

On 28 September 1997, a few weeks after Athens, Sinéad finished second in the Fifth Avenue Mile, her 4.24.87 (behind Paula Radcliffe's 4.22.96) fractionally faster than when she had won the event two years previously.

Geraldine Nolan

Another fine athlete from Kilkenny who won 800m and 1,500m at U/16 and U/17 level, Geraldine also won Celtic International and Tailteann Games 800m. In 1988 she took up a four-year athletics scholarship at Providence College, USA. Along with many other achievements, she was a member of the 4x1,500m team that set a world record.

She won BLE 800m silver in 1991 and 1992 and gold (2.08.2) in 1993. In the 1994 Helsinki European Championships, she excelled, recording a PB 4.10.84 on the way to the 1,500m final.

Geraldine developed sinusitis in the buildup to Atlanta 96, which wrecked her plans. At the time of writing she is taking a rest from athletics.

Susan Smith

Susan Smith from Waterford comes from an athletic family. She was introduced to running at seven years of age, commenced hurdling at 14, and won a BLOE Athlete of the Year award in 1988. She won European Catholic Schools titles and accepted an athletics scholarship to Brown University, USA, where she spent four years.

In 1989, she won the first of a string of National Senior titles: the 100m hurdles. She won the same title again in 90, 91, 92, and 95, and she won the 400m hurdles title in 92, 96, and 97. Despite her dominance of domestic hurdling, however, her development while at college was delayed by injury; it wasn't until 1996 that she began to fully blossom.

Domiciled in Atlanta since graduation, Susan did most of her preparation for the 1996 Olympics there, travelling home for 400m hurdle races and breaking her own Irish record on five occasions.

She went into the Olympics full of confidence and oozed positivity as she skimmed low over the hurdles to finish third in her heat, her 55.22 just outside her PB 55.08 and fifth-fastest of the 16 semifinal qualifiers.

'Every race for me at this level is an Olympic final. I have been waiting for this race for 12 months – I was just so determined to get through.' she said.

Susan again sparkled in the semifinal: she broke her own national record when placing 5th in 54.93. She had missed the final by a single place.

Susan maintained her brilliant form in post-Olympic races and clocked 55.22 in reaching the semifinal at the IAAF Grand Prix meet in Milan.

In 1997 she went to the Athens World Championships and was the outstanding Irish competitor, becoming only the second Irishwoman to reach a sprint final at a major championships.

In her 400m hurdles heat, she had the third-best reaction time of the 27 competitors, powering away from a field that included the former world champion Kim Batten. The latter caught her in the closing 25m, but Smith still smashed her own Irish record with a scintillating 54.61.

Susan made another great start to the semifinal and was credited with fourth but given the same time, 54.72, as the third placer. The order didn't matter: she had booked her place in the final.

In the final she again exploded from the blocks and actually led over the first four hurdles but started to drift on the final bend and weakened on the run-in to finish seventh (55.25).

'I went for a medal today. I went out really, really hard. I had nothing to lose. I just didn't have the strength over the last 30 yards. But I'm really pleased,' was her justifiably proud verdict.

Catherina McKiernan

Catherina McKiernan, from the village of Cornafean, Co. Cavan, played several sports from an early age. She excelled in camogie, tennis, badminton and basketball, but when she took to athletics in 1986, those other activities took a back seat.

Catherina was immediately successful. She won the Ulster CC Championship in 1987; she won the Irish Schools CC in 1988; she was third in the BLE Senior CC in 1989 and made her World CC debut in Stavanger, Norway.

Her list of achievements is unparallelled. She has been Ireland's foremost cross-country runner for the past eight years and has taken silver in four consecutive World CC Championships: Boston 92, Amorebieta, Budapest, and Durham. She has won Irish track titles at 3,000m (1991,92,93) and 5,000m (1996). She holds the national 10,000m record, 31.08.4. On the road, she has won the Tullamore Two Jack Hartigan five times and set a record 25.43 for the Sportsworld 5, finishing 12th overall, ahead of many accomplished male runners.

Catherina was sidelined with injury for the latter half of 1995 but came back in time for the 1966 World CC at Stellenbosch, South Africa, though she was affected by a pre-race virus, from which she hadn't fully recovered by race day. She fought hard for a creditable 13th place.

In early April 1996 she finished second to, and a second behind, Finland's Anna Marie Sandell (15.11) in a 5,000m at Portsmouth. On 28 April, Catherina won the Saint Denis 15k in Northern France (48.41), shaking off Kenya's Jane Ngotho at halfway and winning by 80 seconds. On 11 May, she won a 5,000m at Osaka, Japan, in 15.07.31, with Kenya's Rose Cheruiyot second. This was excellent by McKiernan, who had flown in only 48 hours before the race.

On May 28 Catherina finally put the injury traumas of 1995 behind her; she ran her fastest ever 5,000m (14.58.65), at Hengelo, Holland, third behind Derartu Tulu and Gete Wami. A few days later she got another PB, 14.55.39, at Saint Denis, with Tulu again winning. In the run-up to Atlanta, Catherina won two fast 5,000m races: 14.55 in Paris and 14.58 in Hengelo.

Catherina's performance in the intense heat of Atlanta was highly commendable; she placed sixth in her 10,000m qualifier. In the final she moved to the front after two laps and for the next six laps looked comfortable. By six kilometres, however, she was struggling and gradually dropped off the pace.

Fernando Ribeiro took the lead at halfway, reached in a swift 15.35. Wang Junxia dogged her footsteps, looking dangerous. But it was the Portuguese world champion who dug deepest on the final lap; she covered it in 63.45 and passed the Chinawoman on the home straight to win gold in an Olympic record 31.01.63.

McKiernan battled bravely to finish 11th in 32.00.28, a splendid effort in the humid heat. 'They were much better and faster. I tried my best and couldn't go with the pace,' she said.

She was, by the way, the only home-based woman in Ireland's squad. Most of her training, coached by Joe Doonan, is done on Cavan Golf Course; track sessions entail long journeys to Lanesborough, Co. Longford, or Claremorris, Co. Mayo.

In March 1997 Catherina finished seventh and led Ireland to team bronze at the World CC in Turin. Three months later she won the Women's Mini Marathon in a race record 32.31 and immediately announced her intention of tackling the full marathon. In her build-up to that debut, she won the Glasgow Half Marathon on 24 August in a record 69 minutes, beating the runner-up, Kenya's Lucia Subano, by two minutes. Two weeks later, on 7 September, she posted the year's second-fastest time, 31.21, in winning a road 10k in London, England.

On Sunday 29 September 1997, in Berlin, Catherina made her entry to the classic distance – and an astonishing entry it was. Her winning 2.23.44 was the eighth-fastest time in history, the fastest-ever female debut, and an Irish record by a mile (Carey May's 12-year-old mark had been 2.28.07).

The most amazing aspect of Catherina's Berlin effort was the apparent absence of effort – she coasted the distance, finished smiling and relaxed, and immediately admitted she could have run faster: 'It was a very easy start to my marathon career – I feel great after it.'.

Coach Joe Doonan confirmed that the race plan – to jog the first 20 miles and race the last six – had worked to perfection. Catherina record a split of 16.59 on the slight climb from 30 to 35k then kicked in with a breathtaking 16.19 to 40k.

The win gave Catherina her biggest pay-packet to date: about £30,000 including bonuses. For the record, Medina Biktagirova finished second in a Belarussian national record 2.24.46. Maureen Renders of Belgium was third (2.26.18).

Whether Catherina now applies her phenomenal talents solely to the marathon – effectively resigning herself to never winning the World CC title – only time will reveal. Whatever the future course of her career, this marvellous athlete has secured her status in running's Hall of Fame.

Catherina's silver streak

(As reported in *Irish Runner* magazine)

1992 World CC, Boston

Sweet-striding Catherina McKiernan more than fulfilled all the great promise that she had shown through the cross-country season with a spectacular run in snow-covered Franklin Field, Boston, on Saturday 21 March.

McKiernan's heart-stopping effort took her agonisingly close to the gold medal and ranks with the very best all-time achievements by any Irish athlete. Only a super late charge by the defending champion, Lynn Jennings, denied McKiernan supreme glory in what was one of the best women's races ever witnessed.

'I thought I had her, but she had that little bit more speed at the finish,' said Catherina.

The Cornafean, Cavan, heroine had run an almost-perfect tactical race, biding her time

Reebok
CORNAFEAN
AC
asics

as the Kenyans Susan Sirma and Helen Chepngeno tried to intimidate the field by surging off the front.

'There were times when I wanted to go away from the leading group but I suppose it was just as well that I saved it for the finish. I am not at all disappointed at missing the gold; you cannot be too greedy – you have to progress naturally. If I got the gold, what would I have to work for in the future?' said the remarkably philosophical Catherina. McKiernan's only request on finishing was for a pair of gloves to protect her frozen fingers, a request which the deliriously happy Irish supporters quickly answered.

Behind Catherina, Sonia O'Sullivan had also done wonders, her seventh place beyond all expectations. Geraldine Hendricken of Carlow (31st) also ran brilliantly. But Monica O'Reilly was just a little too far back (63rd) to secure team bronze for the gallant Irishwomen. Ireland finished fourth, just seven points adrift of third-placed Ethiopia and well ahead of fifth-placed Britain.

There was further joy for Catherina: her second place secured the overall IAAF Grand Prix of $10,000. All in all, a great day for Irish athletics.

1993 World CC, Amorebieta

On a course suited more to track runners than to harriers – flat, hard, and bumpy – Catherina was always in the leading group of 20 led by South African Zola Pieterse.

After three kilometres, Zola's teammate Elana Meyer went clear, taking Pieterse, Albertina Dias, and McKiernan with her and leaving Lynn Jennings struggling to stay in touch.

At four kilometres Dias upped the tempo, and Meyer slipped back; McKiernan was ten metres down; Jennings was improving in fourth, followed by Pieterse and Liz McColgan. The 5k mark was passed in 15.47. At 6k (18.55) Dias was 30 metres clear and stretching away to gold.

On the long home straight Catherina had to summon superhuman reserves to hold off the kicker Jennings and Zola Pieterse. The finishing times strikingly illustrate the closeness of the battle for silver and bronze: McKiernan 20.09, Jennings 20.09, Pieterse 20.10.

Albertina Dias, racing on a course well suited to her, was a worthy and popular winner. But Catherina proved she could stand the heat – because the contrast between this and snow-bound Boston 92 could not have been greater.

Joe Doonan, Catherina's coach, was justifiably proud and declared, 'Today Catherina established herself as world class.'

The Irish team responded well to Catherina's leadership but could manage only 12th of 26 teams, a disappointment after fourth in Boston. Anne Keenan-Buckley fought her way to 44th; Monica O'Reilly ran strongly to take 49th; Teresa Duffy was fourth scorer, in 70th. Breda Dennehy posted 87th of 144 finishers.

1994 World CC, Budapest

Ofter silver in Boston and Amorebieta it was natural that Catherina McKiernan had her sights firmly on gold in Budapest. She had given up her job in October 1993 and under the guidance of Joe Doonan trained twice daily and won three of her six Grand Prix races and finished second in each of the others. She came to Hungary believing she could win.

It was obvious from the start, however, that Catherina was not running with the same freedom as in either Boston or Amorebieta, where she led at crucial places and threatened to break clear. Here she never looked like leading; indeed there was a time about halfway when she seemed to be struggling to make the top ten. Nor could it have helped her confidence to see Chepngeno break away from Merima Denboba of Ethiopia with what was evidently a winning move.

Going past the stands at the end of the first lap, the lead group contained 24 runners. McKiernan was positioned wisely on the inside, and we waited to see her move onto the shoulders of the leaders. But that move never materialised; her way through appeared always to be blocked, and when Chepngeno struck our heroine was in no position to respond.

When Portugal's Dias began to chase the Kenyans, McKiernan was sixth. She managed, with a mighty effort, to get up to third at the bell. But now someone else was in the medal hunt: the other Portuguese, Ferreira, had latched onto the Irishwoman like a leech – this the woman who was fifth in the World 10k final in Stuttgart and had beaten Dias in the Portuguese Championships.

Suddenly Ferreira had opened a ten-yard gap on Catherina. It was crisis time for the Cavanwoman – the 60 supporters who had travelled from Breffni were suddenly almost quiet. But even under extreme duress Catherina was thinking clearly, reading the race. 'I just knew that if Ferreira passed Dias, Dias might give up – it's a bit like one Irish athlete passing another.' How right she was!

Last year Dias sprinted to victory, as did Lynn Jennings in Boston. But now McKiernan had to find real speed to conquer Dias and Ferreira. 'I suppose in the end I timed it perfectly,' McKiernan said, and added with typical understatement, 'It was a very difficult race – I had to work really hard to get up there in the end.'

Yes, this third silver medal was the hardest-won of the lot. And yet within minutes she seemed fully recovered and was all smiles as she stepped onto the rostrum. Yet again she had brought Irish joy on a day when we had little else to cheer about. Teresa Duffy was, by the way, our second finisher, a commendable 74th, 72 seconds behind Catherina.

Meanwhile, McKiernan has achieved much more than the doubters predicted when she turned down a US scholarship back in 1988. Irish athletics is extremely fortunate to have an athlete of her calibre. She has kept the flag flying, is a great ambassador for the country, and with more emphasis on speedwork can someday translate her genius to the track.

1995 World CC, Durham

This was possibly the best race of Catherina McKiernan's career. The first kilometre was covered in 3.03. Little wonder that six were already clear of the field. Catherina was tagged on in fifth, looking comfortable.

With two of the three laps completed, McKiernan moved level with the leaders, Barsosio and Tulu. The bell rang and McKiernan took the lead. Immediately the lead pack broke up; within 400 metres there were only two athletes that mattered: Derartu Tulu and Catherina.

Halfway up the hill Tulu turned to McKiernan and said, 'come on, come on!' McKiernan's only reply was a look of disbelief. They crested the hill side by side. Down the slope they sprinted. We thought now that the race would be decided on the home straight. We remembered McKiernan's sprint for the line at the European Championships – surely she could do it again.

But suddenly, to our disbelief, it was all over. The two athletes touched as Tulu made her bid for home. Derartu opened a ten-metre lead. Then, 600m from home, she kicked again, with devastating effect. The gap widened with every stride; all our hopes of victory were gone.

Catherina McKiernan crossed the line in second place for the fourth year in a row. You would have expected her to be emotionally shattered. But her words proved otherwise: 'I'm absolutely delighted. I gave it everything. I was beaten by a better athlete on the day, and I know I gave every last ounce of energy. It's not like I crossed the line and said I should have beaten her. I got everything out of myself, and we blew away the rest of the field. The support from the crowd was incredible, not just from the Irish but the English as well – I could have been running in Ireland.'

Catherina once again proved that she is among the great distance runners of our time. Sadly, her achievements seem to mean little to the media. Not one feature on her has appeared in any national paper since Durham. Surely this great Cavanwoman deserves better.

In fairness, something should be said about Tulu's pre-race difficulties. She arrived in England after a marathon journey of three days from Ethiopia. As McKiernan relaxed in the grounds of Durham College the day before the race, Derartu was boarding a bus for a seven-hour trip to Newcastle. In this context her victory was astonishing. A truly worthy champion.

European Gold

1994 European CC, Northumberland

Alnwick Castle and surrounding countryside was the setting for the inaugural running of the European Cross Country Championship on a lovely bright day. But only a few enthusiasts turned up to admire the cream of the continent in action.

A sedate start along the bank of the River Aln saw Catherina McKiernan fourth after 700 metres, in a group led by Portugal's European 10,000m champion, Fernanda Ribeiro, and Spain's Julia Vaquero.

The free-running Ribeiro seemed in full control as the field passed the castle for the first time. But McKiernan's presence, if understated, was clear enough to her rivals. Then, dramatically, at 2,000m, Catherina appeared to lose her footing disastrously. Apparently, she had ducked under a rope and jumped a log after the rest of the leaders had run off course, misled by the camera buggy, which, as often happens, was too close to the runners.

McKiernan lost up to 15 metres, but avoided being swallowed by the pack and was able to regain her position within a few hundred metres. Indeed, the adrenalin rush induced by her mishap seemed to inspire her; negotiating the log for the second time, she had moved into second behind Vaquero.

Six hundred metres from home, McKiernan forged ahead of Vaquero, who had taken the brunt of a strong wind for the previous kilometre. But the Irishwoman's determined attack on the steep gradient failed to shake off the Spaniard, who coped noticeably better than McKiernan as the two sought to balance speed with control on the fast downhill; it looked briefly as though our heroine might be caught for pace.

As too seldom happens in cross-country, this one went all the way to the line, Vaquero's brave challenge fading only in the last few metres. And so, Catherina had earned her first major international title. And at last there was gold after her three World CC silvers.

In truth this event probably gained more for her than she from it, for there was little Catherina needed to prove in a 4.4k against those women she beats every other week in the IAAF Cross Challenge. What she did prove was her right to be called the most consistently brilliant grass-runner in the world.

Sonia O'Sullivan

Sonia O'Sullivan joined her local BLE club, Ballymore Cobh, when she was 12 years of age, not so much because she was mad about running, more because of the social possibilities – she was thinking of parties, discos, and the like.

But the cross-country season had barely started when she was winning races. Coach Sean Kennedy immediately detected that the dark-haired, dark-eyed newcomer was a rare talent; he put direction into her training; her progress was phenomenal.

In 1987 Sonia won the National Junior CC Championships at Kilmacow. A week later, at Killenaule, Co. Tipperary, she produced a withering sprint finish to snatch the senior title from Mullingar's Caroline Mullen and Clonliffe's Mary Donohoe. A few months later she won the National Senior 1,500m (4.23.13). Astonishingly, she was still only 17.

Not surprisingly, scholarship offers began to pour in from American universities, each describing the collegiate system in more mouthwatering terms than the last. It was an anxious time for John and Mary O'Sullivan. Should their daughter go west? If so, which institution would best nurture – or least abuse - her precious talent? In the end, it was Sonia's own decision to follow in the spikesteps of John Joe Barry and Ronnie Delany and Eamonn Coghlan – she selected Villanova, Philadelphia, where the head coach was Marty Stern.

It was a huge move for a 17-year-old, and the first year was the hardest. Sonia was under relentless pressure to perform; there were times when she considered giving up.

Home on vacation in July 1988, she produced a sensational last lap and set a national junior record when winning the 3,000m at the Cork Sports. Her next objective was the World Juniors in Birmingham, but she developed a serious injury only a week before the games and had to withdraw. This injury would curtail Sonia's progress for two years. She returned to Villanova on crutches, but after three months of inaction felt under pressure to compete – and broke down again. This pattern would be repeated, until again Sonia was tempted to pack it in altogether.

At last, Sonia got through a winter's training free of injury and began again to show her true form. She became the top college athlete for the next three years. In 1989 she won the Big East 3,000m (9.23.37).

In 1990 she won the NCAA 3,000m (8.56.27), retained her Big East 3,000m title (9.19.24), and won the ECAC 3,000m (8.58.31).

At the European Games in Split, Croatia, 1990, in intense heat, Sonia finished 11th (8.52.65) in the 3,000m, won by Scotland's Yvonne Murray in 8.43.06.

In November 1990 Sonia won the NCAA National CC (5,000m) at Knoxville, Tennessee (Sinéad Delahunty 10th, Geraldine Hendricken 13th, Anita Philpott 19th) and led Villanova to team victory.

Sonia began 1991 with a series of powerful indoor victories. On 12 January 1991, at Gainesville, Florida, she won the mile (4.34.49). A week later she won the New England Mile in a meet record 4.33.49 (Geraldine Hendricken 2nd in a PB 4.35.49). On Jan 26, at the Boston Terrier Classic, she set a world best 15.27.28 for 5,000m indoors. On February 16/17 she dominated the Big East meet, winning mile (4.42.75) and 3,000m (9.14.57) and anchoring Villanova in 4x800m victory.

Then came Sonia's biggest win to date – the 1991 World Student Games 1,500m at Sheffield, England, time 4.12.14.

She won the NCAA Outdoor 5k in 15.49.46 (with Valerie McGovern second), then ended her outdoor college career with victory in the NCAA 3k in 8.56.74 (Geraldine Hendricken second).

She also led Villanova to an emphatic victory over arch rivals Arkansas. *Track and Field News,* the bible of world athletics, told its readers that O'Sullivan and Villanova had entered the history books: *The slender Irishwoman became the first to win consecutive individual titles and her team, Villanova, the first to win three titles in a row.*

In the Feb/Mar 1992 issue of *Irish Runner* Dick Hooper wrote a brilliantly perceptive piece on Ireland's two brightest athletics stars – both women:

Catherina McKiernan and Sonia O'Sullivan have been sent down from Heaven and given to BLE as gifts. Sonia O'Sullivan is a winner. She thinks like one, performs like one, and has the 'presence' of a star – pleasant, personable, confident in her own ability. A pocketful of NCAA titles, World Student Games gold and silver, world indoor records, multiple Irish records. All have come almost ahead of schedule. The best wine is yet to come.

This winter Catherina McKiernan's feats on the Grand Prix cross-country circuit have rekindled the passions of the country's established athletics correspondents after a few years sabbatical from covering the sport, when every story seemed dominated by boardroom battles and infighting.

Quality feature writers, Liam Hayes, Paul Kimmage, David Walsh, and their ilk, have warmed to O'Sullivan and McKiernan. They will become even more interested as the O'Sullivan/McKiernan era gathers momentum over the coming years. As the emancipation of women's sport and the pace of its fight for equality quickens, the face of Irish athletics has already changed.

It is not long since such luminaries as Deirdre Nagle, Louise McGrillen and Catherine Rooney would sigh ruefully that their race would be lucky to garner the last few lines in a report, or a ten-second flash on Saturday Sport. *Now reports of events where Sonia or Catherina compete carry the ladies' race as the main feature. As they continue their inexorable climb to the top, Catherina and Sonia are on the verge of becoming the first real Irish women sporting superstars. Visions of World Championships, Olympic medals and opentopped bus-rides come into view.*

BLE's gift is there for all to see. Two beautiful, talented girls have landed in their laps. Their marketability is mindboggling. The fact of the matter is that if BLE took the opportunity and marketed both women they could earn considerable revenue, not alone for the two achievers themselves, but more importantly for the association. More pertinently, if BLE fail to grasp the nettle on this issue, no doubt some agent will get sole rights on one or both women. On past experience, BLE's ability to show initiative on issues like this has never impressed.

Five years on, and in the light of what happened in Atlanta, Dick Hooper's latter comments about agents and rights still make piquant reading.

The World CC Championships in Boston witnessed the best display to date by an Irish women's team. With Catherina McKiernan taking silver, an agonising two seconds behind Lynn Jennings, and Sonia O'Sullivan also producing one of her greatest ever efforts in seventh, Ireland missed team bronze by a mere seven points.

In her preparations for the Barcelona Olympics, Sonia set Irish records for 1,500m, 3,000m, and 5,000m. She entered the Olympic cauldron and duly won her 3,000m heat in 8.50.08.

On Sunday 2 August 1992 she was back in action in the Olympic 3,000m final – and gave as gallant a display as was ever delivered by an Irish athlete. The 3,000m unfolded as a slow, tactical race which did not ignite until the final third of the distance. At the bell the field was bunched, O'Sullivan lying third on the shoulder of Elena Romanova as Scotland's Yvonne Murray led the charge for home. It was then that Sonia made the tactical error which may well have cost her an Olympic medal.

Sensing that Murray was about to go into overdrive, Sonia moved off Romanova's shoulder and tracked the Scotswoman. It appeared a positive move, except that Murray failed to sustain her effort and with 300 metres remaining 'died' right in front of O'Sullivan. Sonia suddenly found herself leading the pack in the final surge for glory.

She gave everything – and for a while it looked like even gold was possible. Then, on the final bend, Sonia moved wide – and allowed Romanova and Dorovskikh through on her inside.

'I think at that stage I was beginning to pay for what was the wrong decision. I always prefer to come off the last bend in a completely different situation. I had planned it differently, but it did not work out. I think it was lack of experience that cost me a medal, but I went out there with the intention of getting only one colour – gold,' she said.

As the line approached, Sonia was still in bronze position. Then, in those last, desperate strides, the Canadian Chalmers snatched even that consolation.

Two days after that heroic effort, Sonia was back in the Olympic arena, this time in the heats of the 1,500m. She duly qualified for the semifinal, but the bright spark of her Olympic ambition seemed to have faded and, although she gave it everything, a place in the 1,500m final eluded her.

Barcelona was in one sense a huge disappointment not only to Sonia but also to her followers. Nevertheless, the experience was to stand to the brave 22-year-old in her post-Olympic campaign. 'The fear is gone now. It's a different feeling when I go to the line,' she said after soundly beating Romanova over 3,000m in Copenhagen on August 25.

Sonia in fact went on to an amazing series of performances after the Olympics. She smashed a total of five Irish records in Grand Prix meets between August 11 and 21. In Monte Carlo she lowered her 1,500m mark by 3.89 seconds to 4.01.93; in Sheffield she posted a 4.24.23 mile, to reduce Aisling Molloy's record by 3.6 seconds; in Cologne she reduced her own 3,000m figures to 8.37.92 (a 1.7 improvement).

In the Zurich Grand Prix, she again reduced the 1,500m figures, finishing second in 4.01.23. On to Berlin on 21 August; she lopped more than 27 seconds off her 5,000m record, 14.59.11, in finishing second behind South Africa's Elana Meyer.

Sonia's build-up to the 1993 World Championships in Stuttgart, Germany, established her as undisputed world number one over 1,500m and 3,000m. On 13 June, in the Europa Cup at Rotterdam, she trounced the field in a fast 4.03.38. A week later she shattered her own Irish 3,000m record when winning at Hengelo, Holland, in 8.33.40 and leaving Olympic champion Romanova trailing. Later, in Oslo, Sonia outpaced Yvonne Murray and posted 8.28.74, the fastest time since 1988. She was now being hailed as clear favourite for World Championship gold.

After the heats of 3,000m in Stuttgart, however, Irish optimism was a little more cautious. The Chinese, hitherto hardly considered, were looking a real danger.

And so they proved in the final. They stayed off the pace in the first 1,000m, covered in a sedate 2.59.06 with Annette Peters of USA leading the field and Sonia staying out of trouble. Now Yvonne Murray took over; the pace increased; there were eight or nine runners still together with two laps to go.

By the end of the back straight the three Chinese, Yunxi Qu and the two unrelated Zhangs, had made their move and were leading with 700 metres to go. O'Sullivan battling to get by Yvonne Murray, seemed slow to react. Suddenly, the gap to the Chinese, running in single file, was an alarming 25 metres. The predictions of Chinese journalists were now cruelly, from an Irish viewpoint, vindicated. Qu and the Zhangs took the three medals, Qu posting 8.28.71; Sonia again took the dreaded fourth place, in 8.33.38.

Shellshocked, Sonia told reporters, 'I was just ready for the break when it happened. I was feeling fine with no problems and suddenly it happened. I did not believe the sprint would start so early. Suddenly the gap was there and I went after them. I thought I might have a bronze in the last lap, but it was just too much ground to make up.'

The Chinese performances raised many questions, most of them about possible skulduggery in their preparations, but the debate was academic – the medals were gone east, and Ireland mourned for the young Cobh woman.

She herself was defiant: 'Right now I'm angry with myself, but I'm going for a medal in the 1,500m.' It was heartening to hear such fighting words.

Sonia looked relaxed and confident in her 1,500m heat, which she won in 4.05.81, with Yi Lu second. Hassiba Boulmerka of Algeria won the second heat. Dong Lu won the third, in 4.04.36.

On the Sunday, 15 athletes lined up for the 1,500m final. Boulmerka led the Chinese through a 68.2 first lap. O'Sullivan was in close contact, running slightly wide. The second lap was slower, 69.3, but it was apparent that O'Sullivan was very much on her toes, waiting, watching, full of determination.

Yi Liu was the first to go, starting her relentless gallop for home 650 metres from the finish. O'Sullivan and Boulmerka followed closely, and the race for the medals was well and truly on. Liu's faster pace cut the leaders down to four and consolidated her position along the back straight. Behind her, the battle was for silver and bronze, and O'Sullivan's move at 250 metres from the finish was as decisive and brave as you could wish to see. She swept past Boulmerka and the other Chinese, Liu, and drove herself up the finishing straight. Sonia had come back like a true champion to take the silver medal.

The ecstatic Sonia was handed a Tricolour by Sean Callan and joined Boulmerka and Liu on the traditional lap of honour. The German crowd responded with warm and generous applause to the first Irishwoman to win a medal at the World Track and Field Championships. Sonia O'Sullivan had vindicated herself, to the delight of the people back home and her many friends everywhere.

The 1994 European Championships were staged in Helsinki. Once again, Sonia showed wonderful pre-championship form. On July 16 she set new Irish and European figures for 3,000m at Crystal Palace, a sensational 8.21.84.

A stint of training with Marcus O'Sullivan and Bob Kennedy convinced Kennedy, the USA 5,000m record-holder, that Sonia was in form to lower the 2,000m world record. Edinburgh was the venue, and with no wind to combat, she confidently reeled off laps averaging 65 seconds and finished with a 61 to post 5.25.36 and chop 3.31 off the eight-year-old mark.

In *Irish Runner* magazine, Tom O'Riordan compared Sonia to the great Finn Paavo Nurmi, who at his peak ran 2,000m in 5.24.6 and 3,000m in 8.20.4, similar figures to what the Cobh woman was now producing.

Next stop for Sonia was Stockholm, where she won a fast 1,500m in 4.00.46. At the same meeting, Catherina McKiernan knocked 41 seconds off her 5,000m best, with 15.08.1, a few metres behind Yelena Romanova.

O'Sullivan then smashed her 1,500m best with 3.59.10, the year's fastest time.

In a press conference at Helsinki, Sonia announced that she was not planning to run in the 1,500m. By that she meant that her plan was to win 3,000m gold on 10 August. Four years previously, in Split, Yvonne Murray had taken gold and Sonia had fallen back to 11th. Afterwards, through tears, Sonia had vowed that Murray would never again beat her.

And so the pressure was mounting on O'Sullivan as she lined up for the 3,000m. final. It hardly mattered that most people thought she had the beating of the field. What unfolded was beautiful, like a dream come true. We watched history being created in a performance that deserves to be put alongside the greatest Irish sporting achievements.

Yvonne Murray, to her credit, took up the challenge early, almost as soon as Anita

Philpott took the field through the opening 400m in 69.94 seconds. You could see O'Sullivan relax – now Murray would learn how difficult it can be to lead virtually all the way. It was amazing how quickly Murray and O'Sullivan drew away; they reached 1,600m in 4.31.78 and were 80 metres clear of the chasing pack. Twice Murray tried to lift the pace, but O'Sullivan was never going to let her go.

Yvonne looked tired when the bell sounded, and it was only a question of time before Sonia played her trump card. She produced it on the back straight – and the gold medal was decided in a few strides. Covering the last 200m in 29.46 seconds, O'Sullivan sprinted majestically into the pages of history. Her 8.31.84 was a stadium record.

Murray fought bravely to take silver in 8.36.48, a lifetime best. Anita Philpott, in 12th place, also posted a lifetime best – and her 8.54.79 was just two seconds slower than Sonia had run in Split 1990. It had been a great championship for Anita, who had also run a PB, 8.57.74, in her heat.

Sonia was full of smiles in victory and said, 'I had a lot to prove out there. There is never a second chance when it comes to a championship. I've worked long and hard for this moment, and its all very much worthwhile.'

She had in fact looked mentally and physically perfect for the race. By contrast, Catherina McKiernan appeared entirely out of sorts in the 10,000m final, tired and lifeless from the beginning. She dropped out at 6,200m.

Geraldine Nolan also had a magnificent Europeans. She posted a PB 4.10.84 in her 1,500m heat and led for three laps of the final. Sinéad Delahunty ran a brave 4.12.16 PB in her 1,500m heat and was unlucky to miss the final. Longford's Aisling Molloy was not at her best – eighth (2.08.46) in her 800m qualifier, which was run at 8am. Likewise Geraldine Hendricken of Carlow, 9.30.81 in her 3,000m heat.

In September 1994 a banquet organised by BLE and sponsored by Waterford Crystal was held at the Burlington Hotel, Dublin, to mark Sonia's achievements in establishing five national records in the course of a season and becoming the first Irish athlete to win European track gold.

Sonia now began focusing on the 1995 World Championships in Gothenburg, Sweden; her buildup could hardly have been better. She part-wintered in Australia, and in early February became the first Irishwoman to win a race there, a 1,500m. She also won a 5,000m, setting an Australian all-comers record 15.04.05.

Back in Europe, her winning form continued. At the end of May, she won the Bratislava Grand Prix 3,000m in 8.45.50, the fastest time of the year. She took the European Cup 1,500m in Tallin, Estonia, the 1,500m at Cork City Sports (4.07), the Bislett Games 3.000m in 8.34.31. Most satisfying was a 14.47.14 for 5,000m at Crystal Palace, London, the fastest of the year; among those vanquished were Fernanda Ribeiro (Portugal), Rose Cheruiyot (Kenya), and Paula Radcliffe (Britain).

With 15 wins out of 16 races, Sonia now felt fully prepared for Gothenburg. And her plan for the championships was a simple one: 'To win whatever the pace. I came here to win gold.' Clearly, Barcelona and that fourth place were still in the back of her mind.

The 5.000m semis went according to the prepared script: Sonia and Fernanda

Ribeiro won. And so to the final, which got off to a sensational first lap: Gabriela Szabo sprinted it in a crazy 65.28 seconds – the tiny Romanian was on schedule to knock a minute off the world record. Sonia showed new maturity by more or less ignoring the leader. Nor did she panic when a stray long-jumper nearly toppled her six laps into the race. She had enough to concern her in the menacing presence of the 10,000m champion; Ribeiro was right on O'Sullivan's shoulder.

The tension mounted when Fernanda took the lead with three laps remaining. But we need not have worried: a powerful, surging 28.82 final 200m took O'Sullivan clear. Her 14.46.47 was of course a championship record (this was the first staging of the event). Ribeiro was second, Zohra Quaziz third.

How sad that Sonia's greatest moment was now soured by unfair accusations of unpatriotism and even anti-Irishness! Those accusations arose from what transpired on her lap of honour.

When Sonia crossed the finish line she made straight for her father, John, who greeted her with a huge hug and offered her his Tricolour. She declined, telling him she wanted 'one with a pole'. She then began her lap of honour, singled out two of her greatest fans, Sean Callan and Harry Gorman, and asked them for their flag, which was on a five-foot pole. She raised this flag and held it while the world's photographers clamoured to record the moment. Sean Callan explains what followed.

'Sonia then turned back to us and told me the flag was too heavy to carry, and I would have to be in total agreement with her there. She left the flag with me and went on her victory lap. It was ridiculous for anyone to suggest that Sonia did not want to carry the flag. Even after her lap she obliged several photographers by holding up another Tricolour.'

Sonia had been our flagbearer in Stuttgart, Helsinki, and Gothenburg. To now question her commitment to Ireland was unfair, insulting, and begrudging. It is worth noting here that BLE management failed to distinguish themselves in her defence.

Anyway, World Championship gold was still sweet success for Sonia and the Irish nation. Her win was positive, inspirational, laced with courage, conviction, and honesty.

It is important to set the record straight, and that is that Sonia O'Sullivan has always, and will always, be proud to carry the Irish flag and will continue to represent her country with dignity and distinction across the globe. That is the *real* story. During her post-race interviews in Gothenburg, which Sonia conducted with the dignity and direct honesty that we as a nation have long admired in the world champion, Paul Kimmage of the *Sunday Independent* asked her why she refused to accept any of the several tricolours offered immediately after she crossed the line. It was, to say the least, a cheap and highly insensitive shot by a journalist apparently desperate for a story. It was also (as we were later to learn) deeply distressing to Sonia. Nonetheless, she answered with truth and dignity.

Sonia does not owe Paul Kimmage or anyone else explanations. She has always projected a proud, honest, and positive image of Ireland in arenas around the world, and she continues to be an inspiration to both young and old.

Sonia's record-breaking achievements during 1995 earned her the title European

Athlete of the Year. The American magazine *Track and Field News* voted her Number One for 1,500m, 3,000m, and 5,000m.

In May 1996, fresh from training in Australia, Sonia started her countdown to the Atlanta Olympics with two fine race wins in the USA: the 1,500m at Princeton (4.06.99) and the year's fastest 3.000m (8.39.33), in Eugene, Oregon. She then won a 5,000m in Rome, a 3,000m in Moscow, the Irish 1,500m title in Dublin, and the Cork 3,000m (8.40.51). She continued victorious in Oslo, Nice, London, and Atlanta (5,000m on July 16). With ten wins in 62 days, Sonia was entitled to look toward Atlanta 96 with confidence.

Sadly, that confidence, and the high hopes of Sonia's many fans, would wilt drastically in the Olympic cauldron. That trauma has been widely publicised and exhaustively analysed. Whatever the rights and wrongs, the brutal fact is that one of the Games' hottest certainties for glory came away physically if not emotionally shattered and without a medal of any colour.

Sonia had started off well in her 5,000m heat; she won comfortably in 15.15.08. Only the Kenyan Pauline Konga would better that time in the qualifying rounds. The feared Chinawoman Wang Junxia kept a low profile, qualifying fourth in her heat with a modest 15.24.28. Sonia sweated heavily on that humid Atlanta evening but so did many others; we saw no reason to worry.

The final was run in near-perfect conditions: a blue sky over the stadium, skirted by light clouds, a hint of possible showers. But not all was well with Sonia; she looked pale and drawn. We watched with foreboding as she went to the line carrying the hopes of the nation and her own dream of Olympic gold.

The sense of disaster intensified as the race unfolded; Sonia was indeed in trouble. After only 50 metres she was clipped from behind and almost fell. Her body language seemed all wrong; she was not imposing herself. As early as 2,000m she showed signs of drifting.

With six laps remaining Pauline Konga (Kenya) hit the front, bringing the dreaded Junxia with her. We watched in stunned disbelief as Wang sprinted the last 800m to post 14.59.88, a time O'Sullivan had often bettered.

Underneath the stadium the shock was palpable among Irish media and mentors. Sonia had dropped out – but the humidity was only 76 and the temperature only 13. It was a baffling anticlimax to Friday night's semi.

Sonia arrived in the 'mixed zone' tearful and bewildered. She broke down as she embraced her father, John, before disappearing into the Atlanta night with her agent, Kim McDonald, and her physiotherapist, Ger Hartmann.

Big John faced a barrage of questions from the press with dignity and no little wit: 'No one has died – it's only sport. There will be another day. Look, we all have to get up and go to work tomorrow.'

The party that had been planned as celebration was more like a wake, but the O'Sullivan family kept faith. John and Mary and their son, Tony, and daughter Gillian turned up, and like everyone else present tried to unravel the mystery.

Meanwhile, word was filtering through that Sonia would appear at a press conference on the Monday; the OCI would also make a statement. There also came the news that, in a continuation of the feud between the OCI and BLE over sponsorship, Sonia had been required to change gear in the tunnel just before Friday's heat.

The kindest thing one can say about the press conference is that it was a farcical public relations blunder by the OCI, Sonia, and Sonia's advisors if any. A simple typewritten statement would have sufficed. Just a few answers. What went wrong? Was Sonia okay? Would she be running the 1,500m?

O'Sullivan looked pale and at times close to tears as she tried to explain the disaster. She confirmed she had a 'medical problem'. She confirmed she had sought no medical advice. She insisted she was already recovered and ready for the 1,500m. But with the opening rounds of the 1,500m less than 48 hours away, it was hard to share her conviction.

Now the OCI President, Pat Hickey, launched into lengthy details of the row with BLE. The dirty polyester of both bodies was given a very public airing as Sports Minister Bernard Allen looked on.

On the Wednesday, what was left of Sonia's Olympic dream turned to ashes. Looking drained and uncertain, she was tailed off 11th and last in her 1,500m heat. As our distressed and bewildered heroine walked off the track, the full impact of her demise began to register.

Post-Atlanta, Sonia appeared to bounce back. In early 1997 she won World Indoor 3,000m silver, pipped on the line in Paris by Gabriela Szabo of Romania, and posted ninth at the World CC in Turin, where Ireland took a magnificent team bronze.

It was now time to build toward Athens and the World Championships, and Sonia began well with a win over 1,500m (4.06.35) in Oregon in May. She followed this with a 4.06 (second to Russia's Irma Samorokova) in early June in Paris and another 4.06 on June 13 in Nuremburg, this time behind Hotesa Shura of Ethiopia (4.04).

These latter defeats were only slightly worrying; there still seemed reason to hope that she could race herself into worldbeating form in time for Athens.

The Cork City Sports, June 21, boosted that hope. Sonia won the 2,000m in 5.38.9, flying the last lap in 61.97 and disposing with apparent ease of Regina Jacob (USA). It is a certainty that none among the ecstatic Mardyke crowd dreamed then how cruel a revenge the same Regina would exact a few weeks hence.

Sonia's next outing was the Gaz de France Grand Prix at Paris on June 25. This was her first 3,000m of the outdoor season; it proved a minor disaster. She was never able to stay the pace and struggled in fourth, 13 seconds behind Gabriela Szabo (8.40.44).

Five days later at Sheffield things got even worse. Sonia was hopelessly tailed off over 1,500m, tenth in 4.11.52 as Kelly Holmes of England won in a great PB 3.58.07. Shortly afterward, her agent, Kim McDonald, announced that Sonia would not be contesting the Irish Nationals in mid-July but would continue to prepare for Athens with her new coach, Alan Storey.

Sonia took several weeks off racing before the World Championships and arrived in Athens sounding as confident as ever – seemingly she had been flying in training and was about to silence the doubters. Sadly, it was not to be. What we got was a virtual action replay of her Olympic tragedy.

Just as in Atlanta, she started well, dominating her 1,500m heat (4.08.9) on a day when the big shock was the hamstring injury that forced the favourite, Kelly Holmes, to limp off the track, her title hopes shattered.

In the semifinal, Sonia had to produce her fastest time of the year, 4.05.31, to qualify in fourth place but professed herself comfortable and happy – she had been counting bodies on the big screen and saw no need to fight over places. The only nagging worry to her supporters was that this eminently sensible tactic seemed so unlike a woman who had always loved to produce the big finish.

And so to the final, the race that would lay the ghosts of Atlanta – or so we hoped. Sonia stayed in contention for 1,250m, without ever looking totally comfortable much less dominant. We were on the edges of our seats when, on the back straight of the last lap, it all fell apart.

Anita Weyermann (Switzerland), full of running but boxed in, barged between two runners, bumping Regina Jacob toward Sonia on the outside. Knocked briefly out of her stride, Sonia grabbed Regina's singlet and seemed to recover but was losing ground as they hit the last bend and drifted back to finish eighth in 4.07.81.

Meanwhile, Portugal's Carlo Sacramento had made the move that would carry her to gold (4.04.24). Jacob snatched the silver, Weyermann the bronze.

Immediately after the race, embarrassment was added to disappointment when, on camera, the angry Jacob got her own back (somewhat literally) for the vest-pull by thumping Sonia, and Sonia, wide-eyed and barely coherent, tried to rationalise her defeat for RTE's Tony O'Donoghue.

Amazingly, this was not the end of Sonia's campaign in Athens. With typical courage she insisted on tackling the 5,000m. And with typical optimism she actually took an early lead in her semifinal. But then she drifted and lost contact with the lead group on the eighth lap. A fighting final lap lifted her from ninth to seventh, and her 15.40.82, though the slowest of her career, was only fractions off the qualifying time.

Veteran reporter and former Olympian Tom O'Riordan described Sonia's exit as 'one of the most depressing experiences' in a lifetime of athletics. He also echoed popular intuition when he said: 'Perhaps it's just as well she did not make it (to the final), because she is now an athlete who needs to take a long break from running.'

To everyone's relief, Sonia scratched from the remainder of the 1997 Grand Prix season. Despite her continued insistence that for her training and racing were recreation rather than stress, she seemed to be responding to the almost universal call for a period of rest and rehabilitation.

At 27 years of age, Sonia still has time on her side. She could take a year off competition, come back refreshed, and still have two years to prepare for Sydney 2,000 – not to mention the several further years one might reasonably expect her to remain at the summit of middle- and long-distance running.

Whether this brilliant but apparently headstrong lady has the patience and self-discipline for such a long-term strategy is the question only she can answer.

6

Sonia's 1993 races

Jan. 2	Durham International CC	5.2 k	9th	17.16
Mar. 7	Rogaine 5k (road), Los Angeles	5k	4th	15.57
Mar. 28	Home Fed Carlsbad (road)	5k	3rd	15.51
April 24	Penn Relays, Philadelphia (track)	5,000m	3rd	15.47.65
May 29	Nunez Blanca, Spain (track)	1,500m	1st	4.10.60
June 9	Golden Gala, Rome (track)	1 mile	4th	4.22.94
June 12	European Cup, Rotterdam (track)	1,500m	1st	4.03.38
June 20	Paulen Memorial, Hengelo (track)	3,000m	1st	8.33.40
July 2	BNP d'Athletisme, Lisle (track)	1,000m	5th	2.34.66
July 10	Bislett Games, Oslo (track)	3,000m	1st	8.28.74
July 21	Mobil Meet, Nice (track)	1,500m	1st	4.04.36
July 25	Copenhagen Games (track)	1,500m	1st	4.05.19
Aug. 4	Weltklasse, Zurich (track)	3,000m	1st	8.30.12
Aug. 7	Herculis, Monte Carlo (track)	1,500m	2nd	3.59.60
Aug. 14	World Champs, Stuttgart (track)	3,000m (h)	1st	8.30.12
Aug. 16	World Champs, Stuttgart	3,000m (f)	4th	8.33.38
Aug. 20	World Champs, Stuttgart	1,500m (h)	1st	4.05.81
Aug. 22	World Champs, Stuttgart	1,500m (f)	2nd	4.03.48
Aug. 27	ISTF Berlin, (track)	5,000m	1st	14.45.92
Sept. 3	Ivo Van Damme, Brussels (track)	1,500m	1st	4.01.72
Sept. 10	Grand Prix Final, London (track)	3,000m	1st	8.30.86
Sept. 10	Grand Prix Final, London (track)	1 mile	2nd	4.24.91
Sept. 12	Princes St, Edinburgh (road)	1 mile	1st	4.25.00
Sept. 18	Toto Super, Fukuoka (track)	5,000m	1st	14.59.45

Sonia's 1994 races

May 1	Pennsylvania Road Race	5,000m	1st	15.38.00
May 22	Grampian Festival, Aberdeen (road)	5,000m	1st	15.18.00
June 5	Znamensky Memorial, Moscow (track)	1,500m	2nd	4.11.70
June 11	European Cup, Dublin (track)	1,500m	1st	4.05.75
June 25	Dairygold Cork City (track)	1 mile	1st	4.22.95
July 1	Gateshead International (track)	1 mile	1st	4.25.77
July 8	TSB International, Edinburgh (track)	2,000m	1st	5.25.36WR
July 12	DN Galen, Stockholm (track)	1,500m	1st	4.00.46
July 15	TSB International, London (track)	3,000m	1st	8.21.64
July 18	Nice Grand Prix (track)	1,500m	1st	3.59.10
July 22	Bislett Games, Oslo (track)	1 mile	1st	4.17.25
July 25	Goodwill Games, St Petersburgh (track)	1,500m	2nd	4.04.97
July 28	Goodwill Games, St Petersburgh	800m	8th	2.00.69
Aug. 2	Herculis Vittel, Monte Carlo (track)	1,500m	5th	4.03.54
Aug. 7	European Champs, Helsinki (track)	3,000m (h)	1st	8.51.30
Aug. 10	European Champs, Helsinki	3,000m (f)	1st	8.31.84
Aug. 17	Weltklasse, Zurich (track)	1 mile	2nd	4.23.14
Aug. 19	Ivo van Damme, Brussels (track)	1,500m	3rd	4.05.07
Aug. 21	Weltklasse, Cologne (track)	5,000m	1st	15.06.18
Sept. 3	Grand Prix Final, Paris (track)	5,000m	11th	15.12.94
Sept. 4	Sheffield Invitational (track)	2,000m	5th	5.54.10
Sept. 9	World Cup, London (track)	1,500m	1st	4.12.30
Sept. 13	ITC International, Pune Ind (track)	1,500m	2nd	4.15.25
Sept. 15	Toto Super, Fukuoka (track)	5,000m	1st	15.21.02

Sonia's pre-Atlanta races

May 11	Princeton, USA	1,500m.	1st	4.06.99
May 25	Oregon, USA	3,000m.	1st	8.39.33
June 5	Rome, Italy	5,000m.	1st	14.54.75
June 7	Moscow, Russia	3,000m.	1st	8.47.33
June 16	Santry, Dublin (National Champs)	1,500m	1st	4.15.4
June 22	Cork City Sports, Ireland	3,000m.	1st	8.40.51
July 5	Oslo, Sweden	1,500m.	1st	3.59.91
July 10	Nice, France	3,000m	1st	8.35.43
July 12	London, England	5,000m.	1st	14.48.36
July 16	Atlanta, USA	5,000m.	1st	15.15.80

SEIKO
AWARDS
Certificate of Excellence
Sonia O'Sullivan
Excellence in Irish Athletics in 1993

Part three

The elites from A to W

Algar, Ruth
Clubs: Mullingar AC (1970/73); Crusaders
Coach: Paul O'Connor (Raheny)

Ruth won the 1970, 71, 72, and 73 national 100m titles, the 1971 HJ and pentathlon titles, and the 1972 and 73 200m titles. She won NACAI titles in 1974 (100m) and 1975 (200m, 100mH, and pentathlon). International achievements: 10.8.74, Lisbon, Portugal, 3rd 100m; 11.8.74, Lisbon, Portugal, member of winning relay team, 1st 200m, 24.9; 15.6.75, Osijek European Cup, 5th 100m, 5th 400m.
Ruth now lives in France.

Amond (Lawlor), Patricia
Clubs: St Laurence O'Toole; DCH
Coaches: Paudge Ryan; Jim Kilty

Patricia won the 1980 Irish Schools 100m and 200m titles. She won national senior titles as follows: 1981 100m and 200m; 1984 200m (23.88); 1985 400m; 1986 200m; 1988 200m (her PB 23.46 here was a qualifier for the Seoul Olympics, but she was not selected).

International appearances: 1978, 1st in WAAA Intermediate Champion-ships 100m, Crystal Palace; 1979, reached final of the European Junior Championships 100m and 200m in Poland, as did Michele Carroll – the first Irish sprinters ever to reach a major championship final; 1979, second to Merlene Ottey in All-American High School Championships, Chicago; 1980, silver in WAAA Championships 200m, Crystal Palace; 1985, only Irish track winner (400m) in Europa Cup, Reykjavik, Iceland; 1986, 1st 400m (53.99) Barcelona Triangular; 1988, 2nd to Grace Jackson (Jamaica) in pre-Olympic meet, Seoul.

Like her sister, Mary, Patricia feels that in Carlow she was too far removed from BLE's centre so was often overlooked for team selection.

Amond (O´Brien), Mary
Club: St Laurence O'Toole, Carlow
Coach: Jim Kilty

Born 7 March 1964, Mary started athletics in the Community Games 1979, when she won the 100m final. From 1979 to 1981 she was National Champion U/16 and U/17. She posted qualifying times for the European Junior Championships in 100m and 200m, but in the absence of windmeter and electronic timing she was omitted from the team. She was part of the national senior relay team from 1982 to 1988.

Looking back on her career, Mary feels she took running too seriously too early. She reckons teenagers should be encouraged to enjoy their athletics without pressure and without too much early training. Like her sister, Patricia, she believes that living and training far from Dublin was for them a disadvantage.

PBs: 100m 11. 91, 200m 24.00, 400m 55. 94, 400mH 59.90.

Appleby, Jean
Club: Clonliffe Harriers

Coached by her father, Don, Jean (born 14 May 1955) is sister of Patricia (see below) and first cousin of Mary Barnwell (see below). Her events were 800m (PB 2.09.1) and 1,500m (4.28.2). In a short career curtailed by emigration, Jean placed 15th for Ireland at the 1976 International CC at Rawtenstall. In an international meet in Cwmbran, Wales, on 17/7/76 v Wales, Greece, and Spain, she won the 800m in 2.09.2. A qualified physiotherapist, she now lives in the USA.

Appleby (Barnwell), Mary

Mary (born 8 May 1957) won the following national titles: 1976 800m (2.10.8); 1978 400m (55.65) and 400mH (60.59); 1979 400mH (59.5); 1980 800m (2.06.81); 1983 400mH (58.85, which qualified her for the Los Angeles Olympics, but she broke her ankle while training for the Games). Mary won her first Irish vests in 1974, in both relays. She won 25 vests in all on track and country from 1974 to 1983.

International performances: 1977 Europa Cup, Dublin, 3rd 400mH (60.24); 1978 Westathletic, 3rd 400mH (58.40); 1978 European Championships, Prague, 400mH semifinal;1978 British WAAA, 1st 400mH; 1979 Europa Cup, Sittard, 2nd 400mH (57.62); 1979 WAAA, 2nd 400mH; 1980 Westathletic, 2nd 400mH (57.63); 1981 Europa Cup, Frankfurt, 5th 400mH (57.97); 1983 Europa Cup, Dublin, 2nd 400mH (59.10).

PBs: 100mH 14.2, 400m 54.19, 400mH 56.51, 800m 2.04.1.

Educated at Loreto Convent, Crumlin, Mary Barnwell won 47 hockey caps. She played in the 1986 World Cup in Holland and on the Triple Crown winning team in 1987. She captained the Irish team in the 1989 International Cup in India. At the time of writing she is still playing first division hockey with Loreto.

Mary's father, Liam Appleby, was a noted athlete. Her mother, Marie, played camogie for Dublin. Her sister Clare is an athlete and hockey player. Her brother Paul plays golf and soccer.

Appleby (Doherty), Patricia
Clubs: Clonliffe (till 1979); Crusaders
Coach: Geoff Smith, Crusaders

Born in Dublin, Patricia is another member of the remarkable athletics dynasty of Applebys. Career highlights: 1975 National Relays 4x800, 1st club; 1995 and 1996 National CC, 1st club and 1st county; 1977 and 1978 National Relays, silver; 1979 National Relays 4x400, gold; 1980 Dublin CC, 2nd (with Crusaders); 1980 National Intercounties CC, 3rd ind, 1st team; 1981 World CC, Madrid, 39th; 1981 G.V.Ryan Trophy, 1st 3,000m, 2nd 1,500m; 1981 international v Greece and Yugoslavia, 2nd 1,500m; 1982 De Loughrey Cup, 1st (11.02); 1982 Intercounties CC, 1st; 1982 National CC, 2nd; 1982 G.V.Ryan Trophy, 1st 3,000m; 1982 international v Belgium, Brussels, 1st 3,000m; 1983 Louis Vandendries Trophy, 1st 3,000m (9.44).

Patricia's father, Don Appleby, was an international athlete, as was her sister Jean (see above).

Archbold (George), Ann
Club: Clonliffe Harriers
Coach: Pat Bonass

Ann's father was an athlete with DCH; her brother played soccer with Dundalk. Ann took up running in 1970 at school and eventually came to concentrate on the marathon, competing in the first five Dublins: 1980, 3.35; 1981, 2.55; 1982, 2.54; 1983, 2.49 (3rd); 1984, 2.48 (2nd).

She ran a half-marathon PB 77.06 in 1985 and the same year gained her first Irish vest, at the World Cup Marathon in Hiroshima, Japan, where a virus forced her to pull out at 10k. In 1990 she posted 3.18 in Berlin.

Ann is married with one child and lives in Enniskillen, Co. Fermanagh.

Barrett-Condron, Grainne
Disabled athlete, *Les autres* category (does not use wheelchair)
Club: Irish Wheelchair Association
Coach: self

Prior to 1979 Grainne was Kildare shot-putt champion. She also played soccer, basketball, netball, volleyball, and badminton. In 1979 Grainne was one of a youth group hostelling in Wicklow. As they took a shortcut through the Glen of Imaal, one of the group accidentally set off an unexploded shell. Three boys were killed; Grainne's legs were shattered. There followed many years of painful therapy before Grainne again took up athletics and joined the Wheelchair Association.

Achievements: 1988, selected for Seoul Paralympics; set world shot record 7.70. 1992, 4th in shot, 5th in discus, at Barcelona Paralympics; set world shot records 8.36 and 8.41. 1993/94, won NACAI National Veteran titles in shot, discus, javelin, and hammer; won 1994 World Championship silver in shot and bronze in discus. 1995, set Irish shot record 8.68 and javelin record 16.98. 1996, won shot putt bronze at Atlanta Paralympics .

Barry-Murphy, Margaret
Club: Ovens Olympic
Coaches: Sean Kyle; Riobárd O'Dwyer

A highly competent all-rounder, Margaret (born 21 Sept 1944) had the distinction of representing Ireland at Olympic and European Games despite training mostly on her own (six days per week) in rudimentary conditions.

The highlights of her career were the 1971 Helsinki European Championships (5.73 LJ), the 1972 Munich Olympics (27th pentathlon with 3,770 points, 6th 100mH QF in 15.89), and the 1973 Copenhagen European Games (16.5 100mH, 5.74 LJ).

Bollard, Olive
Rush, Co. Dublin
Club: Raheny Shamrocks
Coach: Tom Curran

Olive commenced running with Lusk AC at 16 years of age and won her first race, a 1,500m. She won the Manufacturers Hanover Corporate Challenge New York 5k in November 1986. She won the 3,000m (9.21.56) in the July 1987 triangular v Scotland and Wales. She won National 3,000m silver and bronze and wore the green vest in 15k road races in Portugal and Brazil.

Olive won many road races in the period 1987 to 1991, including the Simon 10k, the Raheny 5, the Ballycotton 10, the Rathcoole Half Marathon, the Claremorris 10k, and the Dunshaughlin 10k.

Bowe, Nuala
Club: Coolcroo, Co. Tipperary
Coaches: her three brothers, all athletes

In 1968 Nuala (born 2 Jan 1953) ran up to Ann O'Brien in the All-Ireland Senior CC but was disqualified for running under her older sister's name (Nuala was underage). She won the All-Ireland U/16 CC in 1969. She won two international singlets: 26th in the 1969 Clydebank International CC 4,000m; 29th in the 1970 Frederick, USA, CC 4,000m.

Buckley, Marie
Club: Leevale AC
Coach: Hugh Parnell

Marie (born Kinsale 26 Oct 1954) won the NACAI 1,500m (5.04.5) and CC titles in 1970. She represented Ireland at the 1973 International CC Championships, at Waregem, Belgium, posting 52nd, and the 1975 Coatsbridge International CC (13th). She disliked track sessions – most of her training consisted of running for an hour or more each day in open fields.

Butler, Mary
Clubs: UCD; Blackrock AC
Coach: Paddy Craddock

Introduced to athletics by Jack Sweeney in UCD, Mary (born 2 June 1955) won the UCD CC title in 1973 and 1974 and the Colours Race in 1974 and captained UCD in 1975. In 1982 she was on the Crusaders team that took Dublin CC silver.

In 1977 the BHAA came into being; their inaugural race was a 10-mile handicap from Bray to Donnybrook. Mary Butler won and became possibly the first Irishwoman to win a ten-miler. That trophy still takes pride of place in her home. She was on the first committee of the BHAA and was PRO for the first Dublin City Marathon.

In 1980 Mary ran her debut marathon, in London. Her 3.26.57 made her the first Irishwoman to break 3.30. Her PB 3.12 came in the 1981 Dublin City Marathon. She continued in good marathon form in 1982, posting second in Belfast.

Mary's first son, Stephen, was born in 1987. Little James arrived in 1988 – but lived only a year (Mary has since published a moving and widely-acclaimed book about his short life). Aengus was born in 1990.

Mary joined Blackrock in 1992 and began to win veteran honours. In 1994 she won the National Veterans 3k walk. Among her cherished memories is her second place to Mary Purcell at Enniscorthy Strawberry Fair 1973. Her prize was a pair of single sheets;

Mary Purcell won two saucepans.

Mary works in RTE as a TV news editor.

Byrne, Kay
Club: Finn Valley
Coach: Patsy McGonagle

Kay ran for Northern Ireland in the 1984 World CC at New Jersey, USA, and posted 90th. She won the Ulster Senior CC in 1993, 1994, and 1995. She finished 130th in the 1994 World CC in Budapest, Hungary, and was fourth in the National CC in 1996. She won the 1995 National League 3,000m (9.50).

Kay formerly played football. Her sister and brother are also athletes.

Cavanagh, Louise
Clubs: University College AC; UCDAC; DCH
Coach: Ray Shanahan

Louise started competing in the Community Games 1980, qualified for finals on four occasions, and won silver and bronze medals. In 1989 at an U/21 international in Wales she won the 1,500m. In 1990 she won an international CC at Breda, Holland. She twice posted fourth in the National CC, and represented Ireland at the World CC at Antwerp 1991, where she was second Irish scorer. She also wore the green vest at the 1995 European CC, Northumberland, England, and was third Irish scorer.

Louise won six consecutive intervarsity CC titles (1989 to 1994) and also represented Ireland in Poland, France, and Limerick. She won varsity titles at 800m and 1,500m. She ran for DCH in European Clubs CC in 1989, 1990, 1991, and 1992. In August 1997 she won the NI 3,000m title (9.50.88).

Her track PBs are 2.12 and 4.26.

Clinton (Shum), Cathy
Clubs: Clonliffe Harriers; Cannock and Stafford
Coach: Dave Sunderland.

Cathy (born 30 May 1961) was a late starter in running at 27 years of age (1988) but made rapid progress. She won her first international vest in the World Half Marathon Championships held in conjunction with the Great North Run, Newcastle, England.

She again ran the World Half Marathon in Oslo 1992 and finished 24th.

She then stepped up to the classic distance and won the 1993 Dublin City Marathon (2.38.14). She ran the 1995 World Marathon Championship, Gothenburg, but 'hit the wall' and posted 2.43. She won Dublin again in 1996 (2.38.35 in strong winds).

By no means a cross-country specialist, she won the 1994 and 1995 Staffordshire, England, CC titles and placed a surprise 3rd in the 1995 BLE Nationals, thereby qualifying for the World CC, where she finished 101st.

Based in England, Cathy won the Staffordshire 10 mile title in 1990 and 1991 and the Midlands 10k title in 1993 and 1995. International appearances have included the Ekiden Relays in Korea and China. She has PBs for 5m of 26.57, 10k 33.17, 10m 54.47, half marathon 72.48.

Cathy's father, Billy Clinton, played soccer for Limerick.

Conlon-Hodder, Maureen

Born in Gravesend, England, and now living in Westport, Co. Mayo, Maureen did most of her running in Kent. She was Kent mile and CC champion from 1963 to 1966 and 880yds champion in 1963 and 1966. Her PBs are 2.12.04 and 5.02.

She represented Ireland at CC in Barry, Wales, 1967, placing 13th.

Cooney, Winifred
Club: St Anthony's
Coaches: Fr Lovell; Philip Conway

Winifred (born Kilfeakle, Co. Tipperary, 15 Dec 1951) achieved 3,511 points in pentathlon (1974) and competed several times internationally at her preferred individual events: 1973 European Cup, Copenhagen, 5th shot (11.96); 1974 v Portugal, Lisbon, 3rd LJ (5.22), 2nd shot (12.63).

Corrigan, Brigid
Club: Dublin City Harriers
Coaches: Oliver Scully; Jim Corrigan (her father)

Brigid (born Dublin 9 Feb 1964) took up high jumping at age 12. She won many schools titles, including, in 1979, the International Schools HJ. It was also in 1979 that, at just 15, she jumped 1.71 to win the first of her five Irish titles (the others 1982, 83, 84, and 85).

At age 16, she became the first Irishwoman to clear six feet (1.84). Her mark would stand for 14 years until bettered by Laura Sharpe (Navan), holder of the present record 1.89.

She won the British Intermediate HJ in 1980 and Irish intervarsity titles in 1983 and 84. She took silver in the 1983 European Clubs Championship, beaten by Germany's Olympic champion Ulrika Meyfarth. She had two notable victories at international meets: Birmingham, England, 1980 and Taipei, Taiwan, 1983. From 1978 to 1988 she collected over 30 international vests.

Now domiciled in Kingscourt, Co. Cavan, Brigid and her husband have four children, ages one to six.

Cotter, Catherine
Cork
Club: Leevale

Catherine (born 9 April 1952) won the BLE 440yds in 1967 but retired early for want of coaching – she felt she was left too much to her own resources.

Coyle, Joan
Club: Dundrum South Dublin

Joan took up running rather late, in 1966, and made her mark as a veteran. She won silver in the National 15k (road) and team gold in the National Intermediates in 1994. Like her husband, Pat, another athlete, she is heavily involved in athletics administration.

Craddock-Smith, Patricia
Club: Blackrock
Coach: Paddy Craddock

Patricia (born 1 May 1958) took up athletics at 11 years of age when Blackrock AC formed a female juvenile section. She achieved considerable success, gaining numerous representative honours with Dublin on track and country. In a career spanning over 21 years she has won races varying from 3,000m to marathon and has competed in every part of Ireland.

In 1977 and 1988 Patricia was a scoring member of the Dublin teams that won national CC titles. On the strength of finishing 9th and 8th in the Championships, she was selected on the panel for the World CC but narrowly failed to make the team. In 1982 she took silver in the Ulster Marathon. She gained her first Irish vest when completing Boston 1990.

Patricia, like her marathon-running coach and father, Paddy, has given trojan service to a great club; she has also been a delegate to the Dublin County Board for many years. And yet she has no thoughts of retiring; no doubt she intends to emulate Paddy, who has clocked over 30 marathons and shows no signs of slowing up at 60.

Cushen, Bridget
Club: Hercules-Wimbledon
Coach: self

Bridget was born in Dublin (16 Sept 1940) but has spent most of her life in England. Among her achievements was third in the English CC Championships and second in the British WAAA 3,000m (1969) in a UK record 9.49.8, behind Clonliffe's Ann O'Brien (9.43.4). Bridget also won the Surrey CC Championships in 1969.

Despite her impressive credentials, Bridget was never selected for Ireland, BLE explaining on several occasions that she had not run trials in Ireland. Oddly, BLE were more lenient with two other women: Brenda Bailey-Robinson (Bury) and Maureen Hodder-Conlon (Dartford Harriers) gained CC vests without ever coming home for a trial. Despite BLE's attitude, Bridget continued with her athletics and became the first Irishwoman to complete a marathon: at Harlow on 28 Oct 1973 she posted 3.37.24 .

Bridget also won veteran medals in many countries and still races occasionally. She is Hon Sec of the English Veterans' Association.

Davoren, Freda
Club: UCC
Coach: Ray Shanahan

Freda, born in Causeway, Co. Kerry (16 Mar 1973) joined North Kerry AC as an 11-year-old and was soon winning races and titles. She won the Munster U/15 800m (in a record 2.16) and the National U/15 1,500m and was second in the National U/15 800m. A year later she was second in the National U/16 400m and 800m.

Around this time, however, Freda incurred a calf injury, which sidelined her for four years. She resumed in October 1993 and, seemingly unaffected by the layoff, was almost immediately back into winning mode – within a year or so she had gained her first senior vests on track (both outdoor and indoor), road, and country.

She won the 1996 National Indoor 800m and 1,500m and the National (outdoor) 800m (2.05.17 PB with Aisling Molloy second). Also in 1996 she ran the World Student Games CC in Portugal, the European Indoors in Stockholm, the Europa Cup in Brussels, and the Ekiden Relay in Seoul.

In 1997 Freda retained her National Indoor 800m and 1,500m titles, won the Scottish National Indoor 800m in Glasgow (2.07) and the Vienna Indoor International 800m (2.08), finished third in the British Indoor 800m, and took silver behind Amanda Crowe in the National 800m (2.07.98).

PBs: 400m 56.6, 800m 2.05.17 (2.05.66 indoor), 1,500m 4.20.00 (indoor).

Delahunty, Sinéad
Clubs: KCH; Providence College; Team New Balance
Coach: John Evans

Sinéad (born 12 Feb 1971) won U/14, U/15, U/16, U/17, All Ireland, Schools Senior CC, and Schools 1,500m track titles before taking up a scholarship at Providence College, USA. While at Providence she was six times All-American NCAA.

She placed 8th (4.12.20) in her 1,500m heat in the 1994 European Championships. She posted 2nd (8.58.33) in the 1995 TAC US Indoor 3,000m. She took silver in the 1995 National 1,500m (4.10.4) behind Sonia O'Sullivan (4.07.09). In September 1995 she won the Fifth Avenue Mile, New York, in 4.25.2; Paula Radcliffe, England, was 2nd, Blodine Bitzner Ducret, France, 3rd. The same year, she was 7th (1st Irishwoman) in the European CC Championships in Durham, England.

In February 1996, while training in Brighton, USA, Sinéad was hit by a car and had to withdraw from the World CC in Capetown, South Africa.

Sinéad reached the 1,500m semifinal in the 1996 Atlanta Olympics. She led that race at the bell, but when the Romanian Szabo led the last-lap charge, Sinéad lacked the necessary acceleration and slipped to ninth place (4.12.52).

In Athens 1997 Sinéad again reached the 1,500m semifinal and ran brilliantly to post seventh therein (4.07.46). Forced to run wide round the last bend, she was brutally unlucky to miss qualification for the final by fractions of a second.

A few weeks after Athens, Sinéad finished second (4.24.87) to Paula Radcliffe (4.22.96) in the Fifth Avenue Mile.

Her PBs include 800m 2.06.9, 1,500m 4.07.27, mile 4.34.4, 3,000m 8.58.33, and 5,000m 15.33.44.

Dockery, Patrice
Clubs: Irish Wheelchair TC; Clonliffe Harriers
Coaches: Carol Hayes; Tom Coyle

Born (28 Mar 1971) with spina bifida, Patrice has been in a wheelchair since she was 14. She trains six days a week, is a marvellous competitor, and has an impressive string of achievements in ten years of competition.

At the 1986 International Junior World Games, Nottingham, she won 100m, 200m, and 800m. At the 1987 International World Games, Stoke Mandeville, she won the 100m and was 3rd in the 200m. At the 1988 Seoul Paralympics she was 4th in the 100m, 5th in the 200m, 6th in the 400m. At the 1989 International World Games, Stoke Mandeville, she won the 100m in a world record 20.33 and was 2nd in the 200m. At the 1990 World Championships, Holland, she was 2nd in the 200m, 3rd in the 800m, 4th in the 400m.

At the 1992 Barcelona Paralympics, she reached the 100m, 200m, 400m, and 800m semifinals, setting Irish records in the latter three. At the 1993 Welsh Nationals she was 2nd in 100m, 200m, and 1,500m and 3rd in 400m, 800m, and 5,000m and set an Irish record in the 5,000m.

At the 1994 World Championships, Berlin, Patrice was 8th in the 100m final and at the BWRA Championships was 3rd in the 100m. At the 1996 Atlanta Paralympics she finished 4th in the 100m, setting an Irish record 18.04.

Patrice won the 1997 Dublin City Marathon women's wheelchair section (2:14:19).

Donohoe, Mary
Club: Clonliffe Harriers
Coach: Kathryn Davis

Mary played hockey and soccer prior to her introduction to running: the first Women's Mini Marathon, 1983.

Her dedication to training was rewarded with an Irish vest at Sidcup, England, in 1985. She won the National CC title at Santry in February 1986 and went on the following month to represent Ireland at the World CC in Neuchatel, Switzerland. She would also run the World CC in 1987 (Warsaw, Poland), 1988 (Auckland, New Zealand), and 1995 (Durham, England).

Mary ran in several international track meets in 1985 and 1986. She won the National 3,000m (9.16.06) in 1986 and a Grand Prix 3,000m (9.12.80) in Bratislava, Czechoslovakia, in June 1987. She suffered recurring injury in the late eighties and early nineties but came back to win the Dublin CC Championship in 1993 and 1994 and to post a 10k track PB 33.25 on 13 June 1993 at the Europa Cup in Rotterdam, Holland. In May 1994 she won the Glasgow International 10k (34.22) and two weeks later the Evening Press Mini Marathon in 33.11.

Doody-Scully, Margaret
Club: Feshanagh, Castlemahon
Coach: self

A natural athlete, Margaret (born 13 Feb 1946) took up running in November 1967 and won over 60 races in the Munster area. She gained her only Irish singlet when posting 23rd in the 1968 International CC at Blackburn. Like many other rural athletes of her era, she felt there was little or no support from officialdom. Her short athletics career was terminated by knee problems.

Dowling (Walsh), Claire
Clubs: Clonliffe Harriers; Calry AC
Coach: self (advised by Harry Cooney and Noel O'Rourke)

Clonliffe Harriers organised their first women's races in November 1963; Claire (born 27 May 1942) won the 600yds. The following February, they organised the first women's cross-country race at Santry; again Claire was the winner (with a certain Ann O'Brien second). For the next decade and more Claire was to be a major force. She won 19 national titles between 1965 to 1973 and represented Ireland from 1964 to 1977.

1970: she was on the Clonliffe team that won Dublin and Eastern Regions CC; she took silver in the WAAA 800m (2.04.9) and was on the Clonliffe 4x400m team that posted second in the WAAA Championships in an Irish record 3.45.8 (unbeaten until 1988).

1971: she reached the European 800m final in Helsinki but was obstructed by falling runners; she helped Clonliffe win the Dublin CC title and the Louis Vandendries T&F Trophy; she helped Clonliffe win the WAAA 4x400m (3.49.1) and 4x800m, the latter in an Irish record 8.48.8 (Jean Appleby 2.16.7, Jean O'Neill 2.14.3, Ann Cummins 2.12.9, Claire Walsh 2.04.9).

1972: she was on the Clonliffe team that won the Eastern Regions CC; she was eliminated in her heat of the Olympic 800m in Munich.

1973: she was second (24.3) in the Europa Cup 200m and helped set a 4x400m national record 3.37.4; she took silver in the WAAA 400m (54.4).

1974: she won the 400m v Portugal in Lisbon (56.00) and was sixth in the Rome European Championships (54.15).

1977: she helped Ireland win the Europa Cup 4x400m in Dublin.

Claire won numerous national track titles: the 1965 AAUE 200m (26.2), 400m (57.6), and long jump; the 1968 BLE 100yds (11.5) and 220yds (26.2); the 1969 100m (12.5), 200m (25.4), and 400m (56.5); the 1970 200m, (24.3 NR), 400m (55.4), 800m (2.10.6), and pentathlon (3,837); the 1971 100m (12.2), 200m (24.6), and 400m (54.4); the 1972 200m (24.5) and 400m (55.4); the 1973 100m (12.2) and 200m (24.3).

Indoors, she took the notable scalp of Hildegarde Falck, winning in Berlin over 800m (2.10.9) in December 1970. In March 1971 she ran 2.07.4 in the European Indoors but failed to reach the final.

During 1967 to 1974 Claire trained close to her home town, Collooney, Co. Sligo, using the clay footpaths by the Dublin-Sligo road. She also used Sligo Racecourse.
Claire held Irish records at 100m (11.9), 200m (24.1 all-comers record,) 400m (53.7), and 800m (2.03.4).

Claire's father was an athlete and played rugby with CYMS, Terenure. Her sisters Jean O'Neill and Anne Manners were both first class athletes. Her daughters Patricia and Niamh won national titles.

Doyle, Mary
Club: St Finbarr's, Cork
Coach: Pat Ryan

Mary (born 17 May 1954) won the BLE National 100m (12.3) in 1972 and went on to represent Ireland at the 1973 European Cup 4x100m in Copenhagen, the 1975 European Cup 200m (4th) and 4x100m (4th) in Copenhagen, and the 1976 Cwmbran International 100m (2nd) and 4x100m (2nd). Like many of her peers, Mary felt that living and training outside Dublin was a huge hindrance.

Duff, Paula
Club: Irish Blindsports
Coaches: Tony Guest; Mick McKeon

Paula took up athletics in May 1986 and represented Ireland at 100m in the 1988 Seoul Paralympics. At the 1991 European Championships, Caen, France, she won javelin silver. At the 1992 Barcelona Paralympics she won medals at shot and relay. At the 1993 European Championships, Dublin, she entered six events and won medals for javelin, shot, and relay. She completed the 1995 Dublin City Marathon.
PBs: 100m 14.09, 200m 32.33, javelin 18.00, long jump 3.40.

Duffy, Teresa
Clubs: Beechmount Harriers; Essex Ladies
Coach: Norman Brook

Teresa represented Northern Ireland at the World CC in Neuchatel, Switzerland, 1986 and Warsaw, Poland, 1987. She represented the Republic of Ireland at the World CC in Aix-les-Bains, France, 1990; Boston, USA, 1992; Amorebieta, Spain, 1993; Budapest, Hungary, 1994; Durham, England, 1995; and Capetown, South Africa, 1996.

She won the National Interclubs CC title in 1994 (Roscommon), 1995 (Naas), and 1996 (Santry). She also won the Northern Ireland CC title in 1994 and 1995, thus becoming the first woman to win double titles two years in a row.

Teresa won the 1995 BLE 5,000m (16.15.94). She has twice posted second in the Women's Mini Marathon, 1995 (34.04) and 1997 (34.12). She holds the Northern Ireland 3,000m record (9.12).

Dunne, Maria
Club: Crusaders
Coaches: Peggy Mullins; Jack Sweeney (sprints); Gay Hogan (discus)

Maria (born 4 Jan 1951) won national titles at javelin in 1971 (83'4.75") and discus in 1972 (116'3.5") and 1973 (125'0.5"). In an international v Portugal at Lisbon on 10.8.74 she placed 3rd (115') in the discus.

Dunne-Fitzpatrick, Cathy
Clubs: Leevale AC; Irish Wheelchair AC

Cathy has competed in four Paralympics: 1980, 1984, 1988, and 1992. Her CV is impressive: 1978, javelin silver at National Championships; 1979, gained first Irish vest, at Stoke Mandeville, England, and won discus and javelin bronze; 1980, won discus and pentathlon bronze at Paralympics in Holland; 1981, won discus and shot gold, javelin silver, and pentathlon bronze at International Games, Stoke Mandeville; 1982, won discus gold and javelin and pentathlon bronze at International Games, Stoke Mandeville.

1984, won discus gold at Paralympics, Holland; 1985, won discus, javelin, and shot silver and pentathlon bronze at European Championships, Belgium, and discus and javelin gold, shot silver, and pentathlon bronze at International Games, Stoke Mandeville; 1988, won discus silver and pentathlon, 200m, 1,500m, javelin, and shot bronze at Seoul Paralympics; 1989, won discus gold at British Paraplegic Games; also won Don Bosco Award; 1990, won discus bronze at World Championships in Holland; 1992, 4th in discus at Barcelona Paralympics, her fourth Paralympics .

Cathy has now retired from athletics (with Irish records for discus and javelin) to concentrate on sailing and water-skiing. In 1987 and 1988 she won National Sailing Championship bronze medals.

English, Una
Clubs: DCH; Zurich, Switzerland; Havering, England
Coach: self

Una (born Cork 14 August 1970) has competed for both Britain, where she resided, and Ireland. She won her first major track title, the National 1,500m, at Santry in 1991. An impressive list of achievements followed.

1993: World Student CC Championships, Dijon, France, 3rd.

1994: British AAA 3,000m, 1st (9.10); World Corporate Games RR, Geneva, 1st; Northern England League CC, 1st; Indoor International 1,500m, Vienna, 2nd.

1995: Scottish National Indoor 3,000m, 1st (9.10); Swiss National CC, 3rd; British

AAA 1,500m, 3rd.

1996: ranked 2nd in Ireland over 800m (2.05), 3rd over 1,500m (4.11), and 3rd over 3,000m (9.01); European CC Championships, Belgium, 31st.

1997: National CC Championships, Whitechurch, 2nd; World CC, Turin, 25th and team bronze.

Selected for the 1997 World Championships in Athens, and drawn in the same semi-final as Sonia O'Sullivan, Una became detached from the main group and trailed in 13th, and outside the qualifying places, in 16.07.09.

PBs: 800m 2.03, 1,500m 4.11, 3,000m 9.01, 5,000m 15.25.57.

Una resides in Zurich, Switzerland, where she works for Nestles. Her brother Des (DSD) is a four-minute miler and Irish international.

Fleming, Joan
Club: St Finbarr's AC

In 1972 Joan won the National BLE 800m in 2.11.6.

Folan (Curran), Jean
Coach: Liam Kavanagh, GCH

While a student in Galway in 1979, Jean Folan (born 15 July 1957) became the official pioneer of women's marathon running in this country: she completed the Tullamore Marathon in a time of 3.37. The following year, she again completed the distance. In 1983 she scored a notable victory (2.59) in the People's Marathon in Stockholm.

Jean was an excellent cross-country runner and won multiple gold with UCG in the early seventies. She also won the Connaught Championships in 1972 and wore an Irish vest in the Home Countries International at Rawtenstall 1976.

She competed for Edinburgh University, Scotland, in 1977 and 1978; she ran with Dundrum and then Bray Runners in the mid-eighties; she orienteered; she was runner up in the National Triathlon Championship; she cycled the Co-operation North Dublin-Belfast-Dublin several times. She won veteran 25k bronze in Israel 1987.

Tragically widowed in the early nineties, when her athlete husband, Dave, died suddenly, Jean lives in Barna, Co. Galway, with her young sons, Enda and Ross.

Foley, Sharon
Club: Lifford AC
Coach: Ben O'Donnell

Sharon (born 20 May 1972) commenced athletics at age 11 and showed immediate aptitude. She won her first National Senior high jump title in 1989 (1.74) and retained it in 1990 (1.76). Injury prevented her contesting the event a couple of times thereafter, but she won it again in 1995 (1.76) and 1997 (1.75).

Sharon jumped 1.75 at the 1990 European Indoors, Glasgow, and again at the 1993 World T&F, Stuttgart. In 1996 she recorded 1.86 indoors, a mark she repeated in 1997 at the AAA Indoors, Birmingham. She won the 1997 National Indoors high jump and long jump and the 1997 NI high jump (1.75).

Foreman (Nagle), Deirdre
Club: Dublin City Harriers
Coaches: Jim Kavanagh; Mick Purcell; Des de Loughrey; Dermot Nagle

Deirdre (born 17 Nov 1949) has been winning races for over a quarter of a century. She represented Ireland 13 times in the International (now the World) CC, with a best placing of 14th, in Chepstow, England. She won the National CC three times: 1974, 1975, and 1976. She was a member of the DCH team that won the European Clubs CC in 1985 and 1986.

She represented Ireland eight times on the track: 1971, Munich 1,500m; 1974, 3,000m and 1,500m v Lisbon and Portugal, 1st and 2nd; 1975, Europa Cup 1,500m, 3rd; 1,500m v Wales and Scotland, 2nd; 1978, European Championship 3,000m, 19th; 1979, Europa Cup 3,000m, 3rd; 1980, Westathletic Meet; 1981, 1,500m v Yugoslavia and Greece. Deirdre also gained singlets for the Hiroshima World Marathon 1985, the Madrid World 10k, and the Gateshead World 15k.

She ran her debut marathon in 1981, finishing second to Emily Dowling (2.48.22) in Dublin. In 1982 she again came second, this time to Mary Purcell in the National Marathon in Limerick. She then went on to represent Ireland in the European Championship Marathon in Helsinki.

In April 1984 Deirdre finished first at the National Marathon in Cork but was disqualified when BLE took offence at the size of the logo on her vest. Christine Kennedy (GCH) came in second and was awarded the gold medal. The consolation for Deirdre was that adidas, whose logo had upset the officials, presented her with their prize.

Deirdre trained hard, averaging eight sessions per week, including hills, intervals, long runs, and a ten-mile cycle. This explains why she could produce a 2.07.02 800m, a 4.14.2 1,500m, and a 2.37 marathon after being in the running game 14 years!

PBs: 800m 2.07.02, 1,500m 4.14.02, 3,000m 8.59.05, 10,000m road, 33.30, marathon 2.37.42 (5th in national rankings).

Deirdre has ceased competing, but still enjoys jogging and has taken up orienteering. She and Dermot Nagle have two teenage sons. Her father, Brendan Foreman, was one of Donore's leading distance runners in the late thirties and forties. One of the longest-serving officers of BLE, he has given a lifetime to athletics.

Gallagher, Deirdre
Clubs: Ballina AC; UCD
Coach: Michael Lane (Mullingar Harriers)

Deirdre (born 13 July 1974) comes from an athletic family; both her father and mother played several sports. Her sister and two brothers are also athletically minded; Daniel (13) is a promising walker, winning an All-Ireland Indoor and National Community Games titles in 1996.

Deirdre started race-walking when she was 11. The judge for her first race was Joe Doonan; he advised her to persist with the discipline. She won Schools walking and CC races in all age-groups.

An international career that began in Hungary 1992, when she was just 17, has had many milestones: 1992 World Junior Championships 5k, Seoul, 25th (24.59); 1994 European Championships, Helsinki; 1995 Penn Relays 5k, 1st (22.51 NR); 1995 World Championships 10k, Gothenburg, 46.00 NR; 1996 Manx Airlines International 10k, 45.12 Olympic qualifier; Penn Relays 5k, 2nd (22.45); National Senior 5k, 1st (22.00); National U/23 5k, 1st (21.35 NR); Atlanta Olympics 10k, 23rd.

Deirdre holds national records at 3k indoor (12.51), 5k (21.35), and 10k (45.12). She trains six days, approx 60 miles, per week.

Good (Murphy), Joy
Clubs: Bandon; St Finbarr's
Coach: George Bennett

Joy (born 14 Jan 1957) took part in schools athletics from age 15. Her first big win was the 1975 NACAI long jump title (16'9.5").

Wonderfully versatile, she won the BLE long jump title in 1975 (5.18), 1976 (5.39), 1978 (5.81), and 1981 (5.80) and the high jump title in 1976 (1.65). She was national pentathlon and heptathlon champion in 1978, 79, and 81 and held the national pentathlon record at 4,794 points. She set PBs for 100m 11.95, 100mH 15.2, 400m 55.5, and 800m 2.14.5 during multi-events.

She wore the green vest in long jump, hurdles, and relays in ten European countries. She was in the Irish 4x100m team (with Nora O'Grady, Caroline O'Shea, and Michele

Walsh) that set a national record 46.9 in the 1978 Westathletic Games at Sittard, Holland. Injuries terminated her career in 1981.

Joy's mother played interpro hockey; her sister was NACAI discus champion.

Now married and living in Carrigaline, she has three boys, David (at 14 the eldest), Peter, and Tony. All enjoy athletics but experience no pressure from Joy, who wisely deplores parental pushiness in this context.

Gorman (Curley), Pauline
Club: Tullamore Harriers
Coach: Robert Denmead

Pauline (born 10 March 1969) had been several years running when, in 1992, she came under the coaching of Robert Denmead. The new regime and her dedication to training paid off when she won the 1994 National Intermediate CC title at Killenaule.

But it has been only in the past couple of years that she has unleashed her real potential. In 1995 she won the Eastern Regions 5k (road), was second in the National Indoor 3,000m (9.55.32), and finished tenth in the National CC.

In 1996 she finished seventh in the National CC and won the Eastern Regions 800m, the Tolerton 10k, and the Ballybrittas Open CC. She also posted seventh in the National Intercounties CC, narrowly missing selection for the European CC.

The year 1997 has been Pauline's best so far. She won the Eastern Regions CC at Ballinakill, Co. Laois, and the National Indoor 3,000m (9.58). She posted a brilliant third in the National CC at Whitechurch, Co. Cork, forcing her way onto the team for the World CC Championships and thereby partaking in Ireland's glory day in Turin, Italy (though she finished 117th and outside the scoring four, she received team bronze alongside Catherina, Sonia, and company).

Pauline has run for Ireland ten times on road and country. Her sister Ann Gorman (Carroll) is also a Tullamore stalwart and an international on track, road, and country who has twice posted fourth in the Women's Mini Marathon, 1993 (35.42) and 1994 (34.31). Remarkably, Pauline and Ann made their international debuts in the same cross-country race, Mallusk 1995.

Greenan, Mags
Club: Dublin City Harriers
Coach: Tom Curran

Mags started running at 16 but was plagued by injuries and switched to horseriding, tennis, windsurfing, and swimming. She returned to athletics at 37 years of age and says it was like being 'born again'.

She was 2nd veteran in the 1994 and 1995 National CC and 2nd in the 1994 British

Nationals. She was on the Irish team that took European 10,000m gold and 5,000m silver at Athens in 1994. She was first veteran in the 1994 Women's Mini Marathon (36.20).

At the 1995 World Veteran Games, Buffalo, USA, she finished 4th (O/35) in the 10k road and led Ireland to team gold. At the 1996 World Veteran Games, Brugge, Belgium, she repeated that feat, again winning team gold and posting 4th individual over 10k. She also won the 25k road.

In November 1996, Mags, now 39, won the Dublin Senior CC and was awarded green singlets (senior) for international races at Belfast and Dunleer. In June 1997 she took 10k gold (36.57) in the European Road Championships (veterans) at Den Haag, Nederland.

Hargan, Dawn
Club: Finn Valley
Coach: Pat Devine

Dawn (born 14 April 1971) played several sports, including swimming and cycling, before concentrating on running and going on to become an international. She gained her first vest with Northern Ireland in a 1987 triangular v Belgium and Scotland, in which she placed 5th in the 1,500m (4,23). Also in 1987, she won a British WAAA 1.500m title (4.33.23). Representing Northern Ireland v Britain at the 1987 Ipswich International, she placed 2nd in the 1,500m (4.32). At Hannover, Germany, in 1987, in a 1.500m v Germany, she posted 2nd (4.31).

Dawn was part of the Finn Valley teams that won the 1993 National Road Relay and the 1994 and 1995 National CC Championship. She won the 1993 National Under/23 1.500m (4.34.36) at Tullamore. She won team gold and individual silver in the Ulster CC Championships. And she finished 3rd in the 800m (2.15) at the 1995 Indoor International at Nenagh.

PBs: 400m 59.00, 800m 2.12, 1,500m 4.23.

Harrington, Maureen
Clubs: Kenmare AC; Olympic AC; An Ríocht
Coaches: Zbigniew Orywal; Eamonn Harvey

Maureen started in the Community Games, reaching Mosney finals U/14 and U/15 and winning the 1983 U/16 1,500m. In 1984 she was on the Holy Cross team that won the All Ireland Schools Senior CC title.

With Kenmare AC she won about 50 NACAI titles before joining Olympic AC and BLE. She took National Intercounties CC silver in 1992 and 1993 and National

Intercounties CC gold at Dungarvan in 1994 and at Killenaule in 1995. Her greatest success to date came, however, in February 1997, when at Whitechurch, Cork, she at last won the National Interclubs CC.

Maureen has a score of international vests. She ran the World CC in Amorebieta 1993, Budapest 1994, Capetown 1996, and Turin 1997 (whence she took home team bronze). She finished 28th in the 1994 European CC Championships.

Hayden, Rosaleen
Clubs: Raheny Shamrocks; DCH
Coach: self

Formerly a cyclist who had represented Ireland at the Women's Tour de France and World Championships, Rosaleen took to athletics in 1983 at 34 years of age. She immediately tasted success, winning the 1983 Leinster CC and representing Ireland in the World CC at Gateshead. She went on to win eight international singlets,

In May 1983 she won the Dublin 3,000m. In 1985 (Madrid) and 1986 (Algarve) she was on the DCH team that won the European Clubs CC. She won the 1987 National Half Marathon, Rathcoole, and the 1989 Belfast Marathon.

Rosaleen produced a PB 2.55.55 for marathon silver at the World Veteran Championships in Buffalo, USA. In the Crete World Veterans she took 4th in 3.23.02. In the Milan World Veterans she posted 3.04.

Hendricken, Geraldine
Club: St Laurence O'Toole
Coach: Jim Harvey

Geraldine attended Providence Rhode Island University from 1988 to 1992, during which period she was seven times All-American at 3,000m and mile indoors and was one of the all-Irish quartet that in 1990 set a US Collegiate 4x800m record 8.38.7 (Geraldine 2.12.1, Sinéad Delahunty 2.10.9, Geraldine Nolan 2.09.8, Siobhán Gallagher 2.05.9).

Her many wins include the 1991 Terrier Classic Boston Indoors 3,000m and the 1991 Oporto International 1,500m (4.18). She also competed in the 1991 World Student Games 1,500m at Sheffield, England, and in 1992 won the NCAA Championships 3,000m (9.14). She contested the 1993 World Indoor 3,000m in Toronto and the 1994 European 3,000m in Helsinki, where she was eliminated in her heat. She made her 10,000m debut in the 1993 Penn Relays, finishing second in an excellent 32.50. In 1994, she won the Harry Jerome Classic 1,500m in Vancouver (4.21) and the Toronto 10,000m (33.30). Also in 1994, she posted second in the Montreal International 3,000m (9.00). She placed third in the 1995 National 5,000m (16.31). PBs: 800m 2.07, 1.500m 4.14, mile 4.34.

Hennessy, Catherine
Clubs: Tulloght, Co. Kilkenny; St Josephs AC; New Ross

Catherine has won 12 Kilkenny county titles at 800m, 1,500m, 3,000m, and CC as well as national titles at outdoor and indoor track, CC, and road (including walking). She joined New Ross in 1984 and was on the Wexford CC team that took team honours in the B section of the National Interclubs CC. In 1984, she ran the Dublin City Marathon when one month pregnant and posted an easy 2.57.19. She represented Ireland at CC in Mallusk and Wales. She contested the World Veterans T&F in Buffalo, USA, winning O/35 gold in 10,000m and team CC and silver in 5,000m.

Catherine finds training in the country difficult. She uses the local tartan track, where the fee is £2 per night and there is no electric lighting unless ten or more athletes turn up. She feels, by the way, that team selection, including that for internationals, should be done by trials.

Hickey, Greta
Club: DCH
Coaches: Jim Kilty; Dermot Nagle

Greta (born 22 Sept 1958) is married to Roy Dooney, former international CC and marathon man. In 1974/75, she made the Schools International CC team. In 1979, she won Intervarsity CC and track titles and was awarded 'pink' by Dublin University Central Athletics Committee. In 1981, she won the British Colleges CC and the International Catholic Universities CC and was third in the Dublin City Marathon (2.53).

In 1983/84, she was on the Irish team at the World CC and the DCH team that ran up in the European Clubs CC. She won the BLE National 10m (road) in 57 mins. In 1985, she again competed in the World CC and was on the DCH team that won the European Clubs CC. In 1986, she captained the DCH team that retained the European CC title. She also captained the Irish team at the World CC.

Greta has won the Evening Press Women's Mini Marathon (34.33) and captained the Irish team at the World 15k Road Championship. She is now retired from racing.

Hickey, Mary
Club: St Benedict's, Arklow.

Mary was introduced to athletics in 1968 by her brother John Nolan, many times a Co. Wicklow CC champion. She ran her first race at 16 years of age, finished second, and was bitten by the athletics bug.

From 1968 to 1993 Mary won dozens of Wicklow track and CC titles. She also excelled on the roads, winning 10k, 10 mile, and half-marathon races all over Ireland and twice posting second in the Clonliffe 20. She completed the Maracycle (Dublin/Belfast/Dublin). She was fifth in the Isle of Man Hill Marathon (39.5 miles) in 1982. She ran the 42-mile Swiss Alpine Marathon in July 1994 (9.14) and was second in the inaugural All-Ireland Triathlon, 28 Sept 1983. She ran the 1980 London Marathon (3.37) and the 1980 National Marathon in Cork (5th in 3.15). She again ran the Cork National in 1984 (7th in 3.12).

The most cherished of all Mary's trophies are, however, her 18 Dublin City Marathon plaques. Her fastest time in the great event was 2.57, for 4th place, in 1981. Her slowest was 6.15 in 1988 – when she was six months pregnant! Three months later she had a bouncing baby boy, 10lbs 8oz, Calvin Seán. In 1987 she won the O/35 category in 3.02. In 1994 she was best O/30 in 3.16. In 1995 she was 2nd O/40 in 3.17.10.

Mary competed in Ireland's inaugural trail race, 50k (approx 32m) over the undulating Wicklow Way on 6 April 1996. She was first woman home, posting five hours and leaving many of the men trailing (pun intended). Some running for a 42-year-old!

Hill, Eleanor
Club: Bray Runners
Coach: Brendan O'Shea

Born in Shercock, Co. Cavan, Eleanor played badminton, football, and basketball before she was introduced to athletics in 1983 at the age of 21. She has won numerous Wicklow CC titles, finished second in Leinster Novice CC and third in Leinster Intermediate CC, and won the 1991 Bray to Donnybrook Ten (58.28).

She has enjoyed most success at marathon. She posted fifth (2.51) in her first attempt at the distance: Dublin 1989. She then went on to win Belfast 1990 (2.50) and to post 2.50 again at Berlin 1991. She was back in Belfast in 1992, finishing 3rd in 2.47, and in 1993 (2nd in 2.49). She achieved her PB 2.45 when posting 2nd at the 1992 National Marathon. She went one better at the 1994 National Marathon, around Dublin Airport, taking gold in 2.57.42.

Eleanor has completed two Belfast/Dublin Maracycles. She is married to clubmate Alan Threadgold, lives in Greystones, and teaches at Newcastle. A very consistent trainer, she has ambitions to improve her marathon best.

Hilliard Murphy, Anne
Club: Dublin City Harriers

Anne (born 7 Mar 1959) showed promise in 1970 when winning the Dublin U/12 CC title but did not take running seriously until the eighties. She represented Ireland in the 1983 Home Countries CC in Dublin (20th) and in the 1983 World CC in Gateshead

(79th and second Irish finisher). In 1984 she again ran the Home Countries CC, in Glasgow, and in December finished second in the National Intercounties CC at Sligo.

1985 was a great year for Anne: she posted fifth in the Home Countries CC, Bexley, England. She finished eighth in the European Clubs CC, helping DCH win team gold. She scored 59th in the World CC, Lisbon, second (74.56) in the Birmingham Half Marathon, and 4th in an international track 3,000m in Norway.

In 1986 she again posted eighth in the European Clubs CC – and again helped DCH secure gold. She ran the World CC, in Neuchatel, Switzerland, and the World 15k Road in Lisbon (30th). And in 1987 she won the Rathcoole National Half Marathon.

Anne is now married, living in Donegal, and running an easy 20 miles per week. She has four girls, aged 7, 6, 4, and 2. Her brothers Brendan and Mel are elite runners.

Hoey, Siobháin
Club: Dublin City Harriers
Coaches: Gerry Ronan; Paul McCauley

Siobháin (born 17 July 1970) took up athletics in 1979 and has won Junior, Inter, and Senior Irish Schools long jump titles, BLOE and Universities titles in long and triple jump, and National Senior triple jump titles. All told, she has won about 80 national titles at various events and age-grades.

She represented Ireland at Celtic Games (1983 through 87), Universities (1993 through 1995), Europa Cup (1994 and 1995), and Five Nations Cup (1996). The first Irishwoman to triple-jump 12 metres, she won the National (outdoor) title for the five years 1993 through 1997. She won the 1997 NI title (12.16). She is national triple jump record-holder outdoor (12.21) and indoor (12.28). Her ambition is to break 13 metres.

Siobháin's younger sister Aoife is an All-Ireland Indoors LJ champion U/13.

Hogan (Mullins), Peggy
Clubs: Crusaders; Hampstead Harriers
Coach: Sean Kyle

Peggy was born 21 Sept 1938 in Riverstown, Co. Tipperary. She took up running in 1962 with Hampstead before coming home to Crusaders. While with Hampstead, she won the British Junior CC title. Back in Ireland, she won the AAUE mile title (5.10.3) and the 1967 BLE CC. She has a mile PB of 4.55.

Her international appearances included: 880yds v Scotland, 8/8/64, Ayr, 4th (2.21.8); 880yds v Belgium, 5/9/64, Brussels, 3rd (2.21.5); 4,000m CC, 18/3/67, Barry, Wales, 3rd; Clydebank International CC, 10th; Frederick CC, 21/3/70, 10th.

Peggy made a comeback in 1973 and won the Dublin CC title. She now keeps fit and plays golf off a 12 handicap.

Hopkins (Dowling), Emily
Clubs: Avondale; DCH; Sports World
Coaches: Tom McCormack; Eddie Hogan; Brendan O'Shea

Emily (born 27 Sept 1950) has been 30 years in athletics. In 1967 she ran the Home Countries CC in Barry, Wales (her brother Tommy ran in the men's race). In 1996 she competed in her 19th National CC Championships, at Santry, alongside her daughter, Lisa (20), on the Sports World team.

While with DCH Emily was ten times a scoring member of the winning National Interclubs CC team. She competed in seven World CC Championships. Her happiest moment was probably her marathon debut in 1981; she won Dublin in a fine time of 2.48.23.

She took 3rd (2.47) in the 1988 National Marathon at Wexford 1988 and just missed selection for the Seoul Olympics. She competed at World 10k and 15k (road) and won Irish titles at 10 miles and half-marathon. PBs:10k 33.53, 10 miles 56.00, half marathon 73.17, marathon 2.47.10.

Emily's father, Tom Hopkins, and brothers Jim and Tommy were all athletes with Donore Harriers. Her husband, Mick Dowling, was an Olympic boxer (Mexico City 1968) and is now best recognised as a TV sportscaster.

Horgan, Terri
Clubs: Mallow AC; DCH
Coach: Oliver Scully

Ireland's best-ever long-jumper, Terri (born Mallow 1966) won seven national senior titles in nine years (1985, 88, 89, 90, 91, 92, and 93), competed many times internationally, and still holds the national record.

She won the National Community Games 100m U/17 in 1983. She won the 1985 National Junior long jump in a record 5.87 and the same year beat her great rival Kathleen Glavin to win the National Senior title (5.79).

She jumped a national record 6.39 at the 1989 Europa Cup in Santry and repeated that distance when winning bronze at the 1990 British AAA Championships in Birmingham. In June 1992, competing in Brussels, she improved that mark to 6.48, which remains unbettered.

Terri trained 90 minutes a day seven days a week and would likely have jumped even farther had she received more official support (a Cospóir grant, for example) when on the verge of world-class.

Hurley, Elizabeth
Club: St Benedict's, Arklow
Coach: Michael Quinn

Elizabeth (born 29 Dec 1958) won the 1975 All Ireland Schools javelin (125ft) and the 1976 National Senior javelin (29.44m) and threw shot and javelin for Ireland. In the 1975 European Cup in Osijek she was fifth in the javelin (34.58). And in 1976 v Wales, Greece, and Spain in Cwmbran she was fourth in the shot (10.36) and third in the javelin (39.26).

Jeffords, Anne
Club: Leevale
Coach: self

Anne (born 6 April 1957) won the National Senior 100m in 1975 (12.2) and 1976 (12.0) and the National Senior 200m in 1976 (25.4) and competed in sprints and relays for Ireland:

1974: v Portugal, Lisbon, 1st 100m (12.00), 1st 4x400m (48.1). 1975: European Cup, Osijek, 4th 100m (12.3), 4th 4x400m (47.4). 1976: v Wales, Greece, and Spain, Cwmbran, 4th 200m (25.4), 2nd 4x400m (48.8).

For the extreme brevity of her career Anne blames the stark deficiency of infrastructure down south, especially in terms of winter training for sprints.

Johnson, Barbara
Clubs: North Cork; Limerick AC
Coaches: Fr Liam Kelleher; Billy Oates

Barbara (born 5 December 1962) came into athletics via the Community Games, competing in U/10 sprints. She won her first BLOE title in 1973, the U/11 high jump.

She won Schools Intermediate and Senior titles in the mid-seventies and represented Ireland at schools internationals in Wales and Scotland. While at UCC in 1982 and 1983 she won varsity titles but only began to apply herself seriously to her favourite event, the 400m hurdles, after a further year of study in London.

The breakthrough came in 1986: Barbara won the National Senior title at Santry (58.91). She retained her title in 1987 (59.06) and made it three-in-a-row in 1988 (57.93). Meanwhile, she had run 400m hurdles and 4x400m at the 1987 World Championships in Rome and posted 57.96, a qualifier for the 1988 Seoul Olympics.

Prior to Seoul, she ran a useful 54.08 400m at the Cork Sports. At the Olympics, she finished sixth in her heat (58.61). In 1989 she moved up to 800m but suffered a chronic knee injury, which led to her retirement from competition.

Barbara and her husband, Billy Oates, live in Cork with their young son, Sam.

Jordan, Kathleen
Club: Old Bawn Meet and Train
Coach: Billy Jordan

Kathleen has no sporting background but married into the Jordan clan of marathon fame. Her first race was the 1983 Women's Mini Marathon; she posted an unremarkable 61 minutes. Soon, however, she had whittled this down to a competitive 40 minutes, thanks to regular training of 50 miles per week. She was now a regular winner in veteran categories at 10k and half marathon.

In 1984 she ran her first marathon and posted 3.32. In 1985 she won Dunboyne O/40 in 3.14 and in 1986 clocked 3.25 in Belfast. For her amazing 1988 Dublin City Marathon, 3.07.32 at 50 years of age, Kathleen won a Seiko/Irish Runner Award.

Joyce, Monica
Clubs: Westport AC; San Diego
Coach: Fred le Platt

Monica, like her sister Regina, declared for Ireland in 1981. In 1981 and 1982 she won national 1,500m titles (4.10.48 and 4.18.90). She represented Ireland in the 1983 Helsinki World Championships and was eliminated in the 3,000m heats. She also went to the 1984 Los Angeles Olympics, where she finished 5th in the first round of the 3,000m (8.54.34 PB).

PBs: 800m 2.05.57, 1,500m 4.06.69, 3,000m 8.49.51, 5,000m 15.27.30, 10,000m 32.21.16, marathon 2.34.39.

Joyce (Bonney), Regina
Clubs: Westport AC; San Diego
Coach: Fred le Platt

Regina (born 7 Feb 1957) commenced running in the 1970s and at 14 set a world age record of 4.36 for 1,500m. She wore the English singlet in the 1979 World CC in Limerick and led the British 1,500m rankings in 1980 and 3,000m rankings in 1981, but the AAA did not select her – they disapproved of athletes accepting American university scholarships. So Regina and Monica Joyce declared for Ireland.

Regina won many 10k races in the USA and Ireland during her short international career. At the 1981 NCWSA T&F Championships at Oregon State University, she became the first-ever collegiate woman to break nine minutes for 3,000m (8.55.05). She won BLE 3,000m titles in 1982 (9.03.83) and 1983 (9.13.15). She won the Fiesta Bowl Marathon in 2.32.56 to beat Carey May's Irish record. She finished 7th in the 1983 Helsinki World Championship marathon. She posted 21st in the 1984 World CC, Meadowland, USA, and 23rd in the 1984 Los Angeles Olympic marathon.

In April 1985 Regina's husband and fellow athlete was told by a doctor, 'There is a structural abnormality in Regina's lower back which just will not hold up under the stress of training and racing long distances.' Twelve years on, however, Regina is still racing and, having recently turned 40, thoroughly fired up about competing as a master (veteran).

In 1994 Regina took American citizenship and thus became eligible to represent a third country – she has since worn the US colours in several road relays. She now lives in Seattle with Alan and their two children.

PBs: 1,500m 4.12.7, mile 4.34.16, 3,000m 8.55.05, 5,000m 15.35.60, 10k 32.35.7, marathon 2.32.57.

Kavanagh, Fiona
Club: St Laurence O'Toole
Coach: self

Fiona (born 19 Sept 1971) is a talented all-rounder with an impressive CV:

1989: National Junior Heptathlon, 1st; National Junior High Jump, 2nd (1.65); National Junior Indoor High Jump, 2nd (1.70); Home Countries Junior Heptathlon, Scotland, 1st.

1990: Schools Heptathlon, 1st; National Junior Heptathlon, 1st; National U/21 Heptathlon, 1st; National Senior Heptathlon, 2nd.

1991: National Multi Events, 2nd; National Senior Heptathlon, 2nd.

1992: National Indoor High Jump, 2nd.

1996: comeback to athletics; National Senior High Jump, 3rd.

Fiona is a sister of Eileen, Mary, and Siobhán, all talented athletes (see below).

Kavanagh, Siobhán
Club: St Laurence O'Toole
Coach: self

Siobhán (born 18 March 1964) excelled as a juvenile, winning the 1978 National Community Games U/16 1,500m and the 1980 Schools Senior CC. She took up an athletics scholarship to Arkansas University in 1982 and while there won the Southwest Conference Indoor 1,000m in 1984 and 1985. She is a sister of Eileen, Fiona, and Mary (see above and below).

PBs: 800m 2.09,1,500m 4.28.

Kavanagh (Kelly), Eileen
Clubs: St Laurence O'Toole; DSD

Eileen started young with St Laurence O'Toole's in Carlow and at age 16 made her first international appearance, at the FISEC Games, where she won a team CC silver. Subsequent career highlights included two silvers (1982 and 1984) and two bronze (1983 and 1986) in the National 400m. There was also gold with DSD in the 1976 National 4x400m.

In 1986 Eileen joined the Garda Síochána and placed second in the 100m and third in the 800m at the European Police Championships in Spain. The same year, running with Mary Nolan, Patricia Walsh, and Aisling Molloy for Team Puma, she helped set a national club record 3.44.73 for 4x400m at the European Clubs in Lisbon. She was fourth in the 1988 European Police Championships CC.

Eileen is married to Eamonn Kelly (St Abban's and London Irish), formerly a National Intermediate CC champion and now a qualified coach. They have two children, Sinéad (7) and Cormac (3).

Kearney, Ann
Club: Clonliffe Harriers
Coach: Tommy Coyle

Ann (born 5 Jan 1949) swam and played football and karate before taking up running in her mid-thirties. 'It's never too late to start,' is her motto. Her first race was a half-marathon; she finished fourth – and the bug had bitten. A good cyclist and swimmer, she was soon attracted to the triathlon, an event at which she has enjoyed tremendous success over 13 years, including third place in the 1988 European Championships in Sweden: a 2.3-mile swim, a 112-mile cycle, and a full marathon.

Other triathlon successes include: 1986 to 1991 Irish Championships, 1st; 1985 Hawaii Ironman, 1st veteran; 1986 European Ironman, 3rd veteran; 1987 European Ironman, 4th; 1988 Swedish Championship, 3rd; 1988 Lyon International, 3rd; 1989 European Veterans, 1st; 1989 Nice International, 1st veteran; 1990 European Veterans, 1st; 1990 French Circuit, 3rd; 1991 European Veterans, 1st; 1991 French Circuit, 2nd; 1992 European Veterans, 1st; 1995 European Veterans, 1st; 1995 Irish Championship, 1st; 1996 Irish Championship, 1st (for 8th time); 1996 European Masters, Hungary, 1st O/45, 2nd overall.

Ann won the O/45 category in the 1995 Dublin City Marathon (3.07.04). She also won gold in the 1997 European Veterans' Half Marathon (O/45), clocking 1.23.40 in extreme heat and wind.

Ann is married to Frank; they have two teenage girls, Edith and Caroline.

Keenan (Buckley), Anne
Clubs: Portlaoise AC; Clonliffe Harriers

Anne (born 7 Jan 1962) was introduced to athletics in 1974 and won U/12 county medals on track and country. She represented Laois at National Community Games in 1974, 75, and 76. Between 1974 and 1978 she won county, Leinster, and national U/17 and Junior CC titles and by 1978 had represented Ireland nine times on track and country.

Transferred to Dublin, she joined Clonliffe and after a few years of relative obscurity finished seventh in the 1983 National CC. Between 1984 and 1995 she wore the Irish vest over 20 times, including seven World CC appearances.

Anne has won numerous Leinster CC titles, the National Intercounties CC, the National 3,000m, and the Manufacturers Hanover Road Race in New York (1987). She has finished second in the National Interclubs CC six times during 22 years of competitive running. The summit of a magnificent career was perhaps her participation in the 1988 Seoul Olympics, where she clocked 9.03.10 for 3,000m.

In April 1997, at BLE's Annual Congress, Ann was co-opted onto the National Selection Committee.

Kelly, Connie
Club: Blackrock AC
Coach: Tom Curran

Clarewoman Connie played camogie, tennis, Gaelic football, and soccer before taking up running in 1984. She won the Clare Senior CC title in 1987, the Dublin Senior CC title in 1988, 89, and 90, and the Kildare Senior CC title in 1992, 93, and 94. She won the Leinster CC title in 1990 and 1994 and the National Veterans CC title in 1993 and 94.

On the roads Connie won the Dunboyne Marathon (2.56) and the Foyle Marathon (2.59) in 1985 and was second in the National (Dublin City) Marathon in 1991 (2.40). She represented Ireland in the 1991 London Marathon (2.42) and won the Ballycotton Ten in 1990, 91, and 92.

Kelly, Margaret
Club: Rathnew

During a brilliant career shortened by injuries, Margaret Kelly excelled in all three branches of distance running (road, track, and country) and was voted Best Home Based Female Athlete of 1983.

Other highlights were the winning of Irish vests for cross-country and wins in the

Gerry Farnan Memorial CC, the Puma Streets of Dublin 10k, and the Ballyshannon 10k. She also won National 3,000m bronze.

Margaret went on scholarship to Arkansas University but found the American way of life uncongenial and returned home.

Kelly (Conroy), Elaine
Clubs: St Finbarr's; UCC
Coaches: Pat Ryan (to 1973); Máire Murphy (1974 to 1978)

Elaine (born 16 Jan 1956) played hockey before taking up athletics in 1969, when St Finbarr's started their women's section. By 1971 the club team of Elaine, Mary O'Sullivan, Mary Ryan, and Joan Fleming had won national honours.

Through the seventies, Elaine gained titles at Schools, County, Province, Varsity, and National level. Her most notable success was the National Senior 800m (2.14.8) on 11 July 1971; at age 15, she was the youngest ever to win a national senior title.
During this period Elaine took the double 400m and 800m at Cork City Sports, recording 2.11.8 on grass, defeating Deirdre Nagle and foreign athletes. She was Athlete of the Year in 1971, winning the W.J. Flynn Memorial Trophy. She won the Universities 400m and 800m in 1974, 1975, and 1976 before illness forced her retirement from competition in 1977.

Elaine's favourite victory was the 1977 National Senior 800m, in which she posted a career best 2.06.07. Now married to Sean, and with two children, Aisling and Niall, she lives in Greystones, Co. Wicklow, and teaches in St David's School.

Kennedy, Christine
Clubs: Galway City Harriers; Racing Club de Paris

Christine (born 29 Dec 1954) took up running at 23 years of age after watching the TV pictures of Emily Dowling win the 1981 Dublin City Marathon. She spent very little time as a jogger (her first marathon being a highly respectable 3.30) and went on to win the 1989 National CC at Killenaule, the 1990 Women's Mini Marathon (34.17), the 1990 National Marathon in Clonmel, the 1990 Dublin City Marathon (2.41.27), and the combined National and Dublin City Marathon of 1991 (2.35.56). She also represented Ireland at World CC and World T&F Championships. Her marathon PB is 2.35.05. Since turning veteran, she has won the O/40 category in Dublin (2.49.05).

Christine and family emigrated in the late eighties, first to England, then to France, and again to the USA. They now live in California, where Christine won the 1997 San Francisco Home Depot Half Marathon (1.17.17).

Kennedy (Phelan), Ursula
Clubs: Raheny Shamrocks; Crusaders
Coaches: Paul Kennedy; Peggy Hogan

Ursula (born 18 Oct 1948) comes from a sporting family, several of whom excelled at bike-racing. She trained up to 70 miles per week, won the 1967 NACAI All-Ireland CC title at Holycross, Co. Tipperary, and achieved one of her ambitions by representing Ireland at cross-country (at Blackburn in 1968 she posted 10th and at Clydebank in 1969 20th). She achieved another ambition when she beat the great Ann O'Brien over 440 yards. Her PBs include 800m 2.12.6 and mile 5.01.00. After a break of 20 years rearing her family, Ursula returned to athletics and, ever enthusiastic, ran several marathons. She now has a coaching certificate.

Kenny, Eithne
Club: Dublin City Harriers
Coaches: Declan Walsh; Dermot Nagle

Eithne was a competitive swimmer and hockey player before she entered athletics. She first made her mark in 1976 with second in the National Intercounties CC and fifth in the National Interclubs CC. For the next 15 years and more she enjoyed much success on track, road, and country, especially as a member of the great DCH team that dominated the national cross-country scene and won European Clubs gold in 1985 and 1986.

She twice (1978 and 1979) took silver in the National 800m before winning the gold (2.13.7) at Santry in 1981. She took individual bronze in the 1982 National CC. In 1985 she was on the Irish team that won the Home Countries CC. And in 1992 she was on the DCH team (with Ursula Noctor and Karen O'Doherty) that won the Northern Ireland Half Marathon.

One of a sporting family (her sisters and brothers are first-class swimmers), Eithne still loves racing and training, often with her longtime mentor, friend, and clubmate, the evergreen Declan Walsh.

Theresa Kidd
Born 18th June 1956
Club: Ballinacreen A.C. Draperstown
Coach: Dick Edwards

Theresa Kidd was the most versatile athlete in Northern Ireland in the 1980's. In that decade she won races from 800m to Marathon. Her career was terminated by two serious lung operations.

Theresa, a dedicated athlete, won two National Marathons 1985, 1987 and took silver in 1986. She won the Belfast City Marathon in 1984 and 1987 and silver in 1985. In 1986 she had a fine win against international opposition in the Amsterdam Marathon in personal best time 2:46:02. During this period she continued to win road races, track races and cross country. She also won countless Ulster Sports Council titles over various distances.

Irish Championship medals won; 2 golds and 1 silver and 5 bronze at Marathon and a bronze at 10 miles road and 5000m track.

Theresa also wore the Irish singlet as representative in Marathons in Scotland, Japan, Korea, Holland and Malaysia.

Lambe, Rosie
Club: Knockbridge AC
Coach: Larry Lambe

Rosie took up running in 1973 at Inver College, Carrickmacross. Almost 25 years later, she has lost count of the number of track and CC titles she has won. Sometimes known as The Barefoot Contessa for her shoeless exploits across country, her dark complexion, and her graceful style, she holds the NACAI records at 1,500m (4.27), 3,000m (9.21.43), 5,000m (16.21), 10,000m (33.44.47), half-marathon (1.15.47), and marathon (2.46.04).

She has won 14 national track titles (NACAI) and 15 CC titles (including the 1997 National, held at Gort, Co. Galway, 15 Feb). She won the CSIT International CC three times (1986, 88, and 94) and won CSIT track gold in 1983, 86, 91, and 93. In 1982 she won the Portuguese 15k in Lisbon.

Since the accord that permitted NACAI athletes to compete in IAAF events, Rosie has represented Ireland in the World CC in New Zealand and Hungary and at the 1987 World T&F in Rome (10,000m). She won the BLE 3,000m in 1988 and the BLE 10,000m in 1987, 88, 90, and 94. She took bronze in the 1990 BLE 15k (road) and silver in the 1993 BLE Half Marathon. She also represented Ireland over 15k at Monaco, Adelaide, and Dublin.

Other wins have included the 1993 Women's Mini Marathon, an event in which she has a remarkable pedigree: 1990 2nd (34.23), 1991 did not run, 1992 5th (34.58), 1993 1st (34.25), 1994 3rd (33.52), 1995 3rd (34.08), 1996 3rd (34.23), 1997 3rd (35.06). She has also won the Guinness Half Marathon (twice), the Belfast Half Marathon, and the Lakeland 15 (twice). She set her marathon PB 2.46.04 in Dublin 1995.

Lambert (O'Brien), Beatrice
Club: St Laurence O'Toole
Coach: John Lambert

Coached by her father, himself an athlete, Beatrice (born 5 Feb 1957) won BLOE 800m and 1,500m titles at U/14,U/15, and U/16 from 1969 to 1971. She also won the Intermediate Girls CC in 1971 and 1972, the Intermediate Girls 800m in 1972, and the All Ireland Schools 800m.

On 19 March 1972 Beatrice made history by becoming the youngest runner ever to gain a senior international vest; the event was at Cambridge, England – Beatrice was 13. She won a second international vest at Clydebank, also in 1972.

Lynch, Bridie
Club: Blindsports

Bridie Lynch, from St Johnston, Co. Donegal, has represented Ireland at European Championships for the Blind, World Championships for the Disabled, and Paralympics since 1983. Talented and versatile, she has won 21 medals for various field events, including pentathlon. She is Donegal BLE record-holder for discus and shot. She held the B3 discus world record from 1990 to 1992. She recently set an Irish indoor discus record, 11.76m.

International medals: 1983 European Championships, Bulgaria, discus bronze; 1985 European Championships, Rome, discus and shot silver; 1986 World Championships, Gothenburg, discus silver; 1987 European Championships, Moscow, discus gold, shot silver; 1989 European Championships, Zurich, pentathlon gold, discus and shot silver.

1990 World Championships, Holland, discus silver; 1991 European Championships, France, discus and shot silver; 1992 Paralympics, Barcelona, discus and pentathlon silver; 1993 European Championships, Belfield, discus silver, shot and pentathlon bronze; 1994 World Championships, Berlin, discus bronze; 1995 European Championships, Spain, discus silver, shot and pentathlon bronze; 1996 Paralympics, Atlanta, gold.

Bridie also won three bronze medals in BLE National Senior Championships.

Lynch, Siobhán
Club: Raheny Shamrocks
Coach: Self

The high point of Siobhán's career was when she posted sixth in the 1968 National BLE CC Championships and thereby helped Raheny and Dublin clinch club and county gold

(Ann Keating, Ursula Kennedy, and Mary McDonnell were her scoring teammates for Raheny). That run gained Siobhán (born 24 Feb 1948) her one and only Irish singlet, for the International CC at Blackburn, England, where she finished 24th.

PBs: 400m 58.00, 800m 2.14, 1,500m 4.45.

Lynch (Kingston), Mary
Club: Raheny Shamrocks
Coach: Roger Kingston

A sister of Siobhán Lynch (see above), Mary won the 1972 National BLE CC title and represented Ireland on track and country. Her CV includes the 1971 San Sebastian International CC (41st), the 1971 European Cup 1,500m, Copenhagen (4th 4.28.00), the 1972 Cambridge International CC (13th), the 1973 Waregem International CC (31st), and the 1974 Monza International CC (29th). Mary (born 17 Oct 1950) held the Irish 3,000m record (9.38.4) from 1973 to 1974.

Other PBs: 400m 59.1, 800m 2.10.3, 1,500m 4.22.5, 3,000m 9.38.4.

McCabe, Brigid
Clubs: Mullingar Harriers; Galway City Harriers
Coach: husband Nicky

Brigid has been competing for more than 20 years and has run in more than 20 Intercounties CC championships, placing as high as 12th and winning two bronze team medals. She has also completed 25 marathons (with a PB of three hours and two seconds!) and won two silver medals in national marathons. She and her husband, Nicky, have run all 18 Dublin City Marathons, a distinction that as far as we know no other husband and wife can boast.

In 1984 Brigid became the first Irishwoman to run 50 miles (7.02). She was on the winning Mullingar team in the 1986 National Road Relays, and she won O/40 gold in the 1995 National Vets. Her sole international appearance was in the Veterans' International CC in Malahide.

McDonnell (Glynn), Mary
Club: Raheny Shamrocks
Coach: her brother Tommy

Mary was a member of the Raheny Shamrocks team that won the 1968 National CC title. Her promising international career (two vests in 1967 and 68) was cut short by injury. She died in July 1993.

McGovern (Young), Valerie
Club: Donore Harriers
Coaches: Eddie Hogan; Don Weber (Kentucky)

Valerie competed in the Community Games in the late seventies and won schools and junior titles before accepting an athletics scholarship to the University of Kentucky.
She was three times National Collegiate champion: she won the 1989 outdoor 5,000m (thus becoming the first Irishwoman to win an outdoor National Collegiate title) and the 1990 indoor and outdoor 5,000m. She was also three times NCAA runner-up: in the 1989 3,000m and the 1991 CC and 5,000m.

She was eight times NCAA All-American and set an NCAA 5,000m record 15.48 in 1989. Also in 1989 she ran for Ireland at the Ekiden Relays, Barcelona, and was on the Kentucky team that won the Penn Relays 3,000m. In 1990 she represented Ireland at the European Championships and Goodwill Games.

In 1991 she represented Ireland at the World T&F 10,000m and won the 5,000m at the SEC Indoor Championships. In 1992 she won the World Cup 10,000m in Finland (33.33) and was fifth in the Parkenburg Half Marathon (74.27). In 1994 she posted third in the Carrera International De La Paz 30k.

Valerie's father was a footballer; her mother competed in athletics as a teenager.

McGrillen, Louise
Clubs: DCH; Blackrock AC
Coaches: Tony Farrell (to 1983); John Kerrane (DCH)

Louise excelled at cross-country, winning the national title in 1983, 1984, and 1985. She led DCH on their great European Clubs CC campaign: second in 1983 and 1984, winners in 1985 and 1986. She wore the green singlet in four World CC Championships and led Ireland to victory in the 1985 Home Countries CC Kent, England.

Louise represented Ireland in the European Championships at Athens (3,000m). She won the De Loughrey Cup several times and set a race record 10.14 in 1984. She won the Liffey Valley Half Marathon (82 mins) and the 1984 BLE 3,000m.

PBs: 1,500m 4.18, 3,000m 9.00, 10,000m 33.16, 10 miles 56.00, marathon 2.56.

McKiernan, Catherina
Club: Cornafean
Coach: Joe Doonan.

During her school years, Catherina played camogie, badminton, tennis, basketball, and any other sport in which she could take part. She commenced running competitively in 1986 and was immediately successful, winning the Ulster CC title. Her CV, both juvenile and senior, is remarkable.

1987: Interprovincial CC, 1st; Ulster and All-Ireland U/20 CC, 1st.

1988: Ulster and All Ireland Senior Schools CC, 1st; Ulster CC, 1st; All-Ireland Senior, 3rd.

1989: Ulster CC, 1st; National CC, Killenaule, 3rd; selected for World CC, Stavanger, Norway; National 3,000m track, 3rd; National Intercounties CC, 1st (the first Cavanwoman to win it).

1990: National Intercounties CC, 1st; National CC, 1st; World CC, Aix-les-Bains, France, 41st; G.V. Ryan 1,500m, 1st (4.21.37); National 1,500m, 3rd (4.21.81) to Sonia O'Sullivan (4.09.44); 3,000m v Iceland and Scotland, 1st (9.27.2); National Intercounties CC, 1st; Jack Hartigan CC, Naas, 1st.

1991: IAAF World CC Challenge, Limerick, 2nd; World CC Challenge, Antwerp, 2nd; National CC, 1st; National 3,000m track, 1st (9.10.93); Jack Hartigan CC, Naas, 1st; World CC Challenge, Antwerp, 1st; National Intercounties CC, 1st.

1992: World CC Challenge, Mallusk, 1st; National CC, 1st; World CC, Boston, 2nd to Lynn Jennings; National 3,000m, 1st (9.04.08); Olympic Games, Barcelona, 3,000m, 8th (8.57.91); Jack Hartigan CC, 1st; National Intercounties CC, 1st.

1993: Mallusk CC, 1st; National CC, 1st; World CC, Amorebieta, 2nd to Albertina Dias; Hengelo 10,000m track, 32.14.74 (NR); Stuttgart World T&F 10,000m final, DNF; Jack Hartigan CC, 1st; IAAF Grand Prix, 1st ($10,000); National Intercounties CC, 1st.

1994: World CC Challenge, Mallusk, 2nd; World CC, Budapest, 2nd to Helen Chepngeno (Kenya); Sportsworld 5, 1st (25.43); Europa Cup 10,000m, 1st (31.19.10 NR); Helsinki World T&F 10,000m, DNF; Berlin Grand Prix 5,000m, 1st (15.13.07); Jack Hartigan CC, 1st; World CC Challenge, Antwerp, 2nd.

1995: World CC Challenge, Seville, 1st; World CC, Durham, 2nd to Derartu Tulu, (Ethiopia); Paris Grand Prix 5,000m, 2nd (14.59.04 PB); Europa Cup, Tallin, 5,000m, 1st (15.37.66); World Games 5,000m, Gothenburg, unplaced in final; injured for six months.

1996: World CC Challenge, 1st; World CC, Capetown, 13th; Osaka 5,000m, 1st (15.07.31); Hengelo 5,000m, 3rd (14.58.65); Paris 5,000m, 2nd (14.55.39); National 5,000m, 1st (15.27.10); Olympic Games, Atlanta, 10,000m, 11th (32.00).

1997: World CC, Turin, 7th (and led team Ireland to bronze); Women's Mini Marathon, 1st (32.31 RR).

After winning the 1997 Mini Marathon, Catherina announced her intention of tackling the full marathon in the autumn. In her build-up to that debut, she won the Glasgow Half Marathon on 24 August in a record 69 minutes, beating the runner-up, Kenya's Lucia Subano, by two minutes. Two weeks later, on 7 September, she posted the year's second-fastest time, 31.21, in winning a road 10k in London, England.

On Sunday 29 September 1997, in Berlin, Catherina made her entry to the classic distance and posted an amazing 2.23.44, the eleventh-fastest time in history and the fastest-ever female debut. Looking fresh and relaxed throughout the race, she finished smiling and confirmed afterward that she could have run faster if pressed. The win was worth almost £30,000 in prize money and bonuses.

McNicholl, Jane
Club: Dublin University Harriers
Coaches: Michael McDonagh; Frank Duffy

Jane (born 2 Feb 1947) ran for Ireland twice in the International CC Championships: she finished 17th and won team bronze (in the company of Ann O'Brien, Peggy Hogan, Deirdre Foreman, and Nuala Bowe) in 1970, at Frederick, USA, and she finished 45th in 1973, at Waregem, Belgium. Her PBs are 2.15 (800m) and 4.38 (mile).

McShane, Kay
Clubs: Leevale AC; Dublin Wheelchair Sports Club
Coach: Carol Hayes.

Formerly from Cobh, Co. Cork, now residing in Drimnagh, Dublin, Kay got polio as a baby and has been in a wheelchair all her life. She was introduced to athletics in 1982 and proved to be an exceptional athlete. Coached by Carol Hayes, Kay did eight hours track training, an hour of weights, and 70 miles pushing her wheelchair each week. Such dedication brought rewards.

1983: Dublin Marathon (Wheelchair Ladies), 1st.

1984: National 400m, 800m, 1,500m, and 5,000m, 1st; Paralympics, Stoke Mandeville, Marathon, 2nd; Dublin City Marathon, 1st.

1985: National 400m, 800m, 1,500m, and 5,000m, 1st; Stoke Mandeville Games 800m and marathon, 1st; 1,500m, 2nd; European Championship 5,000m and marathon, 1st; Vienna International 800m, 1,500m, and 5,000m, 1st; London Marathon, 1st.

1986: National 400m, 800m, 1,500m, and 5,000m, 1st; London Marathon, 1st.

1987: National 400m, 800m, 1,500m, and 5,000m, 1st; London Marathon, 1st; competed in 800m wheelchair demonstration race at IAAF World Championships, Rome.

1988: National 400m, 800m, 1,500m, and 5,000m, 1st; Paralympic, Seoul, 800m and marathon, 3rd.

It is fair to say that Cobh, Co. Cork, has given us not one but two world-class women! Kay also won many road races, including the Evening Echo Mini Marathon and the Evening Press Mini Marathons of 1987, 88, and 89. Now working in the Civil Service, she has given up athletics but still swims to keep fit.

Malone, Christine
Club: Crusaders
Coach: Tony Farrell

Christine, from Piltown, Co. Kilkenny, gained one Irish singlet, at the 1976 International CC, Chepstow.

Marnell (Champion), Sheila
Club: Sports World AC

Like her twin, Dorothy, Sheila (born 11 Sept 1935) is an all-rounder: tennis, golf, swimming. In athletics she has completed over 20 marathons and is a champion (no pun intended) vet. She set a European O/55 record in 1993 for 2,000m steeplechase. She holds the following Irish records: 100m O/50, 17.36; 100m O/55, 16.90; 400m O/50, 1.31.83; 400m O/55, 1.26.90; shot O/55, 6.92; discus O/55, 10.88; javelin O/55, 21.78. She is joint world-record-holder for indoor pole vault O/60 (1. 90).

Marnell (McLennan), Dorothy
Club: Hounslow AC
Coach: Chris Joosiffe

Dorothy (born 11 Sept 1935) is twin of Sheila Champion, with whom she has run over 20 marathons. Introduced to athletics in 1983, she specialises at pole vault; she holds the indoor and outdoor world records O/55 and is joint world indoor record-holder O/60 (1.90). She won world titles O/55 in Finland 1991 and Japan 1993 and British titles in 1991, 92, 93, and 94. She is currently Middlesex senior pole vault champion.

Dorothy trains every day and has reaped the dividends. She will continue to win titles and break records in her new category: O/60.

May (Edge), Carey
Club: Dundrum
Coaches: Eddie McDonagh; Patrick Shane

Carey was introduced to athletics at Wesley College by Dan Kennedy in 1971. She ran her first marathon, the National at Letterkenny, in August 1980, in a record 2.53.43, to become the first Irishwoman under three hours. Two months later she won Dublin City in 2.42.11. In June 1981 she won the National Marathon (2.42.39). Also in 1981, she won the Phoenix Fiesta Bowl Marathon and was Irish orienteering champion. In 1982 she ran the European Championship Marathon, in Athens.

In 1983 Carey made the breakthrough to world class, winning Osaka in 2.29.23. In 1983 she competed at the Helsinki World Championships and won Toronto. In 1984 she ran the Los Angeles Olympic Marathon and again won Toronto. In 1985 she again won Osaka, in 2.28.07, a national record that would stand until September 1997. In 1986 she won Shanghai (2.43).

In 1987 she wed Dave Edge, a Commonwealth Marathon silver-medallist. They have twins, a girl, Brittany, and a boy, Nicholas.

In April 1995 Carey posted 2.53 in Seattle and in June 1995 clocked 2.45 in Los Angeles.

Meagan (Watts), Carol
Club: Dundrum
Coach: Eddie McDonagh

Carol burst into prominence when she won the British WAAA Intermediate 1,500m in 1978, defeating the talented Sandra Arthurton of England in a tense battle; her 4.21.02 was an Irish age-group record. At senior level, she shocked her more experienced rivals in the 1980 Intercounties CC, in the Phoenix Park, leaving behind such as Deirdre Nagle, Fionnuala Morrish, and Carey May. This great run qualified her to wear the Irish senior singlet for the first time. The following year she confirmed her form by winning the BLE National CC title.

Despite, or maybe because of, her brilliance, Carol abruptly gave up running, to the surprise and disappointment of the many who saw her as a potential worldbeater. She is now happily married and living near Liverpool, England.

Carol's father, Mick Meagan, was a professional footballer with Everton and played for Ireland many times. Her brother played with Shamrock Rovers.

Midleton-Gross, Janet
Club: Crusaders
Coach: Louis Vandendries

Janet (born 14 May 1948) won National BLE High Jump titles in 1968 and 1969 (1.42 both times) and has high jump and shot PBs of 1.50m and 9.54m. A true amateur who trains in moderation and also plays hockey, badminton, and tennis, she dislikes the influence of money on athletics and as far back as 1970 was warning against 'the tendency in international sport toward professionalism'.

Molloy, Aisling
Club: Dublin City Harriers
Coach: Norman Poole

Aisling is a PE teacher at Loreto Abbey, Rathfarnham, who comes from a sporting background in Ballymahon, Co. Longford. Her father, Martin, played Gaelic football with Longford and Roscommon. Her mother played tennis and badminton. Her sisters, Siobhán, Deirdre, and Emer, have all run at juvenile and junior level, Emer winning a scholarship to and competing for Villanova in the mid-nineties. Aisling herself has played basketball and showjumping.

From the early age of 12, she competed with distinction in cross-country and long jump (2.16 at age 14). In 1979 and 1980 she won All-Ireland 800m U/16. In 1981, when just 17, she won the Cork City Sports 800m in 2.09 and reached the semifinals of the European Junior Championships. In 1982 she took up a scholarship at Brigham Young University, Provo, USA. In 1983 she won the NCAA Indoor Mile and the Los Angeles Times Indoor Mile and reached the final of the US Collegiate Outdoor 800m. Between 1985 and 1995 she won the National BLE 800m six times. In 1990 she finished sixth in the final of the European Indoor 800m and set an Irish indoor record 2.02.8. She reached the semifinals of the 1990 European Championship 800m in Split, Croatia (2.01.14). In 1991 she reached the semifinals of the World Indoor 800m (2.03).

Also in 1991 Aisling scored perhaps her most famous victory, beating Sonia O'Sullivan over a mile at Cork City Sports in a national record 4.27. In 1992 she posted 3rd (2.01.4) in the WAAA (British) 800m championship. 1992 and 1993 were written off by injury, but Aisling came back in 1994 to win the Westathletic 800m in Scotland. At the European Championships, Helsinki, however, she could manage only eighth (2.08.46) in her heat. In 1995 she won the Europa Cup 800m, the Kilkenny International 800m, and the AAA Indoor 800m before going to the Gothenburg World Championships (2.04.15 and 6th in heat).

PBs: 800m 2.01.14, 1,500m 4.01.1, mile 4.27.

Moroney (Davis), Kathryn
Clubs: Avondale; Raheny; Clonliffe
Coach: Eddie Hogan

Kathryn won the National 3,000m (track) in 1977 (9.24.6) and the National CC title in 1978 and gained several international vests: 1971 San Sebastian International CC (34th); 1976 International Track Meet, Cwmbran, Wales, 2nd 3,000m; 1977 International CC, Mullingar (15th). She is married to the BLE official Nick Davis and works as a freelance athletics reporter.

Morrish, Fionnuala
Club: Leevale

Fionnuala won Community Games and BLOE titles on track and country in the early seventies. She won the 1976 Schools Home Countries Championship, the 1976 Intermediate Home Countries International at Mullingar, and the Home Countries CC in Lancashire, England.

In 1980 she posted second in the National CC Championship, won the Intervarsity 3,000m (9.20), and defeated Mary Purcell in the Louis Vandendries 3,000m at Belfield. Dundrum hosted Ireland's first ever women's 5,000m track race; Fionnuala won from Louise McGrillen, Deirdre Nagle, and Carey May.

The National CC champion of 1982, Fionnuala wore the Irish singlet 21 times.

Morrison (Dowdall), Aideen
Club: Crusaders
Coach: Eddie Hogan

Aideen (born 2 Oct 1953) joined Crusaders in 1968 and was a winner from the start. She collected national titles at U/14 100m (13.4) 1968; U/15 100m (12.8) and 200m (26.7) 1969; U/17 200m (16.1) and 400m (62.8) 1970.

She won all-Ireland schools titles at inter 100m (12.2) and 200m (25.1) 1970; senior 200m (25.7) 1971; senior 100m (12.2) and 200m (25.00) 1972; senior 400m (56.7) 1974; and national junior titles at 100m (12.6), 200m (26.3) and 100mH (17.3) 1971; 200m (25.00) and 400m (57.6) 1972.

She won national senior titles at 100m (12.5) 1970 (at age 16); 400m (55.00) 1973; 200m (25.8) 1974; 800m (2.06.77) 1982; 800m (2.06.5) 1983. She also won 1982 National Road Relay gold with Crusaders. PBs: 100m 12.00, 200m 24.2, 400m 54.1, 800m 2.06.5, 1,500m 4.25.5.

Aideen is married to David Dowdall. They have one child, Maria (born 17 Feb 1997).

Morrissey, Sheelagh
Club: Kildare AC

Dublin-born Sheelagh won the 1974 Irish Schools CC Championships. Also in 1974 she took track silver in the BLE 3,000m and the FISEC 1,500m in Spain and posted 58th at the International CC Championships, Monza, Italy.

She finished 11th at the 1975 International CC Championships, Coatsbridge; 9th in the 1976 International CC Championships, Rawtenstall; 40th in the 1977 International CC Championships, Chepstow; and 12th in the 1978 Mullingar International CC.

Mulligan, Sr Andrena
Born Charlestown, Co. Mayo

A sister and now Provincial in the Marist order, based in Abilene, Texas, Andrena was practising physiotherapy in Carrick-on-Shannon when a certain Noel Henry turned up for treatment. Soon the patient's love of marathoning began to rub off on the therapist – and Andrena took to the classic distance in 1979.

She served in Mexico, where she also was physio to a soccer team. In Detroit for a few years, she registered a PB 3.38.13 (and won her veteran category) in 1994. She also won her category in Port Huran.

Now over 50, she posted 4.02 in Boston 1997 and two months later, on 21 June 1997, completed her 25th marathon, the unusual Mayor's Midnight Sun event in Anchorage, Alaska. But she 'will not be satisfied' until she has completed the Dublin City Marathon.

Working a ten-hour day at Hendrick Medical and also giving her religious community long hours, Sr Andrena still finds time to run 50 miles per week. Her philosophy: 'Fitness is a tool in the recovery programme. Running keeps one in tune with one's spirit.'

Andrena's brothers, Francis and Michael, and her sister, Emer, have also run marathons.

Murphy (Richardson), Niamh
Club: Mayo AC
Coach: Liam Moggan

Niamh was a tennis interprovincial and county camogie player before taking up running at 18 years of age when studying at Thomond College, Limerick. She was Intervarsity CC Champion in 1988 and won bronze in the 1989 and 1990 National BLE 3,000m and in the 1990 and 1991 National Interclubs CC.

She wore the green singlet at the 1989 and 1990 Europa Cups, at the World CC in Aix-les-Bains, France, and at the Ekiden Relay, Barcelona, 1990. In 1989 she reached the final of the World Student Games 3,000m, at Duisburg, Germany. She also represented Ireland in several Home Countries internationals and twice finished second in the Women's Mini Marathon (10k), in 1991 and 1993.

Niamh is married to Noel Richardson, a track and CC international.

Naughton, Lindie
Clubs: Collegians; UCDAC; Crusaders
Coach: Jack Sweeney

Lindie (born 11 Jan 1954) played tennis and hockey before taking up athletics in 1971. She tried her hand at many disciplines and had most success in the javelin, winning all-Ireland silver in 1976. Probably even more than that championship medal, however, she enjoyed her marathon PB 3.43 (Dublin 1986) and her second place in the Maulin Hill Run.

Always a five-days-a-week trainer, Lindie has given endless time and boundless energy to coaching countrywide and seems always ready to help and advise newcomers. She is also, of course, a busy newspaper and magazine journalist. Her columns in the *Evening Press* (of fond memory) and the *Evening Herald* have greatly raised the profile of athletics and attracted thousands to that great annual odyssey known as the Mini Marathon.

Lindie has published a popular primer for joggers, *Let's Run,* and was co-author (with Johnny Watterson of *The Irish Times*) of *Irish Olympians* (1992). She has recently completed her first work of fiction, a crime novel, and is now working on her next book, an exploration and celebration of a year in her sporting and journalistic life.

Nicholson, Emma
Club: Dublin City Harriers
Coach: Jim Kilty

Emma took up athletics in 1986 and found her favourite event to be the one-lap sprint. She won the 1992 National 400m Indoor and Outdoor. Her outdoor PB 53.73 was run in a Grand Prix race in South Africa. Her indoor PB and national record 53.63 was set at the 1996 European Indoors in Stockholm. She also competed at the World Student Games at Sheffield 1991 and Buffalo 1993.

Besides running, Emma enjoys swimming and horseriding. She is married to her clubmate T.J. Kearns, Olympian and national record-holder at 110m hurdles.

Noctor, Ursula
Club: Dublin City Harriers
Coach: Jim Kilty

A very promising athlete at school, Ursula was not long making an impression at senior level. Among her wins were: 1982 National Junior 1,500m (4.29); 1982 Jack Hartigan CC, Naas; 1983 Cork Mini Marathon 10k; 1984 BLE (inaugural) 5,000m track; 1988 NI 3,000m track; 1988 Foyle Half Marathon.

For many years part of the great DCH cross-country team, she helped achieve the marvellous European Clubs double of 1985 and 1986. She also represented Ireland at the World 10k in Madrid.

In the early nineties, at a time when she was actually battling terminal illness, Ursula ran a series of magnificent half-marathons and marathons, including the 1990 Columbus Marathon (3rd in a PB 2.39.25), the 1991 Columbus Marathon (7th), the 1991 Chicago Marathon (4th in 2.41.20), and, her last race, the 1992 Chicago Marathon (4th in 2.41.50). Ursula died on 4 April 1993.

(See also the fuller profile and Roy Dooney's appreciation of Ursula in Part Two).

Nolan, Geraldine
Club: Kilkenny City Harriers
Coach: John Dooley

Geraldine began collecting titles in 1986, winning U/16 National 800m (2.10 NR) and 1,500m. She also won the Celtic International 800m, the Schools International 800m, and the Tailteann Games 800m. In 1987 she was U/17 800m champion. In 1988 she accepted a four-year track scholarship to Providence College, Rhode Island.

In 1989 she won the National Junior 800m and was second in an International 800m in Greece.

In 1990 she helped set a world record at 4x1500m and was one of the all-Irish quartet running for Providence that set a US Collegiate 4x800m record 8.38.7 (Geraldine 2.09.8, Sinéad Delahunty 2.10.9, Geraldine Hendricken 2.12.1, Siobhán Gallagher 2.05.9). Also in 1990 she won the National Junior 800m and took silver in the National 1,500m.

In 1991 she again won the National Junior 800m. She was second in the National Senior 800m, which placing she repeated in 1992. In 1993 she at last won the National Senior 800m (2.08.2) and also took 1,500m silver.

In 1994, Geraldine posted second in the National 1500m (4.14), sixth in the WAAA 1,500m (4.13.1), and posted a PB 4.10.84 in reaching the Helsinki European 1,500m final.

Geraldine's father, now deceased, was a top-class cyclist; her brother Ned and sister are also athletes.

Norton, Mary
Club: Clonliffe Harriers
Coach: Harry Cooney

In a short career, Mary won one Irish singlet, at the 1967 International CC, Barry, Wales, where she placed 17th.

Nugent, Doina
Club: Galway City Harriers

Doina lived in Baden-Baden, Germany, as a child until her family came to live in Galway in the eighties. She commenced running long distances at 19 years of age and won the Galway and Castlebar marathons in 1982; she also won many triathlons around that time. She now holds Irish records at distances from 50 miles (Templemore 1985, 6.52.10) to 160 miles. The following are extracts from her amazing ultra-distance CV.

1986: Tullamore 24-hour track, 106 miles 588 yds.

1987: Greystones 24-hour road, 100 miles 394 yds.

1991: Cork to Dublin 160 miles, 3rd (34.42.12); London to Brighton, 2nd (7.03); Nottingham 100k, 2nd (8.37.44).

1992: Madrid 100k, 2nd (8.42.53); Barcelona 100k, 3rd (9.00.46); Women's World Cup, Palermo, Spain, 9th (8.19.17); Intercontinental Cup 100k, Tourhout, Belgium, 5th (8.19.37); IAU 100k, Winschoten, Holland, 4th (8.19.05 NR regardless of sex).

1993: Madrid 100k, 1st woman, 4th of 86 overall (8.28.30); Ultimax 100k, New York, 6th (8.55.20)

1995: Granada to Pica Valeta 50k, Spain, 1st (4.56.10); Triathlon World Cup, Pangvezys, Lithuania, 1st woman, 4th overall (27.48 and Doina's second win at this annual event).

The above are only a few of the many endurance events this extraordinary woman has completed in the past 15 years.

Doina's parents, Elfriede and Jerome, have also been athletes.

O'Brien (Cummins), Ann
Club: Clonliffe Harriers

Ann (born 9 May 1943) comes from a sporting background. Her father, Christy, played Gaelic football with Dublin; her mother wore Dublin colours in camogie. Her sisters, Nuala, Ursula, and Antoinette, were all fine athletes as was her brother Noel. Another brother, Gerald, was an able amateur boxer but was tragically killed in the ring.

Ann took up running in 1963 at age 20 and became one of the leading Irish runners in the era 1966 to 1974. She was the first Irishwoman to break five minutes for the mile (4.59.2 in 1966). She won British WAAA 3,000m titles in 1969 and 1970.
She was the only woman from any country to compete in all eight International CC Championships (the forerunner of today's World CC) from 1967 to 1974. Her placings were: 18.3.67, Barry, Wales, 7th; 23.3.68, Blackburn, England, 8th; 11.3.69, Clydebank, Scotland, 5th; 21.3.70, Frederick, USA, 9th; 20.3.70, San Sebastian, Spain, 19th; 18.3.72, Cambridge, England, 22nd; 17.3.73, Waregem, Belgium, 59th; 16.3.74, Monza, Italy, 46th.

Ann won an amazing total of 18 national senior titles on track, field, and country: the AAUE CC titles in 1968, 1969, 1970, and 1971; the 1966 All Ireland (including NI)

880yds (2.16.1) and mile (5.04.02) and the 1966 AAUE mile (5.04.02); the 1967 880yds (2.29.7), mile (5.32), and HJ (4'7"); the 1968 440yds (59.04), 880yds (2.12.7), and mile (5.04.7); the 1969 880yds (2.12.5) and 1,500m (4.32.3); the 1970 800m (2.10.6) and 1,500m (4.38.6); the 1971 1,500m (4.29.8).

O'Donoghue, Lucy
Club: Leevale AC

Lucy O'Donoghue made an impression on the booming marathon scene of the early eighties before injuries cut short a fine career. In 1982 her debut in the Cork Marathon was a struggling 4.11.44, but with serious training she improved to 3.13.33 in Cork 1983. And in Galway 1984 she won in a PB 2.45.52 (with Galway's Christine Kennedy second in 2.54.25).

O'Dwyer-Moore, Pádraigín
Club: Clonliffe Harriers
Coach: Joe Moore

Pádraigín (born 10 Mar 1945) was a late developer. She gained her first of four Irish vests at 28 years of age in 1973 and won three national titles thereafter: 1974 800m (2.12.8); 1975 400m (56.5) and 800m (2.07.8). PBs: 400m 55.3, 800m 2.07.6.

O'Shea, Caroline
Club: Crusaders
Coach: Mick Purcell

Caroline (born 13 Dec 1960) joined Crusaders at age 10 in 1971 and won her first national title at 14, the 1975 400m (she won the same title again in 1979).

She won the 400m in 1978,1981,1982,1983, and 1984. She ran 53.24 to take the 400m record from Claire Walsh and held it until Claire's daughter, Patricia, clocked 53.06, which still stands. Caroline also held the national 800m record from 1984 to 1994. She represented Ireland at 200m, 400m, and 800m. She reckons her finest performance was her eighth place (2.00.77) in the 1984 Olympic 800m final.

Caroline's last competitive race was in the 1985 Nice Grand Prix. During the race she fell and broke her shoulder. The following year she got achilles tendinitis, which eventually caused her retirement in 1988. PBs: 100m 12.1, 200m 24.60, 400m 53.24, 800m 2.00.70.

Caroline's father played minor football with Kerry and ran with Crusaders.

O'Sullivan, Sonia
Club: Ballymore Cobh
Coaches: Sean Kennedy; Kim McDonald

In terms of races won and records broken, arguably Ireland's greatest and most successful runner of all time. For full biography refer back to Part two.

Parr, Mary
Club: Dundrum South Dublin
Coaches: Hayden Lewis; Tom Curran

Mary was always involved in sport: water-skiing, windsurfing, swimming, cycling, hill-walking, horseriding, tennis, badminton. She took seriously to athletics in 1979 after winning Leinster Schools titles.

She won the National 400m hurdles in 1984 and 1985 and was second in the National 800m in 1988. She was a member of the Irish 4x100m team that set a national record 46.3 and the 4x400m team that set a national record 3.39 in 1983. Her many international appearances from 1979 to 1987 included the 1984 Olympic 400mH in Los Angeles (7th, 61.66, in heat). PBs: 100m 11.8, 400m 54.8, 800m 2.07, 400mH 58.3, LJ 5.90.

Mary is now a practising biotherapist (biotherapy being a form of holistic vibrational medicine) and a member of the International Committee for Biotherapy Testing. She and her husband, Philip Mulligan, have two children, Sarah (7) and Barry (6).

Philpott, Anita
Club: Kanturk
Coach: Liam Kelleher

When only 16, and in only her second season in athletics, Anita (born 24 July 1969) was second in the 1985 Intermediate Women's Home Countries International to England's Wendy Wright. She followed this by winning the 1985 National Junior CC title at Mullingar.

She continued almost unbeatable as a juvenile. For example, she raced Sonia O'Sullivan 25 times underage and won 23 times. But while Sonia went on to become a worldbeater, Anita suffered a series of stress fractures that forced long layoffs from training and seriously damaged her career. Nevertheless, her CV is marvellous.

In 1984 she won the Cork, Munster, and All-Ireland 800m titles, the BLOE 1,500m, and the Celtic International in Scotland. In 1984/85 she won Munster U/16, U/17, U/18, and novice CC titles, the All-Ireland BLOE U/16 CC, and the National Junior

CC. She was second in the Home Countries International CC in England. She won the National 1,500m in 1993 (4.24.36) and was third in 1994 (4.14.89).

Anita reached the final of the 1994 European 3,000m in Helsinki and set a PB 8.54.79 in finishing 12th. She was second in the 1996 National Indoor 1,500m (4.36.2). But her Olympic ambitions for Atlanta 96 were ruined by yet further injury.

Pierce (Evans-Lynn-Heath), Sophie
Club: Kensington Ladies

Born on 17 November 1896 in Ballinderry, Co. Limerick, Sophie emigrated to England at a young age. Married to two Englishmen (in succession, of course), she represented Britain when there was no athletics for women in Ireland and held high offices in world athletics. She also distinguished herself as a pioneer aviator.

The incredibly versatile Sophie set the following marks which may be justly considered all-Ireland records: high jump 4'10.5" (unbeaten from 1923 to 1943); long jump 12'11.5" (unbeaten from 1923 to 1944); shot 30'2.5" (unbeaten from 1923 to 1951); discus 64'3.25" (unbeaten from 1924 to 1951); javelin 107'9" (unbeaten from 1924 to 1958); two-arm javelin 173'2".

Porter-Hogan, Gay
Clubs: Ballymena; Crusaders
Coach: Sean Kyle

Gay (born Co. Armagh 23 Sept 1945) won 17 Northern Ireland titles in discus, shot, javelin, and 220 yds between 1957 and 1972. She won all-Ireland titles in shot, discus (115'10"), and javelin (113'6"). And she won BLE titles in shot (42'5.75") and discus (137'11.5") in 1974, in shot (45'0.5") and discus (143'5") in 1975, and in discus (121'7") in 1976.

In 1965 she set an all-Ireland shot record of 38'4"; she improved this nine times, reaching 48'5.5" in 1970. In 1966 she improved on Thelma Hopkins's discus record, with 128'11"; she went on to eventually reach 162'11". The same year, 1966, she improved on Bridget Dixon's eight-year-old javelin record, with 134'3". In 1971 she added a foot to that mark.

Gay represented Northern Ireland internationally 13 times at throws and high jump between 1964 and 1971, including the 1970 Commonwealth Games in Edinburgh. After joining Crusaders and marrying Sean Hogan, she threw discus, javelin, and shot five times for the Republic in 1974 and 75.

Quinn (Griffin), Patricia
Club: Ballinamore AC
Coaches: Pádraig Griffin; Joe Doonan

Patricia (born 5 Mar 1955) comes from an athletic family: her late father was involved in GAA and athletics; her sister and three brothers were also athletes, but Mickey (Leitrim's first All Star), Thomas, and Seamus favoured football. Patricia played basketball and swimming at school.

She got a taste for athletics in 1967 at Ballinamore Sports, has been winning titles for the past 25 years, and is Leitrim's outstanding sportsperson. Amazingly versatile, she has won County, Provincial, and National titles (30 in all) over distances varying from 400m to 10 miles and has taken silver and bronze in National Pentathlons. In one year, 1989, she won the National 5,000m and 10,000m track and National 15k road and was second in the National 1,500m and 3,000m.

She has represented Ireland 30 times on track and country: in Europa Cup T&F, West Athletic T&F, World CC, World 15k (road), World Half Marathon, World Cup Marathon, Ekiden Relay. In the process she has travelled as far afield as Japan, Brazil, and Australia.

For her the high point was winning the 1988 Dublin Millennium Mini Marathon, first of 15,000 competitors, in a PB 33.57. A few months after that victory she was named Best Home Based Woman Athlete of 1988. She retained her Mini Marathon title in 1989 (34.28).

Patricia made her marathon debut (2.43.50) as part of an Irish team (with Ursula Noctor, Connie Kelly, Brid Murphy, and Bernie Stankard) in London 1991. She was seventh in the 1991 Chicago Marathon (2.42.36), posted third in Dublin 1993 (2.46.08), and won the 1995 Belfast Marathon (2.53.10).

Patricia's husband and coach, Pádraig Griffin, has spent over 30 years as an athletics journalist and administrator.

Real, Mary T
Club: Limerick AC
Coach: Declan O'Donoghue

Mary (born 17 May 1971) took up athletics in 1985 having played basketball, tenpin bowling, and golf. Concentrating on the javelin, she became our best-ever thrower.

She was Munster senior javelin champion from 1987 to 1993, represented Ireland during that same period, and was national senior champion in the four years from 1990 to 1993. She set a national record 50.42 in Waterford on 20 June 1992 which still stands.

Serious injury in 1993 put her out of competition, and at the time of writing (early 1997) she has yet to return.

Reilly-Murphy, Rosemary
Clubs: Crusaders; Sparta
Coach: Paddy Murphy (her husband)

Rosemary (born 2 May 1940) was a versatile and durable athlete who garnered not only a score of national titles in AAUE, BLE, and USC (Ulster Sports Council) competition but also an All-Ireland gold medal for camogie (1964).

AAUE: 1965 shot (10.56) and discus; 1966 shot (11.15) and discus (32.97).

BLE: 1967 shot (10.84), discus (37.36), and javelin (37.38); 1968 discus (35.56) and javelin (28.41); 1969 shot (10.25) and discus (31.88); 1970 shot (10.34) and discus (35.08); 1971 shot (10.76) and discus (36.48); 1973 javelin (27.51).

USC: 1973 shot (11.75) and discus (26.59); 1974 shot (11.99) and discus (31.88).

Internationals: 1964 v Scotland, Ayr, 4th shot (9.47), 4th discus (27.19), 4th javelin (31.40); 1973 European Cup, Copenhagen, 5th discus (34.69), 6th javelin (24.90).

Rosemary describes the administration of athletics in her competitive hey-day as 'pathetic', especially in the context of women. Nor does she reckon all the problems have been solved; as recently as 1995 she said, 'I have no good opinions of the present administration in Irish athletics.'

Rosemary now lives in Derry and, with her husband, Paddy, coaches children.

Reynolds, Pamela
Club: Clonliffe Harriers
Coach: Richie Davis

Pam (born 1945), from Garristown, was Ireland's first female international race walker and in 1976 came 5th in the WAAA (British) 5k in London (28.31.2). She competed in over 20 races in Europe between 1976 and 1983. Her proudest achievement was her 2nd place in the Isle of Man 50k (32.5 miles) in a time of 6.44.40.

In 1981 BLE held its first women's 3k championship at Santry. Mary Hennessy (KCH) won in 15.48; Pam was 2nd in 15.55. Now in the veteran category, Pam still races occasionally.

Robinson (Bailey), Brenda
Club: Bury AC
Coach: Vera Duerdin

This Rochdale lass (born 27 Sept 1943), who reportedly never exceeded 35 miles per week in training, was one of the first exiles to represent Ireland. She never ran a trial in Ireland, but her English form was taken into account (3rd in the 1964 English CC Championships). She posted 12th in the 1967 International CC.

Rooney, Catherine
Club: Blackrock
Coach: Paddy Craddock

Catherine (born 19 April 1957) came from Grange, Co. Sligo, to work in Dun Laoghaire and took up running in 1981. Training on her own she ran the 1981 Dublin City Marathon in 4.21 and the 1982 Dublin City Marathon in 3.21. She came under Paddy Craddock's guidance in 1983 – and improved to 3.08.

From here on, improvement was relentless. She took silver in the 1984 National 10, won by Greta Hickey (59.00 to Catherine's 60.05). In August she won the Grange Half Marathon (1.17) and in September the Ballyshannon 10 (59.27), which got her a trip to Boston's famous Bonnie Belle 10k.

In 1986 she represented Ireland in the Home Countries CC at Peterborough, was 2nd in the Bray-Donnybrook 10 (Rosie Lambe 56.25, Catherine 57.01), and won the Claremorris 10k (34.48) and the Bank of Ireland Two (12.04).

In late 1986 she was knocked from her bicycle and sidelined for three months but came back in January 1987 to take silver behind Anne Keenan-Buckley in the Leinster CC. She won the Raheny 5 (27.35) from Emily Dowling and Eleanor Hill. In May 1987 she won the Navan 10k and in January 1988 the Eastern Regions CC.

On 14 February 1988 came Catherine's finest hour: she outstayed and outpaced Anne Keenan, Rosie Lambe, and Christine Kennedy, among others, to win the National CC and qualify for the World CC in Auckland, New Zealand.

In December 1988, she was 2nd to Anne Keenan in the National Intercounties CC. February 1989 Christine Kennedy won the National CC; Catherine was 2nd; a promising youngster called Catherina McKiernan was 3rd. In March 1989 Catherine finished 64th (Catherina McKiernan 76th) in the World CC in Norway.

Catherine's career was terminated by a spinal injury, which after seven years still bothers her. Despite the need for regular medical treatment, she keeps fit by walking.

Ryan, Mary L
Club: Blackrock
Coach: Brendan O'Shea

A late starter at 31 years of age, Mary prospered from steady training and won many cross-country medals with her club. She won National Marathon bronze in 1985 and clocked a marathon best of 2.59.20. Her 10-mile PB is 59.40.

Mary's greatest achievement was winning the 1984 European Veterans' Marathon (O/35) at Brighton. In intense heat she clocked 3.01.21 in becoming the first Irishwoman to win European gold. Besides running, she enjoys hillwalking, climbing, and caving.

Ryan (Jennings), Mary B
Club: Waterford
Coach: Frank Leahy

Mary (born 18 Feb 1955) is an all-rounder who has been competing for over 20 years. She won juvenile races at 100m and 200m before progressing to cross-country. She has won the Dublin pentathlon title and numerous Waterford track and CC titles. The following PBs show her astonishing range: 100m 12.6; 200m 26.9; 800m 2.20; 100mH 16.84; 400mH 63.5; long jump 5.10; high jump 1.42; 10k 36.50; 10 miles 60.10; half marathon 80.5; 20 miles 2.05; marathon 2.51.30.

She has completed a score of marathons, winning two national titles: Tralee 1986 and Sligo 1995. Her marathon CV reads as follows: 1986 National, Portlaoise, 4th, 3.02; 1986 Dublin, 16th, 3.13.14; 1987 National, Galway, 2nd, 3.00.2; 1987 Dublin, 8th, 2.58; 1988 Belfast, 2nd, 2.54; 1988 Dublin, 8th, 2.51.30; 1989 Milan (World Cup), 3.00.12; 1989 National, Tralee, 1st, 2.53; 1990 Dublin, 7th, 2.58; 1990 New York, 3.09; 1993 Dublin, 4th, 3.04; 1994 Potteries, England, 3rd, 3.09; 1994 Dublin, 10th, 3.01; 1995 National, Sligo, 1st, 3.00.45; 1995 Belfast, 3rd, 3.03.03; 1995 Finglas, 1st, 2.59.42; 1995 Dublin, 1st O/40, 3.06.4; 1997 National, Derry, 2nd, 3.26.15; 1997 Belfast, 3rd, 3.07.03. Her ambition at the time of writing is to enter ultramarathons.

Mary is married to Brian Jennings, a former international athlete. They have four children: Cian (b 24 April 90), Emmet (b 28 Aug 91), Ryan (b 20 March 93), and Emily (b 23 June 96).

Scallan, Carmel
Club: St Benedict's, Arklow
Coach: Michael Quinn

During her short career, Carmel (born 21 Sept 1958) won the 1975 National Senior high jump title (1.67) and jumped in three internationals (1.60 each time), v Wales, Greece, and Spain, all in 1976 .

Scanlon, Dorothy
Club: Blindsports AC
Coach: Tony Guest

From 1989 to date Dorothy has consistently won the National 100m and 200m. She first represented Ireland in New York, winning medals at 100m and 200m. In the 1994 Eurochampionships at Belfield she took relay bronze. In the 1995 British Nationals in London she took silver at 200m and bronze at 100m, long jump, and shot. The versatile Dorothy trains three times per week and works as a landscape gardener in Arklow.

Shankey (Kyle), Maeve
Club: Ballymena
Coach: Sean Kyle

Maeve (born 6 October 1928) was introduced to sport at the early age of nine. She had two sportsmen brothers (Brian, who played cricket for South Africa and hockey for Northern Rhodesia and Dermot, a good all-rounder) and an athletic sister (Deirdre, who played tennis and interpro hockey).

Kilkenny College (where Maeve's dad was headmaster) catered for all sports; Maeve ran against the boys and won U/13 100 and 200 yards. Highly versatile, she also excelled at hockey and while still at school was selected for the Leinster Senior squad. She went on to collect 58 international hockey caps over 20 years, which included the Triple Crown triumph of 1950.

In 1953 Maeve met Sean Kyle and began to concentrate on athletics. In 1954 Sean and Maeve married and the following year founded Ballymena AC. In 1956 Maeve won the British WAAA 100yds and 200yds in London, setting NI records. She was selected for the Melbourne Olympics, where she was eliminated in the first round of both sprints. In 1958 she ran for Northern Ireland in the Cardiff Commonwealth Games and was on the 4x100 team that made the final. In 1960 she went to her second Olympics, in Rome, but was again eliminated in both sprint heats.

In 1962 she moved up to 440yds, won the WAAA title, and set a British all-comers mark of 54.9. She qualified for the European Championships and reached the final. In 1963, she took silver in the WAAA 880yds, her 2.09.5 a NI record. In 1964 she qualified for her third Olympics, Tokyo. It was her most successful Games; she reached the 400m and 800m semifinals.

In 1970, at 42 years of age, she competed in the Edinburgh Commonwealth Games and qualified for the 400m final; she was also on the squad that made the relay final. Between 1974 and 1987 she competed in veteran championships all over the world, set many age-group records, and won over 30 medals.

Maeve's contribution to athletics has not been only competitive; from 1957 to date she has served as committee member, secretary, treasurer, chairman, and president of the Joint Federation. She has been a Great Britain team manager and selector. She and Sean are master coaches.

Her major achievements include: bringing women's athletics to Trinity College Races in 1960; helping to get women organised in both Crusaders and Clonliffe in 1963; serving on the working group to rationalise athletics in Ireland; coaching Sharon McPeake, Northern Ireland's first 1.83 (6ft) high-jumper, and Ricky Robinson, Northern Ireland's first 2.14 (7ft) high-jumper.

Shakespeare, Dara
Club: Dundrum South Dublin
Coach: Dan Kennedy

Dara (born 3 June 1963) has performed several sports at high levels; among other exploits, she captained Ireland's handball team at the 1984 Los Angeles Olympics and played intervarsity table-tennis.

She burst upon the athletics scene in 1980 when taking Community Games, All-Ireland Schools, BLOE, and National Senior javelin titles. Perhaps surprisingly, she failed to repeat her National Senior win in any of the following four years (Linda Kennedy, Brenda Walsh twice, and Kay McGovern preventing her) but returned to dominance in 1985 and 1986 with great throws of 46.72 and 47.20 and won again in 1988 (43.76) and 1989 (43.98). During some 15 years she gained 30 international vests. She still trains but has virtually retired from competition.

Dara's father, Dick Shakespeare, played hockey with the Guinness club and Leinster; her brother Geoff won a National Junior triple jump title.

Sherry (Duffy), Vera
Club: Glaslough Harriers

Between 1968 and 1977 Vera (born 13 Mar 1953) won 21 Ulster Sports Council titles at distances from 100m to 1,500m. She also won the 1975 BLE 3,000m (9.54.2) and retained it in 1976. A versatile runner who nevertheless preferred cross-country, she represented Ireland seven times: 1971 San Sebastian 3,000m, 1974 Monza 5,000m, 1975 Coatsbridge 3m (2nd), 1976 Rawtenstall CC, 1976 Chepstow CC, 1976 Cwmbran, Wales, Triangular 3,000m (1st), 1977 Mullingar CC (1st).

PBs: 800m 2.07.5, 1,500m 4.34.4.

Smith, Catherine
Club: Dublin City Harriers
Coach: Jim Kilty

A classic 10k road-racer, Catherine posted top ten in the Women's Mini Marathon on eight occasions and scored a great victory in the event in 1991 (34.29), leaving behind such big names as Niamh Murphy, Cathy Shum, and Patricia Griffin.

Catherine also excelled at the marathon and in the early nineties made Belfast her own with a marvellous hat-trick of wins: 1992 (2.42.41), 1993 (2.45.00), 1994 (2.44.42). She took third in the 1995 Dublin City Marathon (2.47.02).

Smith, Susan
Clubs: Waterford AC; Brown University, USA
Coach: David Smith

Susan boasts an excellent sports pedigree: her granduncle John Keane was a famous hurler; her father, David, was a sprinter and played hurling, soccer, and cricket. She was introduced to athletics at the age of seven and started to make a reputation as a hurdler when she was 14.

She won All-Ireland Schools 80mH in 1985, 86, 87, and 88. She won the 1988 FISEC (European Catholic Schools) 80mH title. She won the National Senior 100mH in 1989, 90, 91, 92, and 95 and the 400mH in 1992, 96, and 97.

Susan has steadily improved each year (including the four years she spent at Brown University, Providence, Rhode Island) and in 1996 blossomed into true world class at 400m hurdles with the series of record-breaking runs that culminated in the Atlanta Olympics, where she brought her own Irish record down to 54.93 and reached the semi-finals.

In 1997 she went to the Athens World Championships, and there confirmed her world class by lowering her national record to 54.61 and reaching the 400mH final, where she finished seventh (55.25). She thus became only the second Irishwoman to reach a sprint final at a major championships.

Smyth, Ailish
Clubs: DCH; Sportsworld AC
Coaches: Jim Kilty; Emily Dowling
Marathon advisor: Brendan O'Shea

Ailish commenced athletics at Community Games level, joined Good Counsel AC in 1976, and in 1978 started to train seriously under Jim Kilty's coaching.

She won the 1986 Dublin City Marathon (2.47.30), the National 3,000m track (9.29.27), and the 1987 National 5,000m track. She was 2nd in the 1987 National 10,000m track and the 1988 National Marathon, Wexford (2.45.18). The latter race qualified her for the Seoul Olympics.

She was a member of the DCH CC teams that won European Club gold in 1985 and 1986. She was 8th (2.39.36 PB) in the 1987 Berlin Marathon. She wore the Irish singlet at the 1985 World Cup Marathon, the 1987 Ekiden Relay, Japan, the 1987 World 15k, Gateshead, the 1988 Olympic Marathon (46th in 2.44.17), the 1995 Irish and British Veterans' CC Championships (1st in 10k, 2nd in 15k).

Ailish's father played Gaelic football for Louth. All her brothers and sisters have also played sports.

Smyth, Róisín
Clubs: Sparta AC; DCH; Loughborough College
Coaches: Paddy Devine; John Dooley; George Gandy

Róisín took up athletics in 1976 (her father and brother were athletes, her father winning many Louth titles). In May 1984, running for University College, she won the Intervarsity 800m (2.09.4) and 3,000m (9.20). She qualified for the 1984 Olympics by posting 2nd (8.57.94) in the 3,000m trial. She also won the National 800m in a PB 2.06.01. In a warmup race for Los Angeles, she did a PB 4.14.7 for 1,500m. In the intense heat of the Olympic stadium, she clocked 9.01 in her heat but failed to progress.

In 1985, Róisín again did an Intervarsity double: 800m (2.10.1) and 1,500m (4.36). In July she won the National 1,500m (4.16.5). In January 1986 she took three third places: Mallusk CC International, Cosford Indoor 3,000m (9.22.07), Cosford 1,500m (4.16.61). In March she won the Intervarsity CC and in May confirmed her dominance of Academe by retaining the Intervarsity 800m (2.17.2) and 1,500m (4.45). Also in 1986, she won the National 1,500m (4.19.52). She won the 1989 National 3,000m.

In a period of eight seasons, 1984 to 1991, Róisín represented Ireland in over 20 internationals, including the Olympics and the European T&F Championships in Split, Yugoslavia. Dogged by injuries, she retired from competition at the end of 1991. She now teaches and lives in Dublin.

Spence, Jacqueline
Club: Crusaders AC
Coach: self

Jacqueline won the 1965 AAUE 100yds (11.1), the 1966 AAUE 100yds (11.5) and 220yds (26.4), the 1966 All-Ireland 100yds (11.6) and 220yds (25.8), and the 1967 BLE 100yds (11.4) and 220yds (27.8). In a 1963 match v Belgium she was 4th in the 100yds (11.9) and on the winning 4x100 team (48.2). In a 1964 international at Ayr, Scotland, she was 4th in the 100yds (11.8) and 3rd in the 220yds (26.4). Also in 1964, at a triangular meeting in Brussels, she was 2nd in the 100m (12.6) and helped win the 400m relay (47.7). And in the 1973 European Cup, Copenhagen, she was 3rd in the 100m (12.0).

Jacqueline's running career was cut short by a knee injury sustained while playing hockey.

Stokes, Jacqui
Club: Ferrybank
Coach: Drew Harrison

Jacqui (born 1 April 1967) has a great sporting pedigree. Her grandfather P.J. Stokes played rugby for Ireland in the twenties. Her father, also P.J. Stokes, was a successful amateur jockey. Her brother John played rugby with the Irish Youths and is a member of Garryowen. Another brother, Nick, is an amateur jockey.

Jacqui took up athletics at age nine and soon became proficient in sprints and jumps. She took national BLOE and schools titles in many events from U/11 to U/17, setting a number of records along the way. She also won Tailteann Games titles. At age 14 she gained her first Irish singlet, at the 1980 Celtic Games, Glasgow, winning long jump, high jump, and 4x400m. She represented Ireland at schools competition up to 1985 and was captain that year. She set a national junior LJ mark of 5.72 in 1984.

She gained her first senior singlet at 16 in 1983. In 1987 she took up a four-year athletics scholarship to Providence, Rhode Island. She won State and All East 200m and LJ titles in each of her four university years. In 1989 she was a member of the medley relay team that set a world best for 400m/800m/1,200m/mile.

Jacqui won Irish National LJ (indoor and outdoor) titles in 1994, 95, 96, and 97 and took 200m gold in 1996. Also in 1996 she won the Scottish National Indoor LJ, the Welsh Games LJ, the Westathletic LJ, and the Pappendal Games, Holland, LJ. And as Irish captain at the Europa Cup in Belgium, she won 200m, LJ, and relay.

This versatile athlete has also found time and energy to play international schools hockey and first-class senior hockey, with Hermes, Waterford, and Kilkenny (while in Providence, she starred on the university hockey team, the best in the country). She also holds an amateur jockey's licence.

PBs: 100m 11.80, 200m 24.02, 400m 56.01, LJ 6.27, HJ 1.75.

Stuart, Heather
Club: Kavanagh Striders

Heather, from Sligo, did not take up athletics until after her 21st birthday but has made up for lost time. Most marathoners are content with two or three marathons per year. Heather has often run 15 and an ultra-distance race for good measure. All on only 25 to 30 miles weekly training – she uses races to get fit!

She ran her first marathon in Letterkenny 1981. She ran her 100th Marathon in October at the Dublin City Marathon – a great many more than any other Irishwoman. She has run London to Brighton (53 miles) and the South African Comrades' Marathon (57 miles) three times (PB 8.28). She took second in the Tourhout, Belgium, 100k (62 miles) and thrice won gold (1993, 94, and 95) at the Corporate World Games Half Marathon.

She has run marathons in America, South Africa, Malta, Majorca, France, Spain, Hawaii, England, Isle of Man, Turkey, and Germany. She now competes as a veteran (O/35) and wins a medal every time she races.

Career highlights: 9 Oct 1994 World Corporate Games Half Marathon, South Africa, 1st; 16 Oct 1994 Sun City Marathon, South Africa, 4th; 19 Oct 1994 Brackan 15k, South Africa, 2nd. 29 Oct 1994 Dublin City Marathon, 8th; 27 Dec 1994 Carraroe Marathon, 1st; 20 March 1995 Larne Half Marathon, 3rd; 27 March 1995 Omagh Half Marathon, 1st; 2 April 1995 Taunton Marathon, 2nd; 21 April 1995 National Marathon, 2nd; 2 May 1995 Belfast Marathon (British Vets Championship), 3rd; 17 July 1995 Portaferry 10, 1st; 21 July 1995 World Veterans, 4th; 27 July 1995 Kilavea Crater Marathon, Hawaii, 4th; 9 Sept 1995 World Corporate Games 10k, Geneva, 3rd; 13 Sept 1995 World Corporate Games Half Marathon, Geneva, 1st; 30 May 1995 Comrades' Marathon, South Africa, 1,100th (of 14,000); 20 April 1997 National Marathon, Derry, 3rd (3.29.40).

Heather works with AIB in Belfast.

Tennison-Little, Hazel
Club: Crusaders
Coaches: Louis Vandendries; Sean Kyle

Hazel (born 6 Sept 1942) did exceptionally well on very little training. Her best ever performance was finishing second to the then world 800m record-holder, Judy Pollock, in Santry (now Morton) Stadium on 27 June 1966. Her national record 2.11.1 stood until 1968, when Ann O'Brien (Clonliffe) ran 2.10.2.

During her entire career there were only three international T&F matches for women. As she said herself (1967), 'The administration in athletics in Ireland has always treated women as second-class citizens.' Her expressed hope (also in 1967) was to see an Irishwoman win European or Olympic gold. Happily, that hope has been fulfilled in the nineties, thanks to Sonia O'Sullivan.

Hazel won national AAUE titles at 880 yds in 1965 (2.18.3) and 1966 (2.17.2). She won the National (BLE) Long Jump title in 1967 (16'6"). She is married to Ivan Little, a Crusaders clubmate.

Thompson, Brenda
Club: Slaney Olympic
Coach: Paul Kinsella

Brenda (born Enniscorthy 13 May 1975) is one of a sporting family and has been in athletics since she was nine. Her father played hurling, her mother squash, rowing, and athletics (including the Dublin Marathon); her sister Clara (born 10 Nov 1979) represented Ireland at the 1976 European Youth Olympics, won BLE junior discus and hammer, and in 1997 emulated Brenda by taking the National Senior hammer title (48.82); another sister, Gina, won Leinster U/16 shot and discus.

Brenda herself is ideally built for throws: six feet tall and a fit 12 stone. She first came to national prominence in summer 1993, when she won the national junior (32.07) and national senior (35.20) hammer titles and gained her first Irish vest v English and Russian selections at Cork City Sports.

Other highlights to date:

1994: BLE Games, Tullamore, 1st hammer (41.28); National Seniors, 1st hammer (39.98); National League Finals, 1st hammer (42.72 NJR).

1995: Intervarsity Games, Cork, 1st hammer (42.26); BLE Games, Tullamore, 1st hammer (42.26); Irish Universities v Harvard and Yale, Belfield, 2nd hammer (43.62); National U/23 Champs, Tullamore, 1st hammer (43.74), 2nd discus (33.80); National Seniors, Santry, 1st hammer (44.28); National League Finals, Tullamore, 1st hammer (44.00); International v Belarus and English Southern Counties, 1st hammer (44.14).

1996: BLE Games, Santry, 3rd hammer (42.42); Westathletic, Santry, 5th hammer (44.48); National Seniors, Santry, 4th hammer (45.22); National U/23 Champs, Tullamore, 3rd hammer (44.80), 2nd discus (44.80); National League Finals, 1st hammer (46.20 PB).

Brenda underwent physiotherapy for back problems in 1996, and though she competed well and actually improved her PB, her throwing was affected.

Like many another athlete, Brenda sees the Dublin Syndrome as a problem in BLE – she suspects some national coaches dislike venturing outside the Pale. She also reckons many athletes of international class don't get enough financial help. It costs the Thompson household about £1,300 per year to have two such athletes.

Tracey (Purcell), Mary
Clubs: Guinness; Crusaders
Coach: Peter Purcell

Mary (born 22 May 1949) held national records for 800m (2.02.8), 1,500m (4.08.63), and 3,000m (9.07.98) during the period 1972 to 1976. She represented Ireland for many years and built a fine record of six wins in 11 starts against elite international opposition.

She won BLE titles at: 800m 1973; 1,500m 1972, 1973, 1974, 1975, 1976, 1978, and 1980; cross-country 1973 and 1980; marathon 1982. She won British WAAA titles at 800m in 1972 and 1973 and took silver at 800m in 1984 and 3,000m in 1975 and 1976. She won the 1983 Dublin City Marathon.

She competed in the 1972 Olympics, Munich, reaching the 800m QF (4th in 2.04.2) and the 1,500m QF (6th in 4.16.4). In the 1976 Olympics, Montreal, she was 5th (4.08.2) in her 1,500m heat. She was selected for the 1980 Moscow Olympics but declined.

Mary won numerous international track races: 1973 Copenhagen European Cup 800m (2.02.9); 1973 Pretoria, South Africa, Open 800m (2.05.2); 1973 Frankfurt International 800m (2.04.03); 1974 Ostrava Golden Spike 1,500m (4.16.4); 1974 v Lisbon and Portugal 1,500m (4.28.8), 800m (2.07.6), 1,600m relay 3.44.2 (57.3); 1975 Osijek European Cup 800m (2.06.05); 1975 Den Haag Sparta Games 1,500m (4.16.4); 1976 Padendal Games 800m (2.04.5).

Mary was fourth in the 1976 Helsinki World Games 1,500m (4.13.4). And in cross-country she won the 1976 Rawtenstall International.

Treacy, Siobhán
Club: Dublin City Harriers
Coach: Jim Kilty

Siobhán (born 13 Sept 1956) commenced athletics at the 1971Community Games and went on to represent Ireland on track and country from 1978 to 1981. But after a very promising marathon debut in 1983 (2.52 in Dublin) she gave up competing to concen trate on work and family. Her PBs include 2.22.2 800m and 4.41.9 mile.

A successful physiotherapist, Siobhán was part of the Irish medical team for the Barcelona Olympics 1992. She is married to another former athlete, Liam Treacy; they have four children, two boys and two girls.

Treacy (Bullen), Liz
Club: Villierstown AC

Liz won underage CC titles in Co. Waterford before leaving the sport in 1974 to take up nursing in England. She returned to running in 1986 and in 1988 ran her first marathon, the Dublin City, finishing ninth in 2.53. She improved to second and 2.46 the following year, then improved again, to 2.40, in the National Marathon at Clonmel, winning silver and qualifying for the European Championships in Split (2.53 and 18th). She won the Cork Evening Echo Mini Marathon (5 miles) in 1989. She also posted 18th (2.44) in the Boston Marathon. Injuries terminated her career.
She now coaches with Cappoquin Ballinamela AC.

Liz is a twin of John Treacy, the 1984 Olympic Marathon runner-up.

Vaughan, Valerie
Clubs: Blarney Inniscarra; Costa Mesa, USA
Coach: John O'Riordan

Valerie (born 1 Nov 1966) commenced her career by winning nine Schools titles at National level in the years 1981 to 1984. At only 13 she won bronze in the Senior 3,000m. In 1984 she won the National Junior 1,500m. While in UCC from 1984 to 1988 she won several National Intervarsity track and CC titles.

In 1989 she availed of a three-year scholarship to Western Kentucky but did not compete for the college, concentrating instead on taking her Masters in English and Communications.

In 1991 she was selected for the World CC in Antwerp. In 1992 she wore the green vest at the Europa Cup (track) in Brussels and the Ekiden Relay (road) in Japan. She won the National 1,500m in 1992 and 1997 (4.28.71 and 4.23.50) and the National 5,000m in 1997 (15.44.72).

Valerie has done most of her racing Stateside. In 1995, for example, she won the USI 1,500m, the San Diego State 3,000m, the Fullerton 1,500m, and several big 10k road races. In 1996 her victories included a race record 15.51 in the Cure 5k at Newport Beach (this event supporting breast cancer treatment and research attracts over 10,000 participants).

Despite having posted a qualifying time, Valerie was passed over by BLE for Atlanta 96. She was, however, selected for the 1997 World CC in Turin, and was part of the brilliant team effort that brought home the bronze medals (Catherina McKiernan 7th, Sonia O'Sullivan 9th, Valerie 23rd, Una English 25th). She was also selected for the 1997 Athens World Championships (her first major track championships), where in the semi-final of the 5,000m she stayed with the leaders until halfway but then suffered in the humid heat and finished 14th, and outside the qualifiers, in 15.57.58.

Valerie, whose four sisters are also athletes, lately resigned her job as coach at Mater Dei High to concentrate fulltime on her running.

PBs: 1,500m 4.20.2, mile 4.40, 3,000m 9.17.4, 5,000m 16.02.

Walsh, Catherine
Clubs: Blindsports AC; Fingallians

A physiotherapist in Beaumont Hospital, Catherine has been involved in athletics since winning a Community Games medal in 1987. Her biggest international success was pentathlon bronze at the 1994 World Championships in Berlin.

Catherine has represented Ireland seven times in major games: 1990 Assen, Holland, World Championships; 1991 Caen, France, European Championships (pentathlon bronze); 1992 Barcelona, Spain, Paralympics; 1993 Dublin European Championships; 1994 Berlin World Championships (pentathlon bronze); 1995 Valencia, Spain, European Championships; 1996 Atlanta, USA, Paralympics.

Walsh (Carroll), Michele
Club: Crusaders
Coach: Ronnie Carroll

Michele (born 5 August 1961) began her amazing winning spree in 1977: Dublin Championships 200m, Tailteann Games 100m and 200m, National Junior 100m and 200m (national records 11.80 and 24.90), Europa Cup 100m (11.59 NR) and 200m (24.35 NR), National Senior 100m and 200m, AAA Intermediate 100m and 200m, Bavarian Youth Championships 100m (11.54 NR) and 200m - and so on.

She won 100m and 200m at the 1978 FISEC Games, Leeds; 100m and 200m at the Westathletic, Sittard, Holland (11.43 NR and 23.51 NR); 100m and 200m at the Prague International; reached the semifinals of the European Championship 100m (she was eliminated in the 200m heats).

In 1979, in Edmonton, Canada, she finished second in the 60m (won by Evelyn Ashford). At Winnipeg she was second in the 60m to Brenda Morecraft. At the European Indoor Championships in Vienna she reached the 60m semifinals (7.42).

In 1980 Gothenburg she won a 60m. She missed 1981 due to a hamstring injury.

In 1982 she was second in the 100m and third in the 200m at Athens. In 1983 she won the Donore International 100m.

In 1984 she won 100m and 200m in the triangular v Denmark and England; 100m and 200m in the Eastern Regions USA; 100m, 200m, and 4x100m v Iceland. In 1986 Michele was working in the USA and took a rest from competition. In 1987 she won the Flagstaff, Arizona, 300m; the Cork Sports 100m.

In 1991 she won 100m and 200m at the BLE Games. In 1992 she qualified for the European Indoors 60m semifinals. In 1993 she set a national record 7.38 for 60m and represented Ireland in the World Indoors, Toronto. In the 1995 Europa Cup, at Tallin, she represented Ireland in 100m, 200m, 4x100m, and 4x400m.

Besides all the above, Michele won 31 national track titles from 100m to 800m, a phenomenal total that is unlikely ever to be equalled.

Walsh (Morales), Patricia
Clubs: Waterford De La Salle; University of Tennessee
Coach: Donal O'Keeffe

Patricia (born 16 March 1960) commenced athletics at age 15 and the following year won a Junior Schools shot title (11.62). She won the 1976 All-Ireland javelin U/16 (33.98) and at the 1976 Schools International took second in the shot (12.02) and fourth in the discus (38.76).

Thereafter she carved out a brilliant career and became arguably our greatest-ever thrower. She won 12 national senior titles: nine discus (1977 through 1985), two shot (1979 and 1985), and one javelin (1977); she represented Ireland at the Los Angeles

Olympics 1984; she was five times All American while at Tennessee; her national discus record 57.60 from 1984 still stands.

1976: Trosberg, Germany, 2nd discus (41.12), 3rd shot (11.46).

1977: National BLE Senior Champs, 1st discus (46.34 NR at age 17), 1st javelin (36.66), 2nd shot (12.94); represented Ireland at European Juniors, Kiev, USSR.

1988: FISEC Games, 1st discus (44.68), 1st shot (12.75), 2nd javelin (38.26), 2nd 4x100m; All Ireland Schools, 1st discus (48.08 CR), 1st shot (12.54); National Champs, 1st discus (48.26), 2nd shot (13.89), 2nd javelin (40.32); British AAA Champs, 2nd discus (47.28).

1979: National Champs, 1st discus (49.70); Ireland v Israel, 1st discus (50.12); Ireland v Denmark, 1st discus (50.12), 2nd shot (13.89); British AAA Champs, 2nd discus (50.95).

1980: Eight Nations, Switzerland, 1st discus (54.36 NR)

In 1981 Patricia retained her national discus title before taking up a scholarship to the University of Tennessee.

In 1982 she captained her university's track and field team, set a national discus record 57.06, again retained her BLE title, won her specialty event at an eight-nations meet in Holland, and placed 14th at the European Championships in Athens.

In 1983 she won the Penn Relays discus, the Irish title yet again (54.26), and the Westathletic meet in Dublin.

On July 7 1984, at Morton Stadium, Patricia threw the 57.60 NR that has yet to be bettered. A month later she finished ninth in the Los Angeles Olympic final.

In 1985 she crowned a glorious career by winning the ninth and last of her national discus titles (47.54) and the second and last of her shot titles (13.08).

Patricia now resides in Knoxville, Tennessee, where she is on the coaching and academic staff of the University of Tennessee.

Walsh (Ó Cléirigh), Patricia
Club: Dundrum South Dublin
Coach: Hayden Lewis

Patricia's mother, Claire, was an Olympian; her sister, Niamh, was 1982 Schools 800m champion. Patricia herself amassed titles and set records galore.

In 1982 and 1983 she won Leinster and All-Ireland Schools 200m and 400m, International Schools 400m (56.4), and Junior Westathletic 400m. In 1984 she won Leinster Schools 400m, All-Ireland Schools 400m, and National Junior 400m. In 1986 and 1988 she won the National 400m (53.72 and 54.39).

From 1982 to 1988 she won 20 international singlets. In the 1985 Europa Cup she was a member of the victorious Irish 4x400m team (3.38.12). In 1986 v Catalonia and Scotland she won the 400m. She was eliminated in the 400m heats of the 1986 European Championships.

In 1987 Patricia set a national record 53.06 and was a member of the National

4x400m team that posted 3.32.56. In 1988 she helped DSD set a club NR 3.44.73 for 4x400m. And in the 1988 match v Britain and Switzerland she won the 400m (55.18).

Patricia is married to Aonghus Ó Cléirigh, an international runner and orienteer. Cathal Ronan, their first child (and the first grandchild to Claire and Brian Dowling), arrived on 11 April 1997.

Watters, Barbara
Club: Dundalk Harriers
Coach: self

Barbara won 200m and 400m All-Ireland Schools titles. She gained one Irish vest, at the 1976 Cwmbran Triangular International, where she won the 400m (57.6) and was on the winning 4x400m team (3.52). PBs: 200m 25.9, 400m 57.6, 800m 2.18.

Barbara believes we don't get the best out of our athletes and sums up her own difficulties: 'The facilities in Dundalk are non existent – the athletics administrators should do more for the athletes.'

Williams, Perri
Club: Ferrybank, Waterford
Coaches: Ed Williams (her father); Jim Kilty; Ray Hall

Perri took up cross-country as a 12-year-old and by age 17 had qualified for national finals. She entered a walking race for a dare, was surprised to finish third, and went on to win the All-Ireland 2,000m. In 1986 she started serious walk training – and reaped the rewards with a succession of national titles:

1986 National Senior 3,000m, 1st; 1987 National 3,000m, 1st (14.00); 1988 National 10,000m, 1st (51.52); 1989 National 5,000m, 1st (24.05); 1990 National 5,000m, 2nd (24.00); 1991 National 5,000m, 1st (24.00); 1991 National 10,000m, 1st (50.13); 1992 National 5,000m, 1st (23.30); 1992 National 10,000m, 1st (47.22); 1993 National 10,000m, 1st (47.13); 1993 National 3,000m, 1st (13.09); 1994 UK National 10k road, 1st; 1997 National 5,000m, 1st (24.50).

In the 1992 Barcelona Olympic 10,000m Perri finished 37th in 54.53.

Part four

Results, reflections, records

Heroines of the marathon

In 1972, Australian Adrienne Beanne and American Beth Bonner became the first women to break three hours for the marathon distance. Since then thousands of women have dipped under what was the 'magic' barrier.

By 1982 300,000 women had completed marathon races, and under much pressure the International Olympic Committee gave in and included a women's marathon in the Los Angeles Olympics of 1984.

The first Irishwomen to run a marathon were Bridget Cushen, a cross-country and track runner, and Jean Folan, of Dundrum AC.

Born in Dublin in September 1940, Bridget Cushen did most of her running in England, with the London club Hercules Wimbledon. Her dedication (100 miles per week) paid dividends in cross-country titles and a second place to Clonliffe's Ann O'Brien in the 1970 British 3,000m. But despite all her achievements over ten years in England, she was never picked for her native country.

On 28 October 1973, Bridget was the only woman among 251 entrants in the Harlow Marathon. The weather was atrocious for marathon running, and hardly sympathetic to the little piece of history that was being made. Disregarding the fierce gales, pelting rain, and cramps over the last six miles, Bridget went the distance in three hours, 37 minutes, and 24 seconds.

Bridget still competes in veteran races and officiates in English veteran athletics.

Jean Folan, from Galway, was the first Irishwoman to complete a marathon on Irish roads; on a warm day in Tullamore, Co. Offaly, in 1979 she posted 3.37. A cross-country international, Jean won a signal victory in the 1983 Stockholm People's Marathon; her time was 2.59.

On 3 August 1980 Mary Butler (Crusaders) become the first Irishwoman to officially best 3.30; she returned 3.26.57. But Mary's reign as record-holder was brief; only a fortnight later, young Carey May (Dundrum) ran a sensational 2.53 in the Ulster Women's Marathon in Letterkenny.

Carey improved to 2.42.11 when winning the first Dublin City Marathon, October 1980. Some performances in her first year of running! She further improved the Irish record to 2.36.52 when winning the Fiesta Bowl Marathon in December 1981. By the time Regina Joyce (Westport) recorded 2.32.56 in the 1982 Fiesta Bowl, marathon fever was running wild, and we had 14 women under three hours.

The first women's Olympic marathon was held in Los Angeles 84; the historic date was 5 August. The gun went at 8am, but even at 8am the heat was 75 fahrenheit.

At 15k the American Joan Benoit led the field of 50 by over a minute. She was never challenged thereafter and crossed the line in 2.24.52. The great Grete Waitz (Norway) was second (2.26.18), Portugal's Rosa Mota third (2.26.50).

The first nine in that race bettered 2.30. All 44 finishers recorded times faster than the winners of the 1898, 1900, 1904, and 1908 Olympic marathons. Regina Joyce (23rd in 2.37.57) and Carey May (28th in 2.41.27) became Ireland's first Olympic Marathon ladies.

In 1984, in Osaka, Japan, Carey May set a world best for an all-women marathon of 2.29.23. She repeated the feat in Osaka 1985, posting 2.28.07, an Irish national record that stood for over 12 years.

Emily Dowling (DCH) won the 1981 Dublin City Marathon (2.48.22). The versatile Mary Purcell added the 1983 Dublin Marathon (2.49.09) to her CV. Ailish Smyth (1984) and Pauline Nolan (1989) also won Dublin. Galway's Christine Kennedy powered to victory in 1990 (2.41.27) and 1991 (2.35.56).

Clonliffe's Cathy Shum won Dublin in 1993 (2.38.14), placed second in 1994 (2.44.47), and in 1996 battled wind and rain to post a highly commendable 2.38.35 and become only the second Irishwoman to win the great event twice.

Sadly, after promising so much in the eighties, many of our women seem to lose appetite for the marathon in the nineties. The four Nationals from 1994 to 1997 had small fields and produced winning times around three hours. In Barcelona 1992, Atlanta 1996, and Athens 97 we had no woman marathoner.

Happily, Catherina McKiernan has stepped in to end the famine. She moved up to the classic distance in September 1997, winning Berlin in an amazing 2.23.44, the fastest ever debut.

Let us hope that this wonderful run, besides sending shock waves through the ranks of elite women worldwide, will inspire some of our other cross-country stars to take up the marathon challenge in the near future!

Marathon rankings

2.23.44	Catherina McKiernan	1997
2.28.07	Carey May	1985
2.32.56	Regina Joyce	1982
2.34.49	Monica Joyce	1984
2.35.05	Christine Kennedy	1991
2.37.05	Deirdre Nagle	1983
2.37.55	Marie Rollins	1988
2.38.14	Cathy Shum	1993
2.38.49	Mary Purcell	1982
2.39.25	Ursula Noctor	1990
2.39.36	Ailish Smyth	1987
2.40.51	Liz Mullen	1990
2.42.18	Connie Kelly	1991
2.42.28	Bernie Stankard	1993
2.42.31	Catherine Smith	1992
2.42.36	Patricia Griffin	1991
2.42.57	Pauline Nolan	1990
2.43.00	Brid Murphy	1992
2.43.28	Anne Hilliard	1988
2.45.39	Eleanor Hill	1992
2.46.02	Teresa Kidd	1986
2.46.04	Monica O'Reilly	1994
2.46.23	Mary Brayley	1990
2.47.18	Rosie Lambe	1993
2.47.20	Emily Dowling	1988
2.47.46	Deirdre O'Farrelly	1982
2.48.02	Ann Archbold	1984
2.48.36	Rosaleen Hayden	1987
2.50.04	Noreen Kelly	1988
2.50.33	Teresa Touhy	1992
2.51.30	Mary B. Ryan	1988
2.51.53	Ann Lynam	1991
2.52.07	Lucy O'Donoghue	1984
2.52.52	Siobhán Treacy	1983

BLE National Marathon

1982 Limerick
1. Mary Purcell (Guinness) 2.38.39
2. Deirdre Nagle (DCH) 2.48.53
3. Emily Dowling (DCH) 2.52.41

1983 Letterkenny
1. Theresa Kidd (Ballinascreen) 2.53.11
2. Bridget McCabe (Mullingar) 2.55.42
3. Nuala Logan (Limerick) 2.57.33

1984 Cork
1. Deirdre Nagle (DCH) 2.48.26*
2. Christine Kennedy (GCH) 2.49.46
3. Audrey O'Brien (DCH) 2.58.35

* Disqualified for wearing illegal logo.

1985 Portlaoise
1. Theresa Kidd (Ballinascreen) 2.47.37
2. Bridget McCabe (Mullingar) 3.00.44
3. Nuala Logan (Limerick) 3.07.28

1986 Portlaoise
1. Ailish Smyth (DCH) 2.41.33
2. Theresa Kidd (Ballinascreen) 2.46.13
3. Rose Hayden (Raheny) 2.59.28

1987 Galway
1. Kathleen Looney (Blarney) 2.58.25
2. Mary B. Ryan (Team Puma) 3.00.02
3. Theresa Kidd (Ballinascreen) 3.02.08

1988 Wexford
1. Marie Rollins (Unattached) 2.40.48
2. Ailish Smyth (DCH) 2.45.18
3. Mary Brayley (DCH) 2.48.10

1989 Tralee
1. Mary B. Ryan (Waterford) 2.53.47
2. Marie Morley (St Finbarr's) 3.04.09
3. Jean Folan (Bray Runners) 3.13.01

1990 Clonmel
1. Christine Kennedy (GCH) 2.38.05
2. Liz Bullen (Waterford) 2.40.51
3. Pauline Nolan (DCH) 2.42.57

1991 Dublin
1. Christine Kennedy (GCH) 2.35.56
2. Connie Kelly (Blackrock AC) 2.40.22
3. Mary Brayley (DCH) 2.42.16

1992 Dublin
1. Brid Murphy (Leevale) 2.43.00
2. Eleanor Hill (Bray Runners) 2.43.56
3. Teresa Touhy 2.50.33

1993 Clonmel
1. Brid Murphy (Leevale) 2.51.33
2. Catherine Dowling (DCH) 2.57.29
3. Marie Morley (St Finbarr's) 3.21.36

1994 Dublin Airport
1. Eleanor Hill (Bray Runners) 2.57.42
2. Mary Joyce (Mullingar) 3.38.19
3. Maria Brunton (Bray Runners) 4.07.08

1995 Sligo
1. Mary Jennings (Waterford) 3.00.05
2. Heather Stuart (Sligo) 3.36.12
3. Mary Joyce (Mullingar) 3.57.32

1996 Mallow
1. Brid Murphy (Leevale) 2.52.52
2. Mary Beth Dillon (USA) 3.12.01
3. Eileen Kenny (St Finbarr's) 3.23.08

1997 Derry
1. Donna McNulty (Finn Valley) 3.21.00
2. Mary Jennings (Waterford) 3.26.15
3. Heather Stuart (Sligo) 3.29.40

Dublin City Marathon 1980 - 96

1980
1. Carey May (Dundrum) 2.42.11
2. Mary Walsh (Clonliffe Harriers) 3.02.27
3. Breda Hon (Dallas, USA) 3.03.16

1981
1. Emily Dowling (DCH) 2.48.23
2. Deirdre Nagle (DCH) 2.49.40
3. Greta Hickey (DCH) 2.53.00

1982
1. Debbie Mueller (USA)
2. Deirdre Nagle (DCH) 2.42.08
3. Vreni Forster (USA) 2.46.09

1983
1. Mary Purcell (Crusaders) 2.46.09
2. Julie Gates (England) 2.48.00
3. Ann Archbold (Clonliffe Harriers) 2.48.16

1984
1. Ailish Smyth (DCH) 2.47.30
2. Ann Archbold (Clonliffe) 2.48.02
3. Annette Roberts (England) 2.48.04

1985
1. Julie Gates (England) 2.41.24
2. Josephine Hegarty (An Ríocht) 2.49.24
3. Josephine Murtagh (Dublin) 2.49.46

1986
1. Maureen Hurst (England) 2.46.27
2. Christine Kennedy (GCH) 2.49.34
3. Aastad May Brett (Belgique) 2.49.42

1987
1. Carolyn Naisby (England) 2.42.08
2. Leslie Watson (England) 2.45.17
3. Anne Hilliard (DCH) 2.48.08

1988
1. Moira O'Neill (Belfast) 2.37.06
2. Sandra Branny (England) 2.38.43
3. Linda Rushmere (England) 2.40.02

1989
1. Pauline Nolan (DCH) 2.44.22
2. Liz Bullen (Waterford) 2.46.40
3. Brid Murphy (Leevale) 2.50.30

1990
1. Christine Kennedy (Galway City) 2.41.27
2. Bernie Stankard (Galway City) 2.45.56
3. Brid Murphy (Leevale) 2.48.39

1991
1. Christine Kennedy (Galway City) 2.35.56
2. Connie Kelly (Blackrock AC) 2.40.22
3. Mary Brayley (DCH) 2.42 .16

1992
1. Karen Cornwall (England) 2.41.58
2. Adidas Gazahega (Ethiopia) 2.42.49
3. Brid Murphy (Leevale) 2.43.00

1993
1. Cathy Shum (Clonliffe Harriers) 2.38.14
2. Bernie Stankard (Galway City) 2.42.38
3. Patricia Griffin (Ballinamore AC) 2.46.08

1994
1. Linda Rushmere (England) 2.40.17
2. Cathy Shum (Clonliffe Harriers) 2.42.47
3. Caroline Horne (England) 2.44.48

1995
1. Trudi Thompson (Scotland) 2.38.23
2. Linda Rushmere (England) 2.45.26
3. Catherine Smith (DCH) 2.47.29

1996
1. Cathy Shum (Clonliffe Harriers) 2.38.35
2. Danielle Sanderson (England) 2.41.12
3. Wendy Llewellan (New Zealand) 2.42.06

Belfast City Marathon 1982 - 97

1982
1. Susan Boreham (Belfast) 3.11.27
2. Mary Butler (Crusaders) 3.17.52
3. Bridget McCabe (Mullingar) NT

1983
1. Roma McConville (Belfast) 2.58.09
2. Susan Boreham (Belfast) 3.00.06
3. Bridget McCabe (Mullingar) 3.02.36

1984
1. Theresa Kidd (Ballinascreen) 2.47.33
2. Moira O'Boyle (Belfast Oly) 2.53.54
3. Roma McConville (Belfast) 3.02.10

1985
1. Moira O'Boyle (Belfast Oly) 2.45.40
2. Theresa Kidd (Ballinascreen) 2.51.19
3. Cathy Ward (Derry) 3.00.53

1986
1. Moira O'Boyle (Belfast Oly) 2.43.26
2. Ita Speight (Antrim) 2.54.29
3. Cathy Ward (Derry) 3.00.53

1987
1. Theresa Kidd (Ballinascreen) 2.48.26
2. Una Barry (Co. Antrim) 2.56.34
3. Caroline Cahill (Co. Down) 3.04.45

1988
1. Theresa Kidd (Ballinascreen) 2.49.10
2. Mary B. Ryan (Waterford) 2.54.39
3. Bridget McInerney (Dublin) 3.04.22

1989
1. Rosaleen Hayden (Raheny) 2.58.31
2. Caroline Cahill (Co. Down) 3.05.28
3. Roma McConville (Belfast) 3.07.25

1990
1. Eleanor Hill (Bray Runners) 2.50.07
2. Breda Fogarty (Kildare) 2.58.31
3. Sally Patrick (CIYMS) 3.03.18

1991
1. Brenda McNamara (Ballina) 2.55.25
2. Caroline Jones (Wales) 2.58.45
3. Mary Morley (Cork) 3.11.57

1992
1. Catherine Smith (DCH) 2.42.41
2. Brid Murphy (Leevale) 2.45.59
3. Eleanor Hill (Bray Runners) 2.47.41

1993
1. Catherine Smith (DCH) 2.45.05
2. Eleanor Hill (Bray Runners) 2.49.09
3. Caroline Jones (Wales) 3 .08.09

1994
1. Catherine Smith (DCH) 2.44. 22
2. Eleanor Hill (Bray Runners) 2.53.40
3. Mary Burke (Australia) 2.57.18

1995
1. Patricia Griffin (Ballinamore) 2.53.10
2. Susan Abbis (England) 2.55.14
3. Mary Jennings (Waterford) 3.03.43

1996
1. Trudi Thompson (Pitreavie) 2.44.57
2. Olive Mullan (Dublin) 3.05.00
3. Caroline Jones (Wales) 3.05.00

1997
1. Olive Nolan (Rathfarnham) 2.54.31
2. Barbara Brewer (USA) 3.02.11
3. Mary Jennings (Waterford) 3.07.03

Triathlons and ultramarathons

The women who take on triathlons (run, swim, cycle) and ultra running are a rare breed, and Ireland has produced only a few of them over the past 15 years.

The first to fully embrace ultra distance were the mother and daughter Elfriede and Doina Nugent, from Galway City Harriers. Elfriede comes from Baden-Baden, Germany, where she first took up running. She married athlete Jerome Nugent, and they lived in Germany until 1980, when they moved to Galway City.

Daughter Doina won triathlons in 1980 and 1981; Elfriede also finished these thrice-gruelling events. In 1982 Doina won the Galway and Castlebar marathons.

On Dublin City Marathon weekend 1982, this amazingly fit duo started their massive triathlon in Ballinasloe (Co. Galway) swimming pool. Commencing at midnight, they swam 66 lengths; they then cycled 100 miles in the dark, arriving in Dublin at 8.30am. Both had showers, a massage, and a short snooze. At 11am, they lined up for the third and most trying of the three events, the 26 miles and 385 yards around the wet and windy metropolis. Doina covered the distance in an astonishing 3.34. Elfriede, aged 50, also completed the odyssey.

Ireland's first 50-miler was held in Templemore, Co. Tipperary, in 1983. Well organised by Gerry Ryan and Pat Dolan, two experienced local runners, it attracted 29 entrants, including Mullingar's Bridget McCabe. Bridget became our first 50-mile woman, returning a time of 7.58.51 and placing 19th overall.

The following year Bridget was back in Templemore to improve on her 1984 performance. Running at even pace, she posted 7.02.38 for 11th overall.

In 1986 Doina Nugent made her mark on Templemore, recording the best ever time of 6.52.10 and defeating such experienced ultramen as Don McDonald of Greystones.

Tullamore's fine track was the venue in 1985 for Ireland's inaugural 24-hour race, an event that entails staying on track at all times except for occasional breaks for food, drink, and calls of nature.

Tom McGrath flew in from New York for this event. Tom hails from Fermanagh and owns a bar in New York, where he has won many ultra races. In the seventies he ran from City Hall, San Francisco, to City Hall, New York, a distance of 3,046 miles, in 53 days and seven hours! His record still stands.

Needless to say, Tom won in Tullamore, covering 125 miles and 470 yards. But the revelation of the event was 22-year-old Doina Nugent, who, though suffering from hamstring trouble, posted 106 miles and 588 yards. Some distance behind Doina, her mother, Elfriede, finished strongly with 72 miles and 1,231 yards.

Among many races the Nugents ran in 1987 was the first Greystones 24-hour. Held on a public road near the picturesque seafront and harbour, the event attracted an international entry. Victory went to Wallsend's Paul Bream with a record 158 miles and 539 yards. Doina again struggled against injury but determinedly held on to record 100 miles and 394 yards. Elfriede clocked 81 miles and 111 yards.

Over the next few years mother and daughter would compete with distinction at events all over Ireland. One such event was John O'Shea's memorable Cork to Dublin (160-mile) race in aid of the Third World charity Goal. Thirteen competitors faced rain and wind that would take their toll on some of the world's toughest athletes.

The first casualty was England's Eleanor Adams, one of the race favourites. Badly bitten by a collie near Mitchelstown, Co. Cork, Eleanor ended her race in the ambulance.

Six others would retire from Ireland's longest-ever race, but not the amazing Galway lass Doina Nugent, who showed valiant character as she battled through the dark night on a long and lonely road.

Daylight saw Iran's James Zarei win this gruelling race in the fine time of 24 hours, 34 minutes, 15 seconds. Don McDonald of Greystones was second (32.13.25). Young Doina jogged in third (34 .42.12) - surely a performance that will never be bettered!

Doina was second woman in the 1991 London to Brighton (7.03 for the 52-plus miles).

Now in her mid-thirties, Doina lives in England. She has not competed in Ireland for six years; most of her races are in Europe. She won the 1992 British 24-hour Championship at Coptall, London, covering 111.75 miles. She set an Irish 100k (62m) record 8.19.17 in Palmas, Spain. She won the 1993 Madrid 100k (8.28.30) and was 13th overall of 86 competitors.

August 1995 saw possibly Doina's greatest achievement. In the Ultra World Cup at Panquezys, Lithuania, the Galway amazon was first woman and fourth overall. In this huge event she swam 7.6k in 3.15, cycled 360k in 15.19, and ran 84.4k in 9.14.

The aforementioned are just samples of the type of events Doina has tackled in the past decade. A truly great athlete!

Ann Kearney of Clonliffe Harriers is another of our greatest competitors. Starting in athletics rather late, at 37, she has won the Irish Triathlon and the European Veterans (O/35) Triathlon for the past seven years.

Heather Stuart from Sligo is another ultra woman. She has competed with distinction in the Comrades' Marathon in South Africa (56 miles) and the London to Brighton.

Newer on the scene is Mary Joyce of Mullingar, who recently in the Peace Run (106 miles from Belfast to Dublin) was first woman and eighth overall in 22.22.40 (she was also the first woman ever to complete this course). The Tim Parry Memorial Cup, to the memory of the Warrington boy murdered by the IRA, was presented to Mary by Dublin's Lord Mayor after the race.

The Mini Marathon

The two most prominent landmarks from my many years in athletics were the mass marathon boom of the eighties and the introduction of the Women's Mini Marathon. The Women's Mini Marathon, a 10k run (and walk) around the streets of Dublin, was first sponsored by *The Evening Press* in 1983 and was immediately successful, attracting women from every town and village and townland in Ireland.

One of the prime movers was Lindie Naughton of Crusaders Athletic Club, a sports journalist with the *Press.* Lindie's columns inspired women from all walks of life to take up this exciting new challenge.

'Meet and Train' groups were formed in towns from Letterkenny to Waterford, from Wexford to Galway. Dundrum's Marley Park and Templeogue's Bushy Park saw hundreds of women attend mass training sessions, while at Bray seafront Margaret Dundon put over 200 women through keep-fit classes several nights weekly in preparation for the great event.

The benefits were and are health, fitness, and friendship. But more than that - with an annual entry now averaging 20,000, deserving charities benefit from cash sponsorship of runners.

Margaret Dundon, herself a late starter at 35, managed to cut her own 10k time to a respectable 37 minutes. Recently turned a youthful 50, Margaret still enjoys her daily training spin and, like the Mini Marathon itself, is a great advertisement for the sport of running.

Women's Mini Marathon

1983

1. Kathy Shilly, 34.04
2. Carey May, 34.30
3. Margaret Kelly, 34.57
4. Louise McGrillen, 35.06
5. Deirdre Nagle, 35.16
6. Ann Hilliard, 35.25
7. Mary Purcell, 35.49
8. Ailish Smyth, 36.00
9. Siobhán Treacy, 36.07
10. Edel Hackett, 36.59

1984

1. Regina Joyce, 32.35
2. Carey May, 33.49
3. Laura de Wald, 33.51
4. Kathy Schilly, 33.51
5. Margaret Kelly, 35.49
6. Ursula Noctor, 34.32
7. Greta Hickey, 35.05
8. Emily Dowling, 35.57
9. Deirdre Nagle, 35.59
10. Marese Cullen, 36.01

1985

1. Regina Joyce, 33.31
2. Veronique Marot, 33.52
3. Debbie Mueller, 34.21
4. Ann Hilliard, 34.47
5. Louise McGrillen, 34.47
6. Mary Friel, 34.35
7. Deirdre Nagle, 35.20
8. Kim Webb, 35.11
9. Christine Kennedy, 35.17
10. Ailish Smyth, 35.32

1986

1. Greta Hickey, 34.33
2. Mary Friel, 34.52
3. Sue Collier, 35.11
4. Deirdre Nagle, 35.14
5. Catherine Rooney, 35.34
6. Christine Kennedy, 35.42
7. Ailish Smyth, 36.33
8. Aisling Ryan, 36.28
9. Eileen Prunty, 36.56
10. Nuala Logan, 37.00

1987

1. Sue Collier, 34.02
2. Anne Buckley, 43.24
3. Ann Hilliard, 34.52
4. Catherine Rooney, 35.02
5. Olive Harford, 35.35
6. Ailish Smyth, 35.45
7. Frances Murphy, 35.47
8. Emily Dowling, 35.47
9. Deirdre Nagle, 35.48
10. Nuala Logan, 35.57

1988

1. Patricia Griffin, 33.57
2. Ann Hilliard, 34.35
3. Catherine Rooney, 34.50
4. Olive Bollard, 35.10
5. Sue Collier, 35.18
6. Connie Kelly, 35.22
7. Emily Dowling, 35.34
8. Deirdre Nagle, 35.37
9. Ursula Noctor, 35.41
10. Mary Gallagher 36.00

Veterans (1988)

1. Kathleen Looney, 38.20
2. Evelyn McNelis, 39.00
3. June Comiskey, 39.02

1989

1. Patricia Griffin, 34.28
2. Connie Kelly, 34.51
3. Rosemary Ennis, 35.12
4. Olive Bollard, 35.34
5. Ursula Noctor, 35.51
6. Frances Murphy, 35.57
7. Caroline Mullen, 36.09
8. Ailish Smyth, 36.14
9. Catherine Smith, 36.26
10. Pauline Nolan, 36.36

1990

1. Christine Kennedy, 34.17
2. Rosie Lambe, 34.23
3. Ursula Noctor, 34.31
4. Olive Bollard, 34.31
5. Patricia Griffin, 34.55
6. Karen O'Doherty, 35.07
7. Veronica Colleran, 35.14
8. Catherine Smith, 35.26
9. Regina Joyce, 35.42
10. Eleanor Hill, 36.10

1991

1. Catherine Smith, 34.29
2. Niamh Murphy, 34.40
3. Joanne Power, 34.59
4. Veronica Colleran, 35.13
5. Catherine Shum, 35.2
6. Patricia Griffin, 35.47
7. Louise McGrillen, 36.10
8. Sharon Leon, 36.21
9. Annette Kealy, 36.25
10. Susan Jenkins, 36.36

Veterans

1. Deirdre Nagle, 38.19
2. Evelyn McNelis, 38.58
3. June Comiskey, 39.1

Visually impaired

1. Collette O'Reilly

Wheelchair

1. Mary Keena, 54.53
2. Marie Moylan
3. Carol Cochrane

1992

1. Monica Reilly, 33.41
2. Anne Keenan, 34.14
3. Niamh Murphy, 34.29
4. Catherine Smith, 34.45
5. Rosie Lambe, 34.58
6. Frances Murphy, 35.24
7. Bernie Stankard, 35.45
8. Veronica Colleran, 35.56
9. Joanne Power, 36.03
10. Catherine Hennessy, 36.04

1993

1. Rosie Lamb, 34.25
2. Niamh Murphy, 35.05
3. Catherine Smith, 35.15
4. Ann Carroll, 35.42
5. Susan Jenkins, 35.53
6. Mary Brayley, 36.00
7. Eleanor Hill, 36.02
8. Kay Byrne, 36.17
9. Sharon Leon, 36.19
10. Sue Zinay, 36.42

1994

1. Mary Donohoe, 33.11
2. Catherine Shum, 33.17
3. Rosie Lambe, 33.52
4. Ann Carroll, 34.31
5. Catherine Smith, 34.5
6. Marie Christine, 34.56
7. Niamh Murphy, 35.01
8. Olive Bollard, 35.24
9. Rosaleen Campbell, 35.33
10. Patricia Griffin, 35.42

Veterans

O/35 Patricia Griffin, 37.36
O/40 Mary Jennings, 37.29
O/45 Evelyn McNelis 40.48

1995

1. Catherine Shum, 33.21
2. Teresa Duffy, 34.04
3. Rosie Lambe, 34.08
4. Niamh Richardson, 35.07
5. Catherine Smith, 35.25
6. Kay Byrne, 36.21
7. Mary Brosnan, 36.27
8. P. Morgan, 36.35
9. Pauline Gorman, 36.59
10. Mags Greenan, 37.18

1996

1. Cathy McCandless, 32.44
2. Cathy Shum, 33.53
3. Rosie Lambe, 34.23
4. P. Van Damme, 35.27
5. Catherine Smith, 35.28
6. Niamh O'Sullivan, 35.41
7. P. Morgan, 35.41
8. K. O'Doherty, 35.52
9. C. O'Rourke, 36.05
10. Annette Kealy, 36.18

1997

1. C. McKiernan, 32.31
2. Teresa Duffy, 34.12
3. Rosie Lambe, 35.06
4. T. Swindell, 35.37
5. Ann Carroll, 36.14
6. Kay Byrne, 36.29
7. Mags Greenan, 37.25
8. R. Ferguson, 37.25
9. Olive Nolan, 37.39
10. O. Gormley, 37.51

Olympic women 1956 to 1996

1956, Melbourne, Australia

Maeve Kyle: 100m heat 1, 6th (12.48); 200m round 2, 5th (26.57).

1960, Rome, Italy

Maeve Kyle: 100m round 1, 6th (12.5); 200m round 1, 5th (24.9).

1964, Tokyo, Japan

Maeve Kyle: 400m semifinal, 7th (55.3); 800m semifinal, 8th (2.12.9).

1972, Munich, Germany

Margaret Barry-Murphy: 100mH round 1, 6th (15.89); pentathlon, 27th (3,770). Mary Tracey: 800m round 1, 4th (2.04.18); 1,500m round 1, 6th (4.16.43). Claire Walsh: 800m round 1, 7th (2.08.98).

1976, Montreal, Canada

Mary Tracey (Purcell): 1,500m round 1, 5th (4.08.63).

1984, Los Angeles, USA

Monica Joyce: 3,000m round 1, 5th (8.54.34). Regina Joyce: marathon, 23rd (2.37.57). Carey May: marathon, 28th (2.41.27). Caroline O'Shea: 800m final, 8th (2.00.77). Roisin Smyth: 3,000m round 1, 9th (9.01.69). Mary Parr: 400mH heat,7th (61.66). Patricia Walsh: Discus, qual round (54.42), final, 9th (55.38).

1988, Seoul, South Korea

Anne Keenan-Buckley: 3,000m round 1, 13th (9.03.10). Barbara Johnson: 400mH round 1, 6th (58.61). Marie Murphy-Rollins: marathon, 57th (2.54.37). Ailish Smyth: marathon, 46th (2.44.17).

1992, Barcelona, Spain

Catherina McKiernan: 3,000m round 1, 8th (8.57.91). Sonia O'Sullivan: 3.000m final, 4th (8.47.41); 1,500m semifinal, 11th (4.06.24). Perri Williams: 10k walk, 37th (54.53).

1996, Atlanta, USA

Sinéad Delahunty: 1,500m semifinal, 9th (4.12.52). Deirdre Gallagher: 10,000m walk, 23rd (45.27). Cathy McCandless: 5,000m semifinal, 10th (15.55.66). Catherina McKiernan: 10,000m final, 11th (32.00.38). Marie McMahon: 5,000m semifinal, 14th (15.59.17). Sonia O'Sullivan: 5,000m final, DNF; 1,500m heat, 11th. Susan Smith: 400mH semifinal, 5th (54.93).

The Atlanta Paralympics

Irish athletes have been prominent in international competition ever since the inaugural Paralympics were staged by the city of Rome in 1960. Our wheelchair competitors were first into the fray; many of them have competed abroad and brought home European, World, and Olympic medals.

Irish Blindsports have also consistently flown the flag. The Blindsports women first tasted Paralympic competition in Moscow 1980; not surprisingly, they won no medals that year. Their first gold medallist was Carol Carr; she won the 1,500m in New York 1984. In Barcelona 92 Bridie Lynch took discus and pentathlon silver.

And so to the 1996 Paralympics at Atlanta. And the athletes were handed an appalling insult even before they took the field: the Olympic Committee sold off the 197 national flags used during the Olympic Games, for 6,000 dollars, to the organisers of Sydney 2,000 (it has long been the practice for the flags to be passed from the Olympic Committee to the Paralympic organisers). When the Australians discovered what had happened, they promptly donated the flags to the Atlanta Paralympics.

Fortunately, the greed of the Atlanta Committee did not deter the 3,000 athletes from 126 countries at the Paralympics - Ireland had a record 64 competing.

Bridie Lynch, a visually impaired athlete from Lifford, Co. Donegal, created history when she bettered her Barcelona effort to capture discus gold. Bridie (29) had taken a year off work to prepare for Atlanta. She was third for much of the competition but produced a great fifth throw of 37.14 to overcome Russia's reigning Olympic and world champion, Kimara Sivakova, who had been unbeaten since 1987.

'I'm delighted. It's the first time I've won gold in a major international - it feels fantastic,' said Bridie, the Irish number two in open (non-disabled) competition.

This was Ireland's first Paralympic gold in track and field for eight years. Bridie added a bronze in the shot but was forced out of the pentathlon with food poisoning.

Gráinne Barrett-Condron from Lucan, Co. Dublin, threw the shot 8.07m to win bronze in the Amputee class.

Patrice Dockery, a Dublin civil servant, set an Irish record 18.04 when finishing 4th in the 100m Wheelchair. She also set national records for 200m (32.53) and 400m (1.03), reaching the semifinal of the latter. Patrice, in her mid-twenties, is a member of Clonliffe Harriers and certainly lives by the club motto: *Nil desperandum.*

The team were welcomed home at Dublin Airport by President Mary Robinson. They brought with them a total of ten medals: one gold, three silver, and six bronze.

Gold: Bridie Lynch (Blindsports) discus.

Silver: David Malone (Wheelchair Assn), 100m backstroke; Michael Barry (Cerebral Palsy), 50m backstroke; Tom Leahy (Cerebral Palsy), boccia.

Bronze: Joan Salmon (Blindsports), equestrian kur; Sean O'Grady (Wheelchair Assn), discus; Gráinne Barrett-Condron (Wheelchair Assn), shot; Sharon Rice (Cerebral Palsy), shot; Mary Rice (Cerebral Palsy), 200m; Bridie Lynch (Blindsports), shot.

The Billy Morton Stadium

Billy Morton it was who introduced big time athletics to Dublin. In 1949 12,000 turned up at Lansdowne Road to see Ireland's John Joe Barry, The Ballincurry Hare, score a great victory over the Americans Curtis Stone and Fred Wilt.

A few low key promotions followed in 1952, 53, and 54. Billy, a former national marathon champion, persuaded a promising young miler home on vacation from Villanova University to run on grass at Trinity's College Park. Over 7,000 crammed in to see Ronnie Delany set an Irish record 4.08.8 to beat John Joe Barry's previous mark.

A big athletics stadium in Dublin had long been Billy's dream. He now began to draw up plans for such an arena. A few big meets were held at Lansdowne Road; English athletes Brian Hewson, Derek Ibbotson, and Gordon Pirie became frequent visitors. A nationwide appeal for funds fell largely on deaf ears; politicians were in the main negative about the project. But Billy went ahead undaunted. Work commenced in Santry, the longtime home of Billy's club, Clonliffe Harriers; the stadium was completed in 1958.

Part of the cycle track was badly damaged by an explosion prior to the official opening - persons unknown were announcing their disapproval. But Morton was unperturbed and invited many of the world's best to Santry.

In early July, Australian Albie Thomas set Santry's first world record, 13.10.8 for three miles. A few weeks later 22,000 packed the stadium to watch the greatest mile ever run. Herb Elliott's 3.55.5 smashed the world record; Merv Lincoln (Australia), Ronnie Delany, Murray Halberg (New Zealand), and Albie Thomas all dipped under four minutes, the first time five athletes had broken the magic barrier in one race. Santry Stadium and Billy Morton were now synonymous and world famous.

Herb Elliott and Murray Halberg would win Olympic gold over 1,500m and 5,000m in Rome 1960.

Alas, the debt on Santry Stadium continued to rise in spite of Morton's efforts at fundraising: tennis exhibitions, military tattoos, circuses, and so on. Even Billy's £5,000 Prize Bond win was put in the kitty; Clonliffe's women collected £20,000. Still the debt spiralled. When Billy Morton died in 1969, many wondered what the future would hold.

Years of negotiations followed. Eventually Dublin Corporation took over the stadium now named the Billy Morton Stadium. The stadium has in the nineties been completely refurbished, with new tartan track and new stand incorporating dressing rooms and indoor training track. A splendid restaurant overlooks the track; photos of the man they called Mr Athletics adorn the walls of the bar.

Clonliffe Harriers, Ireland's oldest athletic club, are now life tenants of the Morton Stadium.

Photo: Courtesy of National Library of Ireland

De Valera (above) said it could not be done. Billy Morton (right) did it - he built Santry Stadium (below)

Championship winners

All-Ireland

1966

100yds	Jacqueline Spence (Crusaders)	11.6
220yds	Jacqueline Spence	25.8
440yds	Maeve Kyle (Ballymena)	58.9
880yds	Ann O'Brien (Clonliffe Harriers)	2.16.1
Mile	Ann O'Brien	4.59.2
80mH	Maeve Kyle (Ballymena)	12.3
High jump	Kathleen Killian (Spartan Ladies)	1.535 (5'0.5")
Long jump	Magdalene Glendinning (Ballymena)	5.00 (16'5")
Shot	Gay Porter (Ballymena)	12.51 (41'0.5")
Discus	Gay Porter	35.31 (115'10")
Javelin	Gay Porter	34.60 (113'6")

AAUE

1965

100yds	Jacqueline Spence (Crusaders)	11.1
220yds	Claire Dowling (Clonliffe Harriers)	26.2
440yds	Claire Dowling	57.6
880yds	Hazel Tennison (Crusaders)	2.18.3
Mile	Peggy Hogan (Crusaders)	5.10.3
80mH	Maeve Kyle (Ballymena)	11.9
High jump	Kathleen Killian (Spartan Ladies)	1.575 (5'2")
Long jump	Claire Dowling (Clonliffe Harriers)	5.245 (17'2.5")
Shot	Rosemary Reilly (Crusaders)	10.565 (34'8")
Discus	Rosemary Reilly	ND
Javelin	Patricia Downs (Crusaders)	ND
Pentathlon	Maeve Kyle (Ballymena)	3,956

1966

100yds	Jacqueline Spence (Crusaders)	11.5
220yds	Jacqueline Spence	26.4
440yds	Maeve Kyle (Ballymena)	56.0
880yds	Hazel Tennison (Crusaders)	2.17.2
Mile	Ann O'Brien (Clonliffe Harriers)	5.04.2
80mH	Maeve Kyle (Ballymena)	12.0
High jump	Kathleen Killian (Spartan Ladies)	1.60 (5'3")
Long jump	Maeve Kyle (Ballymena)	4.965 (16'3.5")
Shot	Rosemary Reilly (Crusaders)	11.15 (36'7")
Discus	Rosemary Reilly	32.97 (108'2")
Javelin	Patricia Downs (Crusaders)	25.22 (82'9")

Bord Lùthchleas na hÉireann
National Track & Field and Cross Country

1967

100yds	Jacqueline Spence (Crusaders)	11.4
220yds	Jacqueline Spence	27.8
440yds	Catherine Cotter (Leevale)	67.5
880yds	Ann O'Brien (Clonliffe Harriers)	2.29.7
Mile	Ann O'Brien	5.32.0
80mH	Kathleen Leane (Croke)	12.8
High jump	Ann O'Brien (Clonliffe Harriers)	1.39 (4'7")
Long jump	Hazel Tennison (Crusaders)	5.03 (16'6")
Shot	Rosemary Murphy (Crusaders)	10.84 (35'6.75")
Discus	Rosemary Murphy	37.36 (122'7")
Javelin	Rosemary Murphy	37.38 (122'7.5")
4x440yds	Crusaders	NT
CC	Peggy Hogan-Mullins (Crusaders)	12:51
CC team	Clonliffe Harriers	21

1968

100yds	Claire Dowling-Walsh (Clonliffe Harriers)	11.7
220yds	Claire Walsh (Clonliffe Harriers)	26.2
440yds	Ann O'Brien (Clonliffe Harriers)	59.4
880yds	Ann O'Brien	2.12.7
Mile	Ann O'Brien	5.04.7
80mH	Joan Shaw (Crusaders)	12.8
High jump	Janet Midleton (Crusaders)	1.42 (4'8")
Long jump	Joan Shaw (Crusaders)	5.24 (17'2.5")
Shot	Margaret Barry-Murphy (Ovens)	8.53 (28'0")
Discus	Rosemary Reilly Murphy (Crusaders)	35.56 (116'8")
Javelin	Rosemary Reilly Murphy	28.41 (93'2.5")
CC	Ann O'Brien (Clonliffe Harriers)	13.56
CC team	Raheny Shamrocks	20

1969

100m	Claire Walsh (Clonliffe Harriers)	12.5
200m	Claire Walsh	25.4
400m	Claire Walsh	56.5
800m	Ann O'Brien (Clonliffe Harriers)	2.12.5
1,500m	Ann O'Brien	4.32.2
100mH	Maeve Kyle (Crusaders)	15.1
High jump	Janet Midleton (Crusaders)	1.42 (4'8")
Long jump	Margaret Murphy (Ovens)	5.19 (17'0.25")
Shot	Rosemary Murphy (Crusaders)	10.25 (33'7.5")
Discus	Rosemary Murphy	31.88 (104'7")
Javelin	Patricia Downs (Crusaders)	28.09 (92'2")
Pentathlon	Margaret Murphy (Ovens)	3,608
CC	Ann O'Brien (Clonliffe Harriers)	14:51
CC team	Crusaders	11

1970

100m	Aideen Morrison (Crusaders)	12.5
200m	Claire Walsh (Clonliffe Harriers)	24.3
400m	Claire Walsh	55.4
800m	Ann O'Brien (Clonliffe Harriers)	2.10.6
1,500m	Ann O'Brien	4.38.6
100mH	Margaret Murphy (Ovens)	15.9
High jump	Marjorie Adams (Crusaders)	1.525 (5'0")
Long jump	Margaret Murphy (Ovens)	5.46 (17'11")
Shot	Rosemary Murphy (Crusaders)	10.34 (33'11")
Discus	Rosemary Murphy	35.08 (115'1")
Javelin	Patricia Downs (Crusaders)	26.59 (87'3")
Pentathlon	Claire Walsh (Clonliffe Harriers)	3,837
CC	Ann O'Brien (Clonliffe Harriers)	14.41
CC team	Clonliffe Harriers	13

1971

100m	Claire Walsh (Clonliffe Harriers)	12.2
200m	Claire Walsh	24.6
400m	Claire Walsh	54.4
800m	Elaine Kelly (St Finbarr's)	2.14.7
1,500m	Ann O'Brien (Clonliffe Harriers)	4.29.8
100mH	Margaret Murphy (Ovens)	15.6
High jump	Marjorie Adams (Crusaders)	1.59 (5'2.625")
Long jump	Marjorie Adams	5.36 (17'7")
Shot	Rosemary Murphy (Crusaders)	10.76 (35'3.75")
Discus	Rosemary Murphy	36.48 (119'8")
Javelin	Maria Dunne (Crusaders)	25.42 (83'4.25")
Pentathlon	Margaret Murphy (Ovens)	3,997
4x100m	Crusaders	50.3
CC	Ann O'Brien (Clonliffe Harriers)	14.20
CC team	Raheny Shamrocks	11

1972

100m	Mary Doyle (St Finbarr's)	12.3
200m	Claire Walsh (Clonliffe Harriers)	24.5
400m	Claire Walsh	55.4
800m	Joan Fleming (St Finbarr's)	2.11.6
1,500m	Mary Tracey (Guinness)	4. 20.5
100mH	Margaret Murphy (Ovens)	15.0
High jump	Marjorie Adams (Crusaders)	1.55 (5'1")
Long jump	Margaret Murphy (Ovens)	5.51 (18'1")
Shot	Winifred Cooney (St Anthony's)	11.22 (36'9.75")
Discus	Maria Dunne (Crusaders)	35.45 (116'3.5")
Javelin	Margaret Pasquetti (Birchfield H)	32.67 (107'2")

Pentathlon	Margaret Murphy (Ovens)	3,718
4x100m	Clonliffe Harriers	49.5
4x400m	Clonliffe Harriers	3.48.4
CC	Mary Lynch (Raheny Shamrocks)	14.43
CC team	St Laurence O'Toole	25

1973

100m	Claire Walsh (Clonliffe Harriers)	12.2
200m	Claire Walsh	24.3
400m	Aideen Morrison (Crusaders)	55.0
800m	Mary Tracey (Guinness)	2.08.0
1,500m	Mary Tracey	4.25.4
100mH	Winifred Cooney (St Anthony's)	16.3
High jump	Yvonne O'Brien (Carrick-on-Suir)	1.625 (5'4")
Long jump	Margaret Murphy (Olympic)	5.71 (18'8.75")
Shot	Winifred Cooney (St Anthony's)	12.05 (19'6.5")
Discus	Maria Dunne (Crusaders)	38.11 (125'0.5")
Javelin	Rosemary Murphy (Crusaders)	27.51 (90'3")
Pentathlon	Margaret Murphy (Olympic)	3,171
4x100m	Crusaders	49.2
4x400m	Clonliffe Harriers	3.51.8
2,400m relay	Avondale	7.11.0
CC	Mary Tracey (Guinness)	11.45
CC team	Guinness	22

1974

100m	Ruth Algar (Crusaders)	12.1
200m	Aideen Morrison (Crusaders)	25.8
400m	Aideen Morrison	56.7
800m	Pádraigín O'Dwyer (Clonliffe)	2.12.8
1,500m	Mary Purcell (Crusaders)	4.27.0
100mH	Bridget Ruttledge (Bristol)	14.5
High jump	Sheelagh Flatman (Crusaders)	1.62 (5'3.75")
Long jump	Bridget Ruttledge (Bristol)	5.40 (17'8.5")
Shot	Gay Porter-Hogan (Crusaders)	12.95 (42'5.75")
Discus	Gay Hogan	42.05 (137'11.5")
Javelin	Sandra O'Toole (Lozells H)	40.48 (132'9.5")
Pentathlon	Winifred Cooney (St Anthony's)	3,511
4x100m	Crusaders	48.8
4x400m	Clonliffe Harriers	3.56.0
2,400m relay	Clonliffe Harriers	6.43.2
CC	Deirdre Foreman (Guinness)	13.42
CC team	Grange-Fermoy	36

1975

100m	Anne Jeffords (Leevale)	12.2
200m	Ruth Algar (Crusaders)	24.8
400m	Pádraigín O'Dwyer (Clonliffe)	56.5
800m	Pádraigín O'Dwyer (Clonliffe)	2.07.8
1,500m	Mary Tracey-Purcell (Crusaders)	4.19.9
3,000m	Vera Sherry (Glaslough Harriers)	9.54.2
100mH	Ruth Algar (Crusaders)	15.3
High jump	Carmel Scallan (St Benedict's)	1.675 (5'6")
Long jump	Joy Good (Bandon)	5.18 (17'0")
Shot	Gay Hogan (Crusaders)	13.73 (45'0.5")
Discus	Gay Hogan	43.71 (143'5")
Javelin	Sandra O'Toole (Lozelle Harriers)	39.07 (128'2")
Pentathlon	Ruth Algar (Crusaders)	3,240
4x100m	Crusaders	49.0
4x400m	Clonliffe Harriers	3.59.8
2,400m relay	Clonliffe Harriers	NT
CC	Deirdre Nagle (Guinness)	13.59
CC team	Guinness	32

1976

100m	Anne Jeffords (Leevale)	12.0
200m	Anne Jeffords	25.4
400m	Caroline O'Shea (Crusaders)	56.6
800m	Mary Appleby (Clonliffe Harriers)	2.10.8
1,500m	Mary Purcell (Crusaders)	4.22.3
3,000m	Vera Duffy -Sherry (Glaslough)	10.02.8
100mH	Kathleen Glavin (Midleton)	16.2
400mH	Kathleen Glavin	73.6
High jump	Joy Good (St Finbarr's)	1.65 (5'5")
Long jump	Joy Good	5.39 (17'8.25")
Shot	Marita Walton (Kilkenny)	13.08 (42'11")
Discus	Gay Hogan (Crusaders)	37.06 (121'7")
Javelin	Elizabeth Hurley (St Benedict's)	29.44 (96'7")
Pentathlon	Lucy Moore (Crusaders)	2,844
4x100m	Clonliffe Harriers	50.5
4x400m	Clonliffe Harriers	3.55.1
2,400m relay	Clonliffe Harriers	6.49.5
CC	Deirdre Nagle (DCH)	14.21
CC team	Clonliffe Harriers	29

1977, Belfield

100m	Michele Walsh (Glen Abbey)	12.11
200m	Michele Walsh	24.38
400m	M. Fleming (Midleton)	56.23
800m	Elaine Kelly (St Finbarr's)	2.06.07
1,500m	Jean Appleby (Clonliffe)	4.22.7
3,000m	Kathryn Davis (Clonliffe)	9.24.6
100mH	Ruth Algar (Crusaders)	14.56
400mH	M. Moroney (Nenagh)	66.26
Shot	Marita Walton (KCH)	14.11
Javelin	Patricia Walsh (Waterford)	36.76
Discus	Patricia Walsh	46.34
Long jump	Kathleen Glavin (Midleton)	5.79
High jump	F. Kennedy (Crusaders)	1.69
Pentathlon	M. Hetherington (DCH)	3,294
CC	Sheelagh Morrissey (Kildare)	13.11
CC team	Dublin City Harriers	30

1978, Belfield

100m	Michele Walsh (Glen Abbey)	11.52
200m	Michele Walsh	23.97
400m	Mary Appleby (Crusaders)	55.65
800m	Patricia Quinn (Ballinamore)	2.11.1
1,500m	Mary Purcell (Crusaders)	4.14.3
3,000m	Vera Duffy (Glaslough)	9.33.4
100mH	Ruth Algar (Crusaders)	14.58
400mH	Mary Appleby (Crusaders)	60.59
Shot	Marita Walton	14.16
Javelin	Linda Kennedy (Dundrum)	41.86
Discus	Patricia Walsh (Waterford)	48.26
Long jump	Joy Good (St Finbarr's)	5.81
High jump	A. Long (Glen Abbey)	1.69
Pentathlon	Joy Good (St Finbarr's)	3,553
CC	Kathryn Davis (Clonliffe)	17.46
CC team	Dublin City Harriers	30

1979, Belfield

100m	Michele Walsh (Glen Abbey)	11.67
200m	Michele Walsh	23.52
400m	Caroline O'Shea (Crusaders)	54.43
800m	Deirdre Nagle (DCH)	2.07.2
1,500m	Vera Duffy (Glaslough)	4.24.2
3,000m	Vera Duffy	9.31.7
100mH	N. O'Grady (Nenagh)	14.54

400mH	Mary Appleby (Crusaders)	59.5
High jump	Brigid Corrigan (DCH)	1.71
Long jump	J. Murphy (St Finbarr's)	5.94
Shot	Patricia Walsh (Waterford)	13.54
Discus	Patricia Walsh	49.70
Javelin	Linda Kennedy (Dundrum)	41.52
CC	Cathy Ward (London)	19.07
CC team	Dublin City Harriers	45

1980, Belfield

100m	Michele Walsh (Glen Abbey)	11.85
200m	Michele Walsh (Glen Abbey)	23.67
400m	Linda McCurry (Shorts)	55.65
800m	Mary Appleby (Crusaders)	2.6.9
1,500m	Mary Purcell (Crusaders)	4.14.4
3,000m	Deirdre Nagle (DCH)	9.18.8
100mH	Nora O'Grady (Nenagh)	14.75
400mH	Kathleen Glavin (Midleton)	61.37
High jump	W. Phillips (Belfast Ladies)	1.76
Long jump	Kathleen Glavin (Midleton)	5.58
Shot	Marita Walton (Crusaders)	14.71
Discus	Patricia Walsh (Waterford)	51.42
Javelin	Dara Shakespeare (South Dublin)	41.26
CC	Mary Purcell (Crusaders)	17.13
CC team	Dublin City Harriers	23

1981, Santry

100m	Patricia Amond (SLOT)	11.96
200m	Patricia Amond (SLOT)	23.6
400m	Caroline O'Shea (Crusaders)	55.95
800m	Eithne Kenny (DCH)	2.13.75
1,500m	Deirdre Nagle (DCH)	4.23.5
3,000m	Deirdre Nagle (DCH)	9.27.0
100mH	N. O'Grady (Nenagh)	14.76
400mH	S. Cobbe (Limerick)	62.84 NJR
Shot	Marita Walton (Crusaders)	16.23 NR
Discus	Patricia Walsh (Waterford)	53.8
Javelin	Linda Kennedy (Dundrum)	41.90
Long jump	Joy Murphy (St Finbarr's)	5.80
High jump	W. Phillips (Belfast Ladies)	1.70
3,000mW	Mary Hennessy (St Josephs)	15.48.2
CC	Carol Meagan (Dundrum)	17.35
CC team	Dublin City Harriers B	37

1982, Santry

100m	Michele Walsh (Glen Abbey)	12.42
200m	P. Mullins (DCH)	24.2
400m	Caroline O'Shea (Crusaders)	55.92
800m	Aideen Morrison (Crusaders)	2.06.77

1.500m	Monica Joyce (Westport)	4.10.48
3,000m	Regina Joyce (San Diego)	9.03.83
100mH	M. Hetherington (DCH)	14.30
400mH	C. Maher (Nenagh)	61.75
Shot	Marita Walton (Crusaders)	15.83
Discus	Patricia Walsh (Waterford)	51.00
Javelin	Brenda Walsh (Limerick)	43.54
Long jump	B. Fitzgerald (DCH)	5.65
High jump	Brigid Corrigan (DCH)	1.75
3,000mW	G. Robertson (Guest, USA)	15.32
CC	Fionnuala Morrish (Leevale)	22.12
CC team	Dublin City Harriers	38

1983, Santry

100m	Michele Walsh (Crusaders)	12.32
200m	Michele Walsh	24.16
400m	Caroline O'Shea (Crusaders)	53.92
800m	Aideen Morrison (Crusaders)	2.06.58
1.500m	Monica Joyce (Westport)	4.18.90
3,000m	Regina Joyce (Westport)	9.13.15
100mH	Olive Burke (Limerick)	13.93
400mH	Mary Barnwell	58.52
Shot	Marita Walton (Crusaders)	16.19
Javelin	Brenda Walsh (Limerick)	45.64
Discus	Patricia Walsh (Waterford)	54.26
Long jump	M. Coogan (SLOT)	5.77
High jump	Brigid Corrigan (DCH)	1.70
3,000mW	Catherine Hennessy (St Josephs)	16.25.33
CC	Louise McGrillen (DCH)	18.14
CC team	Dublin City Harriers B	36

1984, Santry

100m	Michele Walsh (Crusaders)	11.98
200m	Patricia Amond (DCH)	23.88
400m	Caroline O'Shea (Crusaders)	54.41
800m	M. McKenna (DCH)	2.06.01
1,500m	Roisin Smyth (Sparta)	4.20.30
3,000m	Louise McGrillen (DCH)	9.10.20
100mH	Olive Burke (Limerick)	14.28
400mH	Mary Parr (South Dublin)	58.74
Shot	Marita Walton (Crusaders)	16.15
Javelin	Kay McGovern (Gateway TC, USA)	45.62
Discus	Patricia Walsh (Waterford)	57.60
Long jump	M. Coogan (SLOT)	5.93
High jump	Brigid Corrigan (DCH)	1.77
CC	Roisin Smyth (Sparta)	17.42
CC team	Dublin City Harriers	26

1985, Cork RTC

100m	Michele Walsh (Crusaders)	11.80
200m	Michele Walsh	23.68
400m	Patricia Amond (DCH)	54.29
800m	M. McKenna (DCH)	2.05.39
1,500m	Roisin Smyth (Sparta)	4.16.50
3,000m	Ailish Smyth (DCH)	9.29.77
100mH	J. Rodgers (Lisburn)	13.83
400mH	Mary Parr (South Dublin)	59.81
High jump	Brigid Corrigan (DCH)	1.76
Long jump	Terri Horgan (Mallow)	5.79
Shot	Patricia Walsh (Waterford)	13.08
Discus	Patricia Walsh (Waterford)	47.54
Javelin	Dara Shakespeare (S. Dublin)	46.72
CC	Louise McGrillen (DCH)	16.46
CC team	Dublin City Harriers	16

1986

100m	Mary Amond (SLOT)	12.23
200m	Patricia Amond (DCH)	24.01
400m	Patricia Walsh (Puma)	53.72
800m	Aisling Molloy (Lough Ree)	2.05.99
1,500m	Roisin Smyth (Sparta)	4.19.52
3,000m	Mary Donohoe (Clonliffe)	9.16.06
100mH	Brid Hallissey (Ferrybank)	14.29
400mH	Barbara Johnson (N. Cork)	58.91
3,000mW	Perri Williams (St Senan's)	15.29.4 NR
Long jump	Kathleen Glavin (Midleton)	6.14
High jump	C. Scott (Belfast Ladies)	1.75
Shot	Marita Walton (Crusaders)	15.22
Discus	Marita Walton	48.70
Javelin	Dara Shakespeare (Team Puma)	47.20
CC	Mary Donohoe (Clonliffe)	17.51
CC team	Dublin City Harriers	16
25k road	Nuala Logan (Limerick)	1.36.36

1987, Tullamore

100m	Michele Carroll (Crusaders)	12.33
200m	Michele Carroll	24.02
400m	Michele Carroll	53.75
800m	Aisling Molloy (Unattached)	2.05.84
1,500m	Sonia O'Sullivan (B'more Cobh)	4.23.13
3,000m	Anne Keenan (Clonliffe)	9.29.45
3,000m.W	Perri Williams (St Senan's)	14.57.88
10,000m	Rosie Lambe (Knockbridge)	33.57.13
100mH	Olive Burke (Limerick)	14.46
400mH	Barbara Johnson (N. Cork)	59.06

Shot	Marita Walton (KCH)	14.18
Discus	P. Carolan (Fr Murphy's)	45.00
Javelin	S. Wigesundra (Raheny)	46.00
Hammer	V. Cosgrave (An Ríocht)	34.06
Long jump	Kathleen Glavin (Midleton)	5.90
High jump	C. Scott (Belfast)	1.80
CC	Sonia O'Sullivan (Cobh)	16.20
CC team	Dublin City Harriers	42
10k walk (road)	S. McGranaghan (Finn Valley)	55.19
Half marathon	Anne Hilliard (DCH)	76.35

1988, Santry

100m	Michele Carroll (Crusaders)	11.86
200m	Patricia Amond (DCH)	23.47
400m	Patricia Walsh (Puma)	54.39
800m	Aisling Molloy (Puma)	2.05.48
1,500m	Monica Joyce (Westport)	4.20.43
3,000m	Rosie Lambe (Knockbridge)	9.22.77
100mH	Olive Burke (Limerick)	14.00
400mH	Barbara Johnson (N. Cork)	57.93
Javelin	Dara Shakespeare (Puma)	43.76
Shot	Marita Walton (KCH)	14.89
Long jump	Terri Horgan (Mallow)	6.27
Hammer	B. Wall (Ferrybank)	39.78
Discus	Marita Walton (KCH)	47.64
10,000mW	Perri Williams (St Senan's)	51.52.2
3,000mW	Perri Williams	14.21.72
CC	Catherine Rooney (Blackrock)	19.28
CC team	Dublin City Harriers	30

1989, Cork RTC

100m	Michele Carroll (Crusaders)	12.24
200m	Michele Carroll	24.88
400m	Michele Carroll	54.39
800m	U. Mc Kee (Lisburn)	2.09.2
1,500m	Valerie O'Mahony (Togher)	4.24.20
Shot	Marita Walton (KCH)	14.42
Javelin	Dara Shakespeare (DSD)	43.98
3,000m	Roisin Smyth	9.27.39
3,000mW	M. Walsh (DSD)	14.27.9
100mH	Susan Smith (Waterford)	14.04
400mH	D. Harvey (Finn Valley)	69.08
High jump	S. Foley (Lifford)	1.74
Discus	Ailish O'Brien (West Waterford)	41.78
Hammer	N. Linehan (Eagle)	36.84
Long jump	Terri Horgan (Mallow)	5.95
CC	Christine Kennedy (Galway City Harriers)	25.56
CC team	Dublin City Harriers	40

1990, Tullamore

100m	Marisa Smyth (Boyne)	12.11
200m	Marisa Smyth	24.9
400m	Bernadette Kavanagh (Lucan Hrs)	55.16
800m	Bernadette Kavanagh	2.07.59
1,500m	Sonia O'Sullivan (Ballymore-Cobh)	4.09.44
3,000m	Catherina McKiernan (Cornafean)	9.16.60
100mH	Susan Smith (Waterford)	14.41
400mH	Lisa Nicholson (DCH)	59.46
High jump	Sharon Foley (Lifford)	1.76
Long jump	Terri Horgan (DCH)	6.19
Shot	Mary Mahon (West Dublin)	12.13
Javelin	Mary Real (Limerick)	45.74
Discus	Lorraine Shaw (Gloucester)	45.24
Hammer	Elaine Hayes (North Laois	42.40
3,000mW	Marie Walsh (SDS)	51.14.79
10,000mW	C. Walsh (SDS)	55.35.00
CC	Catherina McKiernan (Cornafean)	20.11
CC team	Dublin City Harriers	26
25k road	Connie Kelly (Blackrock)	1.52.37

1991, Santry

100m	Michele Carroll (Crusaders)	11.79
200m	Michele Carroll	24.18.2
400m	Emma Nicholson (DCH)	54.93
800m	Aisling Molloy (DCH)	2.02.08
1,500m	Una English (DCH)	4.22.69
3,000m	Catherina McKiernan (Cornafean)	9.10.93
100mH	Susan Smith (Waterford)	14.00
400mH	Lisa Nicholson (DCH)	60.75
Long jump	Terri Horgan (DCH)	6.31 CBP
High jump	Laura Sharpe (Navan)	1.78
Triple jump	M. Rea (Annadale Striders)	11.70
Javelin	Mary Real (Limerick)	47.38
Shot	Marita Walton Lannigan (KCH)	14.02
Hammer	E. Hayes (North Laois)	43.32
Discus	Lorraine Shaw (Gloucester)	49.98
10,000mW	Perri Williams (St Senan's)	50.43.40
CC	Catherina McKiernan (Cornafean)	24.55
CC team	Dublin City Harriers	43

1992, Belfield

100m	Michele Carroll (Crusaders)	11.54
200m	Michele Carroll	23.89
400m	Michele Carroll	54.51
800m	Sonia O'Sullivan (Ballymore-Cobh)	2.05.63
1,500m	Valerie Vaughan (Blarney)	4.28.71
3,000m	Catherina McKiernan (Cornafean)	9.04.08
100mH	Susan Smith (Waterford)	13.88
400H	Susan Smith	60.31
High jump	Lorna Sharpe (Navan)	1.75
Long jump	Terri Horgan (DCH)	6.05
Triple jump	Jocelyn Hanrahan (Limerick)	11.06
Shot	Mary Mahon (West Dublin)	12.85
Discus	Lorraine Shaw (DCH)	46.32
Hammer	Lorraine Shaw	44.9
Javelin	Mary Real (Limerick)	47.74
10,000kW	Perri Williams (St Senan's)	49.33.93
CC	Catherina McKiernan (Cornafean)	20.48
CC team	Dublin City Harriers	54

1993

100m	Michele Carroll (Crusaders)	11.74
200m	Michele Carroll	24.25
400m	Stephanie McCann (Lisburn)	55.68
800m	Geraldine Nolan (Kilkenny City Harriers)	2.08.12
1,500m	Anita Philpott (North Cork)	4.24.36
3,000m	Catherina McKiernan (Cornafean)	9.13.40
100mH	Patricia Naughton (Nenagh)	14.31
400mH	Stephanie McCann (Lisburn)	60.21
5,000mW	Elizabeth Paoline (DCH)	23.05.1
High jump	Sharon Foley (Lifford)	1.75
Long jump	Terri Horgan (DCH)	6.29
Triple jump	Siobháin Hoey (UCD)	12.02
Shot	Kelly Kane (Blackpool)	13.01
Discus	Mary Mahon (West Dublin)	42.60
Hammer	Brenda Thompson (Slaney Olympic)	35.20
Javelin	Mary Real (Limerick)	47.48
CC	Catherina McKiernan (Cornafean)	20.04
CC team	Finn Valley	57

1994, Santry

100m	Terri Horgan (DCH)	12.18
200m	Marisa Smith (Clonliffe)	24.36
400m	Stephanie McCann (Lisburn)	54.81
800m	Aisling Molloy (Dundrum South Dublin)	2.04.50
1,500m	Sinéad Delahunty (Kilkenny City Harriers)	4.14.63
3,000m	Geraldine Hendricken (St Laurence O'Toole)	9.35.62
5,000mW	Deirdre Gallagher (UCD AC)	23.34.00
100mH	Patricia Naughton (Nenagh)	14.47
400mH	Mandy Bloomer (Mountmellick)	60.77
High jump	Laura Sharpe (Navan)	1.85
Long jump	Jacqui Stokes (Ferrybank)	6.00
Triple jump	Siobháin Hoey (UCD AC)	12.10
Shot	Kelly Kane (Sheffield)	13.68
Hammer	Brenda Thompson (Slaney Olympic)	39.98
Discus	Ailish O'Brien (West Waterford)	42.46
Javelin	Dara Shakespeare (DSD)	50.26
CC	Teresa Duffy (Beechmount)	23.04
CC team	Finn Valley	53

1995, Santry

100m	Michele Carroll (Crusaders)	11.83
200m	Michele Carroll	24.46
400m	Michele Carroll	54.18
800m	Aisling Molloy (DSD)	2.03.51
1,500m	Sonia O'Sullivan (Ballymore-Cobh)	4.07.09 CBP
5,000m	Teresa Duffy (Beechmount Harriers)	16.15.94
10,000m	Rosie Lambe (Knockbridge)	34.13.15
100mH	Susan Smith (Waterford)	13.99
400mH	Mandy Bloomer (Mountmellick)	60.50
5,000mW	Deirdre Gallagher (UCDAC)	23.14.24
High jump	Sharon Foley (Lifford)	1.76
Long jump	Jacqui Stokes(Ferrybank)	6.17
Javelin	Dara Shakespeare (DSD)	46.26
Triple jump	Siobháin Hoey (UCDAC)	11.38
Shot	Emma Gavin (Limerick)	12.65
Discus	Ailish O'Brien (West Waterford)	42.10
Hammer	Brenda Thompson (Slaney Olympic)	44.28
CC	Teresa Duffy (Beechmount)	22.07
CC team	Finn Valley	61

1996, Santry

100m	L. Barry (Emerald)	12.35
200m	J. Stokes (Ferrybank)	24.46
400m	Emma Nicholson (DCH)	54.79
800m	Freda Davoren (UCC)	2.05.65
1,500m	Sonia O'Sullivan (Ballymore-Cobh)	4.15.24
5,000m	Catherina McKiernan (Cornafean)	15.27.10
100mH	P. Naughton (Nenagh)	14.44
400mH	Susan Smith (Waterford)	56.01 NR
Shot	Emma Gavin (Limerick)	12.45
High jump	B. Tierney-Browne (Nenagh)	1.73
Long jump	Jacqui Stokes (Ferrybank)	5.97
Triple jump	Siobháin Hoey (UCDAC)	11.95
Discus	Anne O'Brien (West Waterford)	41.06
Hammer	J. Kirkpatrick (Lisburn)	48.90
Javelin	Alison Moffitt (North Down)	49.10
CC	Teresa Duffy (Beechmount)	22.00
CC team	Finn Valley	85

1997, Santry

100m	Aoife Hearn (Waterford)	11.88
200m	Ciara Sheehy (West Dublin)	24.31
400m	Karen Shinkins (DCH)	56.20
800m	Amanda Crowe (Lisburn)	2.07.46
1,500m	Valerie Vaughan (Blarney Inniscarra)	4.23.50
5,000m	Valerie Vaughan	15.44.72
100mH	Gráinne Redmond (Cushinstown)	14.29
400mH	Susan Smith (Waterford)	56.56
5,000mW	Perri Williams (St Senan's)	24.50.08
Shot	Emma Gavin (Limerick)	12.85
High jump	Sharon Foley (Lifford)	1.75
Long jump	Jacqui Stokes (Ferrybank)	5.77
Triple jump	Siobháin Hoey (DCH)	12.12
Discus	Ailish O'Brien (West Waterford)	45.02
Hammer	Clara Thompson (Slaney Olympic)	48.82
Javelin	Alison Moffitt (North Down)	45.48
CC	Maureen Harrington (An Ríocht)	22.00
CC team	Finn Valley	85

Gaedheal-Cumann Lúthchleas agus Rothuidheacta na hÉireann (NACAI)

1967

CC	Ursula Kennedy (Co. Dublin)	NT
CC team	Co. Dublin	23

1968

100yds	Emily Hallinan (Newcastle)	11.0
CC	Imelda Rice (Tracton)	NT
CC team	Co. Cork	NT

1969

100m	Emily Hallinan (Newcastle)	13.2
800m	Imelda Rice (Tracton)	NT
1,500m	S. O'Keeffe (Ballytarsna)	4.50.9

1970

100m	Ruth Algar (Mullingar)	13.1
400m	Carmel Higgins (Bros Pearse)	64.4
1,500m	Mary Buckley (Dunderrow)	5.04.5
High jump	Rosaleen Clarke (Mullingar)	1.27 (4'2")
Long jump	Ruth Algar (Mullingar)	4.725 (15'6")
Pentathlon	Ruth Algar	3,208
4x100m	Co. Dublin	NT

1971

100m	Ruth Algar (Mullingar)	13.4
200m	Deirdre Higgins (Bros Pearse)	28.6
400m	Carmel Higgins (Bros Pearse)	64.6
800m	Ruth Algar (Mullingar)	NT
1,500m	Carmel Higgins (Bros Pearse)	5.02.0
High jump	Carmel Higgins	NH
Long jump	Sandra Doyle (Naomh Mhuire)	4.98 (16'4")
Shot	M. Curran (Clonmel)	9.01 (29'6.75")
Javelin	Joy Glennon (Gainstown)	19.20 (63'0")
Pentathlon	Ruth Algar (Mullingar)	NP
4x100m	Co. Westmeath	NT

1972

100m	Ruth Algar (Mullingar)	12.2
200m	Ruth Algar	NT
400m	Deirdre Higgins (Bros Pearse)	NT
800m	E. Sheehan (Millstreet)	2: 25.0
1,500m	Sheelagh Flatman (Bros Pearse)	NT
High jump	Sandra Doyle (Naomh Mhuire)	1.445 (4'9")
Long jump	Joy Glennon (Gainstown)	5.22 (17'1.5")
Shot	Joy Glennon	ND
Discus		27.15 (89'1")
Javelin	Joy Glennon (Gainstown)	21.68 (71'1.5")
Pentathlon	Sheelagh Flatman (Bros Pearse)	2,572
4x100m	Co. Westmeath	NT
CC	Carmel Higgins (Bros Pearse)	NT
CC team	Co. Cork	NP

1973

100m	Ruth Algar (Mullingar)	12.3
200m	Ruth Algar	26.0
400m	Mary Buckley (Fossa)	60.9
800m	Sheila Lonergan (Bros Pearse)	2.24.0
1,500m	Sheila Lonergan	5.14.0
100mH	Ruth Algar (Mullingar)	18.1
High jump	Stella-Marie Murphy (Bros Pearse)	1.47 (4'10")
Long jump	Joy Good (Riverstick)	5.12 (16'9.5")
Shot	O. Maher (Mullingar)	8.93 (29'3.5")
Discus	Joy Glennon (Gainstown)	29.26 (96'0")
Javelin	Joy Glennon	25.64 (84'1.5")
4x100m	Co. Dublin	NT
CC	Mary Kearney (Donard)	NT
CC team	Co. Louth	NP

1974

100m	Anne Hoey (Knockbridge)	13.8
1,500m	Mary Kearney (Donard)	5.0 2.0
100mH	Ann Tuite (Castlebellew)	16.8
High jump	Denise Maher (Bros Pearse)	1.395 (4'7")
Long jump	C. Ring (Ballydaly)	4.63 (15'2.25")
Shot	A. Kelly (Brow Rangers)	8.62 (28'3.5")
Discus	Joy Glennan (Gainstown)	25.42 (83'4.75")
Javelin	Joy Glennan	26.71 (87'7.5")
Pentathlon	Mary Conry (Grangebellew)	NP
4x100m	Co. Louth	NT
CC	Mary Kearney (Donard)	NT
CC team	Co. Louth	54

1975

100m	Ann Tuite (Castlebellew)	12.8
200m	Ann Tuite	28.5
400m	Ann Tuite	62.3
800m	Martina Cronin (Killorglin)	2.21.6
1,500m	Ann Berne (Grangebellew)	4.48.6
100mH	Maria Hetherington (Bros Pearse)	16.5
High jump	Maria Hetherington	1.57 (5'1.875")
Long jump	Mary Buckley (Fossa)	5.08 (16'8")
Shot	Pauline Carolan (Bohermeen)	10.01 (32'10")
Discus	Pauline Carolan (Bohermeen)	27.91 (91'6.75")
Javelin	Barbara Gartland (Connolly)	27.02 (88'7.75")
400mH	Co. Louth	NT
CC	Ann Berne (Grangebellew)	NT
CC team	Co. Louth	29

1976

100m	Carolyn McCoy (Bros Pearse)	12.6
200m	Carolyn McCoy	26.5
400m	Ann Tuite (Castlebellew)	61.0
800m	Martina Cronin (Killorglin)	2.28.2
1,500m	Rose McDonnell (Knockbridge)	4.58.5
3,000m	Maria Hetherington (Bros Pearse)	11.10.0
100mH	Maria Hetherington	15.6
High jump	Dolores Wallace (Navan)	1.565 (5'1.75")
Long jump	Maria Hetherington (Bros Pearse)	4.865 (15'11.5")
Shot	A. Kelly (Brow Rangers)	10.61 (34'9.75")
Discus	Pauline Carolan (Fr Murphy)	30.15 (98'11")
Javelin	Catherine O'Sullivan (Dunleer)	25.63 (84'1")
4x100m county	Co. Dublin	51.2
4x100m club	Bros Pearse	53.3
4x400m club	Bros Pearse	4.21.1
3,200m relay club	Newry Shamrocks	10.33.3
Pentathlon	Maria Hetherington (Bros Pearse)	3,035
CC	Rose McDonnell (Knockbridge)	NT
CC team	Co. Louth	54

BLE National Cross Country

1969 Mallow
1. Ann O'Brien (Clonliffe) 14.51
2. Ursula Kennedy (Raheny) 15.13
3. Nuala Bowe (Moycarkey) 15.33
Team: Crusaders (11)

1970 Thurles
1. Ann O'Brien (Clonliffe) 14.41
2. Nuala Bowe (Moycarkey) 14.59
3. Deirdre Foreman (Guinness) 15.01
Team: Clonliffe Harriers (13)

1971 Mallow
1. Ann O'Brien (Clonliffe) 14.20
2. Kathryn Moroney (Clonliffe) 14.26
3. Mary Lynch (Raheny) 14.42
Team: Raheny Shamrocks (11)

1972 Mountmellick
1. Mary Lynch (Raheny) 14.43
2. Deirdre Foreman (Guinness) 15.06
3. Ann O'Brien Cummins (Clonliffe) 15.22
Team: St Laurence O'Toole (25)

1973 Holycross
1. Mary Tracey (Guinness)
2. Deirdre Foreman (Guinness)
3. Jean McNicholl (Dublin)
Team: Guinness (22)

1974 Mountmellick
1. Deirdre Foreman (Guinness) 13.42
2. Mary Lynch (Raheny) 14.03
3. Mary Mellerick (Grange) 14.21
Team: Grange-Fermoy (36)

1975 Mountmellick
1. Deirdre Nagle (Guinness) 13.59
2. Vera Sherry (Glaslough) 14.31
3. Ann Cummins (Clonliffe) 14.48
Team: Guinness (32)

1976 Ballinasloe
1. Deirdre Nagle (DCH) 14.21
2. Vera Duffy (Glaslough) 14.31
3. Sheelagh Morrissey (Kildare) 14.45
Team: Clonliffe Harriers (29)

1977 Ennis
1. Sheelagh Morrissey (Kildare) 13.11
2. Vera Duffy (Glaslough) 13.39
3. Marion Staunton (St Finbarr's) 13.40
Team: Dublin City Harriers B (30)

1978 Ballyfinn
1. Kathryn Davis (Clonliffe) 17.46
2. D. Mellerick (UCC) 17.56
3. Siobhán Lonergan (DCH) 18.10
Team: Dublin City Harriers (30)

1979 Multyfarnham
1. C. Ward (London Olympiade) 19.07
2. Fionnuala Morrish (Leevale) 19.39
3. Deirdre Nagle (DCH) 19.52
Team: Dublin City Harriers (45)

1980 Phoenix Park
1. Mary Purcell (Crusaders) 17.13
2. Carol Meagan (Dundrum) 17.23
3. Deirdre Nagle (DCH) 17.29
Team: Dublin City Harriers (23)

1981 Killeshin
1. Carol Meagan (Dundrum) 17.35
2. Fionnuala Morrish (Leevale) 18.13
3. Deirdre Nagle (DCH) 18.29
Team: Dublin City Harriers B (37)

1982 Mullingar
1. Fionnuala Morrish (Leevale) 22.12
2. Patricia Appleby (Crusaders) 22.20
3. Eithne Kenny (DCH) 22.41
Team: Dublin City Harriers (38)

1983 Rathkeale
1. Louise McGrillen (DCH) 18.14
2. Deirdre Nagle (DCH) 18.22
3. Greta Hickey (DCH) 18.43
Team: Dublin City Harriers B (36)

1984 Kilmacow
1. Roisin Smyth (Sparta) 17.42
2. Louise McGrillen (DCH) 17.51
3. Mary Friel (Crusaders) 18.01
Team: Dublin City Harriers (26)

1985 Killenaule
1. Louise McGrillen (DCH) 16.46
2. Anne Keenan (Clonliffe) 17.07
3. Deirdre Nagle (DCH) 17.14
Team: Dublin City Harriers (16)

1986 Santry
1. Mary Donohoe (Clonliffe) 17.51
2. Greta Hickey (DCH) 18.01
3. Anne Hilliard (DCH) 18.12
Team: Dublin City Harriers (16)

1987 Killenaule
1. Sonia O'Sullivan (Cobh) 16.20
2. Caroline Mullen (Mullingar) 16.31
3. Mary Donohoe (Clonliffe) 16.33
Team: Dublin City Harriers (42)

1988 Ballyhaise
1. Catherine Rooney (Blackrock) 19.28
2. Anne Keenan (Clonliffe) 19.35
3. Rosie Lambe (Knockbridge) 19.37
Team: Dublin City Harriers (30)

1989 Killenaule
1. Christine Kennedy (GCH) 25.56
2. Catherine Rooney (Blackrock) 26.31
3. Catherina McKiernan (Cornafean) 26.32
Team: Dublin City Harriers (40)

1990 Limerick
1. Catherina McKiernan (Cornafean) 20.11
2. Roisin Smyth (DCH) 20.15
3. Niamh Murphy (Westport) 20.30
Team: Dublin City Harriers (26)

1991 Plassey
1. Catherina McKiernan (Cornafean) 24.55
2. Anne Keenan-Buckley (Clonliffe) 25.45
3. Niamh Murphy (Westport) 25.56
Team: Dublin City Harriers (43)

1992 Santry
1. Catherina McKiernan (Cornafean) 20.48
2. Una English (DCH) 21.40
3. Teresa Duffy (Beechmount) 21.46
Team: Dublin City Harriers (54)

1993 Phoenix Park
1. Catherina McKiernan (Cornafean) 20.04
2. Anne Keenan-Buckley (N. Laois) 20.54
3. Teresa Duffy (Beechmount) 21.09
Team: Finn Valley Harriers (57)

1994 Ballinlough
1. Teresa Duffy (Beechmount) 23.04
2. Rosie Lambe (Knockbridge) 23.36
3. Maureen Harrington (Olympic) 23.49
Team: Finn Valley Harriers (53)

1995 Naas
1. Teresa Duffy (Beechmount) 22.07
2. Anne Keenan-Buckley (N. Laois) 22.16
3. Cathy Shum (Clonliffe) 22.26
Team: Finn Valley Harriers (61)

1996 Santry
1. Teresa Duffy (Beechmount) 22.00
2. Anne Keenan-Buckley (N. Laois) 22.30
3. Maureen Harrington (Olympic) 22.54
Team: Finn Valley Harriers (85)

1997 Whitechurch
1. Maureen Harrington (An Ríocht) 22.35
2. Una English (DCH) 22.52
3. Pauleen Curley (Tullamore) 23.28
Team: Finn Valley Harriers

Teams

Since 1977 the competition has been dominated by two clubs: DCH won it 16 years on the trot, 1977 to 1992; Finn Valley have won it in the five years since.

National records at 30 Sept 1997

Event	Mark	Holder	Venue	Date
100m	11.43	Michele Carroll	Sittard	17.6.78
200m	23.51	Michele Carroll	Sittard	18.6.78
400m	53.06	Patricia Walsh	Morton Stadium	3.8.87
800m	2.00.69	Sonia O'Sullivan	St Petersburgh	28.7.94
1,000m	2.34.66	Sonia O'Sullivan	Lille	3.7.93
1.500m	3.58.85	Sonia O'Sullivan	Monte Carlo	25.7.95
Mile	4.17.25	Sonia O'Sullivan	Oslo	22.7.94
2,000m	5.25.36	Sonia O'Sullivan	Edinburgh	8.7.94
3,000m	8.21.64	Sonia O'Sullivan	London	5.7.94
5.000m	14.41.40	Sonia O'Sullivan	Berlin	1.9.95
10,000m	31.08.4	Catherina McKiernan	Lille	17.6.95
100mH	14.28	Olive Burke	Santry	1987
400mH	54.61	Susan Smith	Athens, Greece	5.8.97
4x100m	45.60	National Team*	Morton Stadium	11.6.94
4x100m club	47.8	Nenagh Olympic**	Tullamore	1.5.80
4x400m	3.32.56	National Team***	Rome	5.9.87
4x400m club	3.44.73	Puma TC****	Lisbon	5.6.88
High jump	1.89	Laura Sharpe	Morton Stadium	3.7.94
LJ	6.48	Terri Horgan	Brussels	14.6.92
TJ	12.21	Siobháin Hoey	Limerick	17.7.94
Shot	16.99	Marita Walton	Stanford, USA	2.4.83
Discus	57.60	Patricia Walsh	Morton Stadium	7.7.84
Javelin	50.42	Mary T. Real	Waterford	20.6.92
Hammer	50.42	Olivia Kelleher	Belfield	8.6.96
Pentathlon	5,236	Brid Hallissey	Hasselt	11.7.93
Marathon	2.23.44	Catherina McKiernan	Berlin	28.9.97
3,000mW	13.06.15	Lisa Sheridan	Tullamore	22.8.93
5.000mW	21.35.62	Deirdre Gallagher	Philadelphia	23.6.96
10,000mW	47.43.7	Marie Walsh	Softeland, Norway	24.5.90
10,000mW road	45.12	Deirdre Gallagher	Isle of Man	24.2.96

* Karen Shinkins, Nicola Moore, Marisa Smith, Terri Horgan.

** Fidelma White, Brid Naughton, Noelle Morrissey, Nora O'Grady.

*** Michele Carroll, Barbara Johnson, Patricia Walsh, Patricia Amond.

**** Mary Nolan, Eileen Kavanagh, Patricia Walsh, Aisling Molloy.

Part five

Photo report

Photo report

Jean Folan (Galway City Harriers) winner of People's Marathon, Stockholm 1983

Teresa Kidd (Ballinascreen) the national marathon champion of 1983 and 1985

Maeve Kyle and Noel Henry, at the Belfast Marathon 1996

Photo report

Valerie McGovern (former Donore Harrier) competing in California, USA

Sister Andrena Mulligan (centre) wins the veteran's title at the 1987 Detroit Marathon

Eleanor Hill (Bray Runners), national marathon champion 1994 and winner of the 1990 Belfast Marathon

Aideen Morrison, Crusaders, national 800m champion 1983

Photo report

Maeve Kyle, AAA coach 1968

Ultra runner Heather Stuart, Sligo AC, competes in the World Corporate Games, New York, 1994

Aideen Morrison of Crusaders, the national 800 metres champion of 1983

Photo report

Gráinne Barrett-Condron (Irish Wheelchair AC), bronze medallist at the 1996 Paralympics, Atlanta

Mary Joyce, Mullingar, the first woman to complete the Belfast to Dublin (106 miles) Peace Run (22 hours) and winner of the Tim Parry Memorial Trophy

Ailish Smyth, Olympian and national marathon champion 1988

The last bend at Santry - Ireland's Deirdre Nagle is pipped by her Israeli opponent over 1,500 metres

Photo report

Blind athlete Paula Duff with her friend Gail

Ann Kearney of Clonliffe Harriers, many times Irish and European triathlon champion

No. 1 Cushla Murphy (Marian AC), No. 5 Edel Hackett (Dundrum AC), No. 4 Siobhán Treacy, (DCH), on the final lap of the National 1,500m

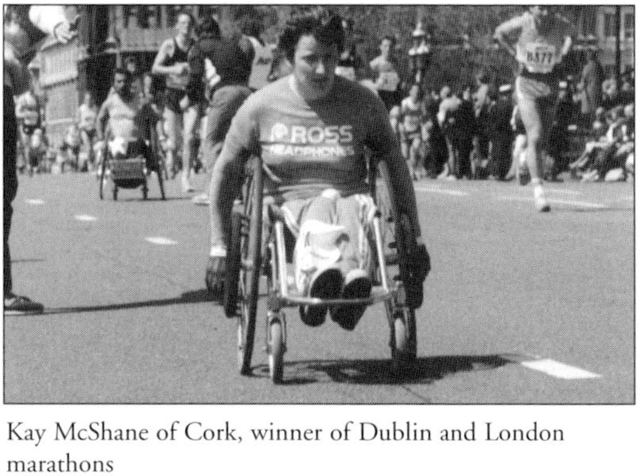

Kay McShane of Cork, winner of Dublin and London marathons

Photo report

Teresa Duffy of Beechmount Harriers, international athlete, national senior CC champion 1994, 95, and 96 and Northern Ireland CC champion 1994 and 95

Dorothy Scanlon (Blindsports AC), winner of many Irish titles and European bronze

Three of the famous O'Brien sisters of Clonliffe Harriers - from left, Nuala, Ann, and Ursula, at Trinity College Sportsground, Santry, 1968

Photo report

Dorothy McLennan, world veteran champion

Dawn Hargan of Finn Valley Harriers wins the Sentinel Half Marathon

Versatile Mary Barnwell, 47 International Hockey Caps, 6 B.L.E. Track Titles

Photo report

Deirdre Gallagher, heel and toe Olympian

Mary B. Jennings 1995 national marathon champion

Perri Williams, Olympic walker Barcelona 1992

Osaka Marathon - left to right, Charlotte Taske, Rita Marchisio, Carey May, Katryn Binns, Laura deWald

Photo report

Pamela Reynolds, Clonliffe Harriers. Ireland' first International Race Walker 1976.

Women's World Cross-Country Team. Bronze medalists, Turin, 1997

The author, Noel Henry, helps his friends beat four hours in Dublin 1989 - No. 1645 Deirdre Parnell (Evening Herald), No. 1234 Anna May Fitzsimons, (Longford)

Photo report

Anita Philpott, flame-haired Cork prodigy

Catherine Rooney, international road and cross-country. Hails from Sligo

Patrice Dockery, World Games sprint champion and Paralympian in Barcelona 1992 and Atlanta 1996

Doina Nugent, our greatest ultra runner, with James Zarei, the world's greatest ultra runner, after the 1991 Cork to Dublin run (160 miles)

Photo report

Finn Valley, National CC champions 1993, 94, 95, 96, and 97. Back row: Peadar McGranaghan, Rosemary Bogle, Margaret Synnott, Rosaleen McGonagle, Kay Byrne, Dawn Hargan, Belinda Carlin, Patsy McGonagle. Front row: Ita Boyle, Catriona McGranaghan, Rosaleen Campbell, Bernie Alcorn

Greta Hickey, Dublin City Harriers

Valerie Vaughan, runner & coach

Connie Kelly winning the Dunshaughlin 10k

Photo report

Rose Hayden, Raheny and Ireland, in the Crete International Marathon 1986

Elaine Kelly (St. Finbars), 800m champion 1971 and 1977

Ann Hilliard, DCH, wins the 1987 BLE 10k championship

Paddy Craddock and his daughter Patricia Craddock Smith

Photo report

Carol Meagan (Dundrum) takes second place behind Sandra Arthurton, who leads, in the British AAA Intermediate Championships at Crystal Palace

Two-lap specialists - Aisling Molloy, Freda Davoren, and Maura Prendiville

Peggy Hogan (Crusaders), 1967 AAUE mile andall-Ireland cross-country champion

Photo report

Patricia Amond (St Laurence O'Toole's, Carlow) winning her 100m heat at the 1972 Community Games, Mosney. Michele Carroll was second, Mary Shannon of Wexford third

Sheila Champion - World Veteran champion by name and nature

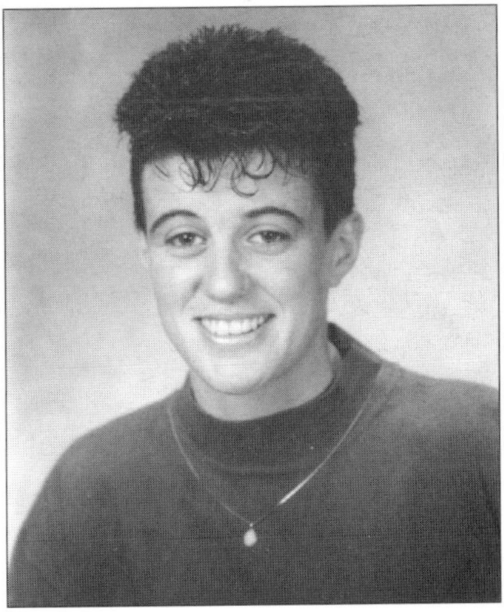

Jacqui Stokes - Irish long jump champion 1995/96 and Irish 200m champion

Photo report

Bridie Lynch - Atlanta paralympics gold medallist for the discus

Patricia Walsh (O' Cleirigh) - 400m national champion 1985 & 1988. Followed in her mothers footprints, Claire Dowling, both Irish sprint champions

Eileen Kelly (Kavanagh) - Dundrum South Dublin AC, 400m runner

Photo report

Joy Murphy (Good) - Irish long jump champion 1976/78/79/81. High jump champion 1976.

Rita Lincoln leads Joyce Smith and Maureen Conlan in the southern womens mile.

Irelands 4 x 400m relay team. Portugal 1992. L to R - Emma Nicholson, Bernie Kavanagh, Marisa Smith and Aisling Molloy.

Left: Deirdre Nagle (26) becomes the first Irish athlete to beat Mary Purcell to the tape in nine years. Santry 1980.

Photo report

Ann Keenan-Buckley, Olympian Seoul 1988.

Rosie Lambe international cross-country, road racing and track athlete for over twenty years.

Photo report

Siobhain Hoey (Dublin City Harriers) - National triple jump champion 1994/95/96

Marie McMahon at the Cork City Sports 1997

Photo report

Una English. World Championships representative in Athens 1997. Member of Women's World Cross-Country team. Bronze medalists, Turin, 1997

Olympic Hurdler, Mary Parr

Club mates - mother and daughter
- Emily and Lisa Dowling

Photo report

Lindie Naughton

(L to R) Anne Buckley-Kennedy, Patricia Griffin and Róisín Smith battling it out at Tullamore.

(L to R) Christine Kennedy and Liz Bullen leave Carrick-on-suir together at the half-way stage in the National Marathon.

Afterword

The highs and lows of our sporting heroines in the Nineties have been thoroughly debated not only by sports-lovers but also by those human vultures in the media who love to feed off the misfortunes of others.

Michelle Smith's marvellous triple gold and bronze in Atlanta may never be surpassed. They were the reward for years of dedicated training, and it was tragic that some American swimmers and journalists had to vent their begrudgery by trying to smear her with talk of drugs - and that even some of our own commentators joined in the unfounded allegations. Happily, the vast majority of Irish people took great pride in Michelle, not only in her heroics in the pool but also in her wonderful dignity, intelligence, and fluency at the press conferences.

As for Sonia O'Sullivan, her Olympic trauma was for many the saddest aspect of the 1996 Games. We heard various theories about her loss of form at this the most important event of her career. My own opinion is that Sonia should have roomed in the Olympic Village with her fellow athletes and sister athletes and, perhaps most important, with our own medical team.

Sonia left Atlanta dejected but knowing that she had to pick up the pieces. After a couple of races in Europe she wisely took time out before embarking on her comeback. She announced the start of her rehabilitation by winning a road-race in Honolulu in December 1996, then travelled to sunny Australia for training and four race wins against local opposition, including a fine 4.10.09 ahead of Kate Anderson.

On 9 March 1997 Sonia contested the World Indoor 3,000m in Paris, France. Looking her former dominant self, she did all the front-running and with 70 metres remaining appeared to have won. But with the line in sight, she was shocked by Gabriela Szabo scurrying through on the blind inside. The tiny Romanian was timed at 8.45.75, Sonia at 8.46.19.

Two weeks later, on 23 March, the 25th World Cross Country was staged in Turin, Italy. The city-centre course had been man-made and woman-made at a cost of one million pounds and was more like track than cross-country.

Sonia, who had not contested the event since running seventh in Boston 92, went into an early lead and headed proceedings for two-thirds of the 6,000 metres. Then, suffering for her bravery, she had to give way to Catherina McKiernan. As the bell tolled the final circuit, Catherina led Britain's Paula Radcliffe and Spain's Julia Vaquero.

Now the Ethiopians Tulu and Wami and the Kenyan Barsosio came through. Catherina began to wilt - clearly, she was paying for the curtailment of winter training by injury. Nevertheless, she hung on gallantly for seventh place.

Sonia also rallied, and posted ninth. Valerie Vaughan was 23rd, Una English 25th. Suddenly we realised we were in the reckoning for team medals. We totted up our sums – and to our great joy confirmed that we had pipped Britain for the bronze (Ethiopia and Kenya having taken gold and silver).

This was our greatest ever team effort at these championships and by any yardstick a colossal achievement (though to read the low-key newspaper coverage it received you might think otherwise). In 1970 our women had taken bronze in Frederick, USA, at what was then called the International Cross Country - but only six teams took part. For the record, the pioneering quintet were Ann O'Brien (9th), Peggy Hogan (10th), Deirdre Foreman (12th), Jane McNicholl (17th), and Nuala Bowe (29th). How gratifying it is to note that our long-distance ladies are now able to compete against the world and can justifiably claim to be the best in Europe, indeed the best outside Africa!

Athens 1997 was the scene of another giant step for womankind - when Susan Smith reached the final of the World Championship 400m hurdles.

Sadly, the same Games provided further disappointment for Sonia O'Sullivan, a virtual action replay of her Olympic disasters. But this latest heartbreak could yet prove a blessing in disguise - if it results in her taking the year of rest and recuperation that almost everyone agrees she needs.

As this book goes to print, Catherina McKiernan has just made a sensational marathon debut in Berlin 97. Her winning 2.23.44 is the best ever by a first-timer and the eighth fastest in history. Given the brilliance of this effort and the reported ease with which it was achieved, we may admit even as we relish it that we are already looking forward with eager anticipation to her next outing over the classic distance. Such is the infinite fascination of athletics.

It only remains to thank again all those who assisted me in this labour of love. Thanks especially to my dear wife, Nano, who put up with all the research, letter-writing, and phonecalls, not to mention the mountains of files cluttering the kitchen table.

Finally, I apologise for errors and omissions. The errors are inadvertent. The omissions (and a few facts and figures and one or two names are, admittedly, conspicuous by their absence) were unintentional: several queries went repeatedly unanswered; some investigations led into cul-de-sacs (or *culs-de-sac*); eventually my publisher called time.

I hope to amend these matters in a future reprinting. In this context all comments, corrections, and contributions are welcome. I can be reached at home: Noel Henry, 61 Rathdown Park, Greystones, Co. Wicklow. Telephone 01-2874429.